W9-BZR-079

Joshua ben Perahyah taught:

"Find yourself a teacher; acquire a colleague for study."

—Pirke Avot 1:6

יהושע בן-פרחיה אומר :

עשה לך רב ; וקנה לך חבר

-פרקי אבות א :ו

FIND YOURSELF
A TEACHER

עשה לך רב

FIND YOURSELF
A TEACHER

עשה לך רב

A Cycle of Divrei Torah
Celebrating Rabbi Joel H. Zaiman's
20th Anniversary at
Chizuk Amuno Congregation

With an Introduction by Professor Jacob Neusner

Compiled and Edited
by
Harriet Helfand
Lee M. Hendler
Judy Meltzer
Larry Shuman

Torah Book Designs by Angela Munitz
Cover Design by Ann Zaiman

Chizuk Amuno Congregation, Baltimore, Maryland
June 2000

Published by Chizuk Amuno Congregation
8100 Stevenson Road
Baltimore, Maryland 21208
or visit our website at chizukamuno.org
email: info@chizuk amuno.org
A member of United Synagogue of Conservative Judaism

Library of Congress Card Control Number: 00-091429
ISBN: 0-9673940-0-7

Printed and bound in the United States of America
by Signature Book Printing, Inc., Gaithersburg, Maryland

Contents

Deuteronomy

Acknowledgements

In May of 1999, president of Chizuk Amuno Congregation, Lee Hendler, came to us with a project. "Rabbi Zaiman will be celebrating his 20th anniversary at Chizuk Amuno next year. . . I have been talking to a number of people about an idea," she said. What followed was an inspiring, thought-provoking, sometimes exasperating, challenging, intellectual experience that has culminated in the following pages of tribute and exegesis in honor of our rabbi, our colleague, our friend, Joel Zaiman.

Bringing together fifty-four varying voices of Torah commentary was a daunting task. *Find Yourself a Teacher* simply would not have come to fruition without the cooperation and support of the following:

To **Professor Jacob Neusner**, whose October 1999 visit and workshop helped to focus contributors on the task at hand. His Introduction to *Find Yourself a Teacher* and published monograph *"How Judaism Reads the Bible,"* reproduced in this volume, adds to the importance of this book as a work of scholarship and as a true testament to our master teacher.

To **Elisheva Urbas** and **Dr. Arthur Lesley**, whose keen eyes, superior knowledge of sacred texts, editorial skill, and commitment to the project, helped to refine *Find Yourself a Teacher*.

To **Ann Zaiman**, whose vision and captivating artwork grace the cover of *Find Yourself a Teacher*.

To **Angela Munitz**, whose original artwork provides the glorious Genesis, Exodus, Leviticus, Numbers, and Deuteronomy illustrations found throughout *Find Yourself a Teacher*.

To the many contributors to *Find Yourself a Teacher*, whose willingness to adhere to tight deadlines and editorial schedules helped to make this project a reality.

And finally, to the underwriters and donors listed on the next page, whose generosity made the publication of this volume possible.

Harriet Helfand
Lee M. Hendler
Judy Meltzer
Larry Shuman
Shavuot 5760

Underwriters

Suzanne F. Cohen
Lee M. and Dr. Nelson Hendler
The Zanvyl and Isabelle Krieger Fund
The Ben and Esther Rosenbloom Foundation

Donors

Ann & Gil Abramson
Linda G. Blumenthal
Dr. Chaim Y. Botwinick
Rabbi Gustav Buchdahl
Carolyn &
  Rabbi Richard Camras
Rabbis Nina Beth Cardin &
  Avram Reisner
Shoshana S. Cardin
Barbara & Dr. Maimon Cohen
Sarina & Stuart Davis
Drs. Gail & Sheldon Dorph
Ellen Friedman
Sharon Bromberg &
  Rabbi Aaron Gaber
Elaine & Dr. Barry M. Gittlen
Florene & Dr. Ronald Goldner
Hadassah & Dr. Levi Gordis
Harriet & William Helfand
Debby & Jesse Hellman
Rebecca Hoffman
Drs. Carol K. & Michael Ingall
Harriet & Alan N. Kanter
Evelyn & Robert Katzoff
Joanne & Dr. Edward Kraus
Barbara E. Leibowitz
Dr. Arthur M. Lesley
Sandee & Dr. Barry Lever
Marsha & Dick Manekin
Judy Meltzer

Alita & Ronald N. Millen
Dr. Andrew J. Miller
June & Stanley I. Minch
Mimi Blitzer & David Mallott
Alison & Michael S. Novey
Janice &
  Hazzan Emanuel C. Perlman
Robyn Perlin
Dorothy Rainess
Deborah & Dr. David Roffman
Nancy & Rabbi James Rosen
Leslie S. Rosen
Rabbi Gila & Dr. Paul Ruskin
Marilyn &
  Dr. Paul D. Schneider
Rabbi Stuart Seltzer
Kathy & Sanford Shapiro
Nancy M. &
  Dr. Moshe D. Shualy
Ruth & Larry Shuman
Rabbi Stuart Seltzer
Drs. Fredelle & Steven Spiegel
Michelle & Jacob Sullum
Lisa & Rabbi Robert L. Tobin
Dr. Anne & David Young
Susan & Shmuel Vick
Rabbi Deborah Wechsler
Judy & Bruce Yaillen
Heller & Ari Zaiman

Preface

In 1996, Chizuk Amuno Congregation marked the occasion of its 125th anniversary by envisioning its future and honoring its past. The congregation came together as a community to develop a mission statement—one that would bridge the generations and give Chizuk Amuno definition and direction. After careful introspection and deliberation, it was decided that the mission statement of Chizuk Amuno Congregation should reflect the words of Shimon Ha Tzaddik in Chapter 1, Verse 2 of Pirkei Avot:

> *"The world rests on three things—on Torah, on Avodah, and on Gemilut Hasaidim."*

These three values, Torah (lifelong learning), Avodah (worship of God), and Gemilut Hasadim (acts of loving kindness), were the ideals that Chizuk Amuno wanted to transmit to its members, as well as to Jewish communities around the world. The mission statement would become the prism by which all endeavors associated with Chizuk Amuno Congregation would be measured.

Shortly following the development of the mission statement, the Stulman Center for Adult Learning of Chizuk Amuno Congregation was established. The presence of the Stulman Center, and the subsequent addition of the Florence Melton Adult Mini-School, have made Chizuk Amuno a beacon of adult Jewish learning in Baltimore. Every morning and every evening, adults of all ages and experiences stream into Chizuk Amuno eager for Jewish study from ancient texts to modern Jewish history. There are courses designed to appeal to an array of interests and levels of study. We have truly become a community of learners.

It is therefore fitting that we choose to honor Rabbi Joel Zaiman on the occasion of his 20th anniversary at Chizuk Amuno Congregation with the publication of this book. Rabbi Zaiman, whose vision propelled the explosion of learning at Chizuk Amuno, has been the master teacher who has guided and inspired us to pursue the path of Torah study. Each of the contributors to this volume has, in some way, been touched by Rabbi Zaiman, either as colleague, as congregant, or as a member of his loving and talented family.

For many, the task of preparing a d'var Torah was both arduous and exhilarating. Long hours were spent researching, discussing, writing and polishing what came to be true labors of love. While honoring our teacher, it was we who were blessed to be able to immerse ourselves in the beauty of Torah and the wisdom of the Sages. It is to Rabbi Zaiman, the teacher and friend who has created our gateway to learning, that we at Chizuk Amuno Congregation dedicate this book.

Harriet Helfand
Project Chair
Shavuot 5760

Tribute

Each year, the Rabbinical Assembly and the Jewish Theological Seminary honor an individual rabbi at the Rabbinical Assembly's annual convention. In 1999, they asked Rabbi Joel H. Zaiman to accept the honor. Since the convention was held in Baltimore and the event would take place at Chizuk Amuno, it was a natural courtesy to invite the President of the congregation to make a few remarks at the ceremony. (Happily, that honor fell to me.) The invitation was extended: wouldn't I like to say a few words about "my" rabbi? I was, in truth, delighted with the request even though it *was* problematic. Not the invitation itself, but the syntax. We call him Moshe *Rabeinu*. Moses, *our* teacher. When exactly did we turn away from all the possibilities suggested by the plural possessive "our," and turn instead to the singular possessive "my?" We've all heard the phrase I'm sure, "So and so is *my* rabbi." The problem with the claim is that it distorts the relationship our tradition celebrates-makes the master servant to the apprentice and places individual above community. There is a *difference* between "my" and "our." And the man honored by his peers at that event and whom we honor with this collection of Divrei Torah knows the difference, has lived his life in the rabbinate modeling the difference, and has taught laymen and colleagues alike to respect and appreciate it.

The truth is that Joel Zaiman is not *my* rabbi. He is *our* rabbi. And 20 years of his leadership attest to the difference. In this context, I mean rabbi in the sense of master. For he *is* master of Chizuk Amuno Congregation: its chief visionary, leader and authority. He assumes the role of our rabbi with remarkable integrity and grace, remarkable because he makes it all look so easy. Yet anyone who has ever tried knows that the last thing it is, is easy. Some of it comes naturally to him and some of it he works at, but the fact remains, he is gifted. Even more remarkable is that while he may occasionally take his gifts for granted, he never takes our congregation for granted. He is as grateful for us as we are for him. We are *his* congregation and he is *our* rabbi. And the evidence of that relationship is all over the place. The tangible evidence is a physical plant that has grown nearly three-fold since his arrival, five schools serving thousands of students, donor walls listing hundreds of contributors, expanded administrative offices, multiple Shabbat services, and a parking lot that is filled day and night throughout the year. The less tangible evidence is, in many respects, the greater achievement because it is such a rarity in synagogue life; but it is the key to his mastery. A dedicated staff flourishes and collaborates under his leadership. Lending new meaning to the word "team," they delight in one another's talents and creativity and find ways to make all the important decisions together. Lay leaders give unstintingly of their time and energy, confident that they are truly valued for their skills, insight and commitment. But the real testament to his vision and leadership lies elsewhere. Joel Zaiman may be *our* rabbi but he is *my* teacher.

Every congregant who has ever studied with him can make that statement. Every child who has ever taken a class with him has felt the power and excitement of his teaching. He is *our* rabbi, *my* teacher. *Hu rabeinu, hu rabi.* Connecting with his students every time he teaches, he understands that whether in the classroom, on the bimah, or in the hallway, *every* moment has the potential to be a "teachable" moment-moments he consistently responds to with wit, warmth and agility. Reading his students as clearly as others read text, he invariably matches the pedagogy to the occasion. And he takes it very seriously, for the occasion is almost always a sacred one. Revelation itself is at stake. There may be a chance to open a heart or mind to the possibilities our tradition contains. A holy moment when he and his students may encounter God together. *Hu rabeinu, hu rabi.*

Our sages teach that Torah is fire. "Fire: Close up to it, one is scorched; away from it, one is chilled; near but not too near, one enjoys it. So are words of Torah; as long as a man labors in them, they are life for him; but when he separates from them, they slay him." Our tradition celebrates rabbis as the primary stokers and guardians of the fire. Then it goes one extraordinary step further. It suggests that in the process of tending the fire, rabbis may enter the fire itself and not be consumed. In the rare alchemy that our theology permits, they become the fire; they become Torah. *He is our rabbi, my teacher.* As *rabeinu*, "our master," he has helped us to create a community in which the fire of Torah burns brightly and safely for all. And as *rabi,* "my teacher," he has beckoned each one of us to draw closer to the fire. Interpreting its meaning with consummate skill and clarity, he has taught us to come near but not too near, to respect its power and its mystery. Sharing his passion for learning, he has taught us to revere and delight in words of Torah. Not to separate ourselves from them but to take responsibility for them-knowing that in them life resides- and that he alone cannot keep the fire burning.

He is our rabbi, my teacher. Hu rabeinu, hu rabi. We are grateful for the many blessings he has bestowed upon us, for all the ways in which he has strengthened our community, expanded our vision and extended our knowledge. And we are grateful to his wonderful wife, Ann, who has made so much of his service possible, and who together with him has lovingly created a Jewish home and family we all admire. We are grateful to his children Elana, Sarina, Ari and their spouses Seth, Stuart and Heller for sharing him with us.

With joy, gratitude and deep respect, we dedicate this book and the year of study it represents to our master, my teacher, Rabbi Joel H. Zaiman.

Lee M. Hendler
President, Chizuk Amuno Congregation
Shavuot 5760

Introduction

This book testifies to what a truly effective rabbi can accomplish in service to a synagogue-community. The choice of the project to honor a rabbi by showing how his congregants, his disciples, have learned to model Torah-study on his teaching—there can be no greater tribute to a rabbi than such an appropriate project.

This book shows how individual members have undertaken to celebrate a rabbi's Torah. No congregation has ever formed a more worthy tribute. The contributors to this book studied Torah with Rabbi Zaiman. Here they show not so much what they learned from him as how he has given them a model for their own learning.

Why is it so appropriate? It is because rabbis are not professors of Jewish studies or social workers in Jewish agencies, though they are learned like professors and organize community affairs like social workers. Unlike professors, they are rightly expected to profess, not merely to inform; to persuade, to advocate, not merely to enlighten, above all, to exemplify and advocate, not merely to preside and analyze. Unlike social workers, they bring to leadership not merely an open-ended agenda of effective action but a very particular set of commitments. Authentic rabbis cannot be mistaken for other Jewish leaders; they are not ethnic cheerleaders but bear a religious message about service to God. They are not Jewish in general, but rabbinical-Judaic in particular.

For rabbis, synagogues and Torah-study form not only means to an end but a well-defined goal, defined out of the resources of Judaism: commandment, not culture. Specifically, rabbis in the community stand for Judaism, the religion, and not merely for Jewish identity, for Torah as God's message and holy Israel's identification, not merely for Jewish ethnicity. For rabbis, as for Judaism, the continuity of a group, the Jewish community, is an end in itself. Rabbis serve through the Torah that they teach, in word and in deed. The measure of their success comes to expression in how their disciples, who are the members of the congregation that they serve, grasp the requirements of Torah.

By that criterion, Rabbi Zaiman may derive satisfaction in his twenty years of service. That Chizuk Amuno asked me to prepare a lesson of Torah—not history, not sociology, not even systematic analysis of theology, but Torah—forms the only tribute that, because he is an authentic rabbi, Rabbi Zaiman could accept. So, too, that this book has been brought into being represents that same impulse of authentic honor to the Torah. That is because the form of this celebration accords with what the Torah requires to bring honor to the Torah, not to oneself. Specifically, "if you have studied much Torah, do not take pride in that fact, for it was to that end that you were created." Rabbi Zaiman has worked for twenty years that, through him, the Torah finds an honorable embodiment, a worthy model for this generation in this time and in this place. You have responded in the only way that matters: as "doing a religious duty brings about doing another religious duty," so study of Torah brings its own reward, which is more and better study of Torah. That defines the challenge set by the Congregation to itself in this project, as much as to me in my address in celebration of the same event.

For this occasion, then, all of us pay tribute to Rabbi Zaiman through what we set forth as a lesson in Torah. For my part, I will not write about him by way of introducing this book; this book bears its own message. About him I will say only this: Rabbi Zaiman comes from the prior Rabbi Zaiman, his father, whom I knew and of whom I can speak, and Rabbi Zaiman's life has been lived as a tribute to the model of that master of Torah who was his father, and as a tribute, too, to his father's counterpart, also an embodiment of Torah, his mother. More praise than that no one has coming in the setting of the nobility of the Torah, from which he descends. If Rabbi Zaiman's father was to pick up this book and read what is written in it, he would be very proud of his son. And he would be equally proud of this congregation of

American Jews. You vindicate his life and struggle, as much as you honor his son.

How, then, to realize your resolve of honoring a rabbi in a rabbinical way? It is to show your rabbi what he has achieved by doing yourself what he, as your model, has done for these twenty years. In this congregation, through these essays, you have determined to celebrate your Rabbi's service by taking up his task and showing what he has taught you by doing the same work on your own. He will then have been your model, just as he drew upon models in Torah-learning. How Rabbi Zaiman studied the Torah in the setting of synagogue worship is how he was taught the Torah in synagogue and in school and in the Rabbinical seminary. And that is, Torah as taught by the sages of the Mishnah, Talmud, and Midrash. Rabbi Zaiman made his anniversary the occasion to act out, to specify how in the synagogue we receive the Torah week by week, lesson by lesson, as our sages mediate the Torah to us. This is what members of this remarkable synagogue do in the pages of this book.

Jacob Neusner is Distinguished Research Professor of Religious Studies, University of South Florida and Research Professor of Religion and Theology, Bard College

Editorial Committee Note

Although we have tried to standardize the text of *Find Yourself a Teacher*, internal footnotes, references to the Five Books, additional commentaries and book titles, and Hebrew transliterations may vary from parashah to parashah. These variations reflect the diversity of the contributors to the project and should not be read as oversights or mistakes in the text.

GENESIS

בראשית

B

E BOLD AS A LEOPARD & LIGHT

AS AN EAGLE AS SWIFT AS A DEER &

mighty as a lion to do the will

of your father who is in heaven

ANGELA MUNITZ. 1999

Bereshit
Rabbi Nina Beth Cardin

*"And God caused to spring forth from the ground all
manner of lovely and tasty trees. And the tree of life
was in the center of the garden. And the tree of the
knowledge of good and evil." (Genesis 2:9)*

*"And God took the human and placed him in the
garden to tend it and work it. And God commanded
him saying: From every tree in the garden you may
eat; but the tree of the knowledge of good and evil, you
may not eat from it, for on the day that you eat it, you
shall die."(Genesis 2:15-17)*

Such a generous, yet troubling, beginning of human life.
The world's bounty is ours for the taking, given to us as a gift from
God. We need simply to care for it. We know our place and our
place is good. But there is something haunting and dark lurking in
this beginning.

Among all the questions that this story raises, we will focus
on two: (1) Why would God prominently place in the garden
something that the human was not to touch? (2) How, in fact, did
the tree of the knowledge of good and evil work? That is, how was
its knowledge imparted?

As every parent of a young child knows, those items that we
do not want little hands to touch are kept locked up or out of
reach. Poisons, drugs, cleansers and fragile items are all kept away
from exploring little fingers. Even as adults, those of us on diets
know not to buy or keep in the house food that we should not eat.
Ex-smokers know they should not have packs of cigarettes lying
around. The best way to resist transgression is to avoid temptation.

Then we are compelled to ask, if the forbidden tree had to
exist, why did God not place it outside the garden out of reach, or
build a fence around it and shield the human from it? Why draw

the human's attention to it and then leave the human, and the tree, unprotected?

We can imagine the human walking around the garden, repeating to himself, "Don't eat from that tree, don't eat from that tree..." much like Dosteovsky's Idiot trying in vain not to break the vase. Such constant tugging at the forbidden is bound to wear away one's coat of restraint.

Perhaps, then, we are to conclude that God wanted us to be attracted to the tree, to be compelled to make a decision about whether to obey or not. And that brings into high relief the paradox, and the ethics, of the command. If the human does not have the capacity to know the difference between good and evil (and the assumption is we don't, or else what would be the need for this prohibition against eating the fruit?) how can *adam* be expected to understand the concept of commandedness and obedience? And if he does not have the capacity to understand the command, how can he be punished if he transgresses it? The answer hinges on the notion of self-awareness, that one characteristic that seems unique to humankind.

Pirkei Avot says: "Beloved is humanity, for they are made in the image of God. Doubly beloved are they, because they were **told** they were made in the image of God."

We humans are creatures endowed with all sorts of gifts. Some are shared among all of us and some are unique to each of us. We can speak, dance, sing, solve problems, make tools. The ability to exercise these gifts is shared by us all; the finesse with which we express these gifts is unique to each of us. Finding our particular talents is the challenge. That is why our parents often encourage us to take piano lessons, or dance lessons; and why schools make us all learn geography and algebra, even if we are never, ever to use such knowledge after our school career. Because if we were never exposed to it, we would never know our capacity to understand it and use it. And we would never be able to stumble upon the gift that is uniquely ours.

Imagine if we were made in the image of God and did not

know it. Imagine if we had the capacity for compassion and did not know it; or the capacity for love and could not recognize it; or the capacity to give and preserve life and never develop it. Imagine if you had won the lottery and did not know it. You would be one thing, and misguidedly think you were something else. You would be rich, but your life would be unchanged. Awareness of reality changes that reality.

So it has always been for humanity. So it was in the garden. The human was born with the capacity for knowledge and discernment; in other words, with the capacity for the exercise of choice and free will. But in an environment which offers no choice, or at the very most, offers choice without consequences, this divine capacity of discernment and choice could not be recognized, or cherished, or utilized. Then the human would be no different from the animals.

But the awareness of the capacity of choice is not one that is taught. Rather, it must be discovered. And the way to discover it is to be faced with a choice that has significant consequences. God was not being a mean-spirited or unprotective parent in placing the tree in the garden and telling the human so. On the contrary, God wanted the human to learn, early on, about the most divine gift that he possessed, the only gift that gives life meaning: choice.

But, we may wonder, did the price have to be so high? *From every tree in the garden you may eat; but the tree of the knowledge of good and evil, you may not eat from it, for on the day that you eat it, you shall die.*

Did God have to barter our lives for the gift of discernment and choice? No. And God did not. In fact, death was already present in the world. The human would have died with or without this self-discovery. We know this because of the presence of the Tree of Life in the middle of garden. If there were no death in the world, there would be no need of The Tree of Life. The Tree only makes sense as an antidote to death. And the precaution taken to prevent the human from eating from the Tree of Life was put in place only **after** he ate from the tree of knowledge, that is, only after he had an intuition of death. When he was ignorant of himself, he had no thoughts of mortality or immortality and hence had no need of the Tree of Life. Though he would have died, he would have taken no measures to prevent it. Only in self-awareness was there a danger, indeed likelihood, that the human would seek the source of immortality. Only then does the prohibition against eating of this tree make sense.

What death, then, does the Torah speak of in verse 17? The death of innocence, the death of ignorance. This phrase, *tov v'ra*, good and evil, occurs only here and in Deuteronomy 1:39, where it says: "Moreover, your little ones... your children who do not yet know good from bad." On the day that we become aware of our divine abilities of discernment and choice, on that day, our innocence dies.

So how does the tree of knowledge of good and evil work? Does the acquisition of wisdom depend on eating the fruit; in touching it; in grasping it? Does the tree possess a quality that is passed on to us?

Not at all. Unlike the Tree of Life, the location of the tree of knowledge is not mentioned. And it need not be, for the power of this tree resides not in the physical properties of the tree itself, but in our awakening to the dilemma and awareness that the command brings on. Any tree, any object, so proscribed, with its related consequences and accountability, can serve as the object of awakening.

If our actions, if our lives, are to mean anything, they must emanate from the exercise of choice. Tradition tells us that one of the things that distinguishes us from the angels, the fawning, alleluiahing chorus of the heavenly court, is that we have choice. God created us not to be angelic, but to be human. And that lesson was the very first that the human had to learn.

*Rabbi Nina Beth Cardin is the Director of Jewish Life at the JCC of Greater Baltimore. Her most recent book is A **Tapestry of Jewish Time: A Spiritual Guide to Holidays and Lifecycle Events**.*

Noah
Sarina Davis

The story of Noah's ark is one that we all too often make into a fairy tale for children. But this story is hardly a fairy tale. It is a dark tale. It is a tale of God's despair over His creation, and His decision to destroy His creation, all except for Noah, his family and a host of animals.

In Genesis, chapter six, we read: "God saw how great was human wickedness on earth, and how every plan devised by the human mind was nothing but evil all the time. And God regretted that He had made humans on earth, and His heart was saddened. God said: 'I will blot out from the earth the people whom I created, men and women, together with beasts, creeping things and birds of the sky; for I regret that I made them.' But Noah found favor with God."

When I read this passage, I think, how could God do this? How could God be so cruel as to destroy all living things? Is this a merciful way for God to behave?

In the Sifre on Deuteronomy the rabbis tell us that if God destroyed the wicked, that is how it was meant to be. We should not question God's actions. Fascinating that the rabbis were not troubled in this context by the question of God's mercy. They believed that God's actions were just, that those people who were punished deserved to be punished.

We learn later in Genesis that questioning God is okay. Abraham takes God to task about His decision to destroy Sodom and Amorah. Abraham says to God: How can You destroy an entire city? What if there are people within it who are righteous? Abraham questions God's actions, but Noah did not. He very well could have.

For years I was angry at God when I read this story. I found God's behavior thoroughly reprehensible. How could I believe in a God who would destroy the very creatures He created? Was that a God I could trust?

The only positive outcome of God's decision to destroy the world as far as I can tell can be found at the end of the Noah story. When the waters of the flood had subsided, and when God smelled the pleasing odor of the sacrifices Noah offered up to Him, God said to Himself: "Never again will I doom the earth because of human beings, since the devisings of the human mind are evil from youth; nor will I ever again destroy every living being, as I have done. So long as the earth endures, seedtime and harvest, cold and heat, summer and winter, day and night shall not cease."

We get a glimpse of God's feeling about His actions. God realized that He had done wrong. He repented of His mistake. He stated that He would never act this way again. God had much to learn. After all, it was the beginning of His relationship with the world.

On the one hand it is disconcerting for us to think of God as one who makes mistakes. We want God to be perfect. We assume that God is perfect. Isn't that part of what makes God God?

On the other hand, I find it comforting in a way to think of God as one who can make mistakes, because it makes God more accessible, and it allows me an explanation that I can comprehend for some of God's actions which I would otherwise find difficult to understand.

Maybe it was through His experience that God learned about the importance of giving human beings the opportunity to repent. Maybe it was by making this mistake, and by experiencing how awful it felt to have made such a mistake, that God learned to have a greater sensitivity toward His creatures. There is something to be said about how experiencing something first-hand makes us more understanding and more attuned to those around us who are going through something similar.

Another understanding of God in the Noah story comes from Byron Sherwin, a professor of Jewish Theology and

Mysticism. Sherwin understands God as a "young artist," who is unsatisfied with His creation, and therefore has to make some sort of change in the picture He has created. God responded as any young artist would.

It is not unusual for artists to continually work to perfect their creations. In the magazine Art News in an article entitled: "The Second Time Around," Milton Esterow writes: "Degas couldn't keep his hands off his paintings even after they had left his studio. One collector reportedly chained several Degas pastels to his living-room wall when he knew the artist was coming to dinner."

Picasso once said, "To finish a picture, what nonsense." Isaac Bashevis Singer noted what Picasso left unsaid regarding the internal frustration in the heart of every artist. "Every creator painfully experiences the chasm between his inner vision and its ultimate expression." God, Singer maintained, is no different.

And God had an added kink in His system—a kink which He, Himself, had built into the system. God was dealing with a living picture, a dynamic universe. His creations had free will to act within their environment in whatever way they wanted and thus dramatically change the world God had created, for good, but also for bad.

Having given human beings free will, God had to come to terms with the fact that He could not control His creatures. He would just have to accept them in spite of their flaws, or even perhaps, because of their flaws. And that was precisely the recognition that God came to after the flood: that He would have to learn how to deal with His creatures in a compassionate manner, even when they disappointed Him.

This is our responsibility as parents- to accept and love our children for who they are, not who we want them to be. A very successful doctor once joked that his father never pressured him at all. When he was growing up, his father told him that he could be any kind of doctor he wanted to be. My goal as a parent is to give my children the strength to make their own decisions and allow them to grow through their mistakes, not mine.

So do I feel comfortable believing in a God who makes mistakes? Yes, more comfortable than I feel believing in a God whose behavior seems reprehensible and unjustifiable. And yes, I am comforted by God's recognition of His own mistakes, His acceptance of responsibility for His mistakes, and His decision not to act in the same way in the future. If we are made "Betzelem Elohim," in God's image, then we too should have that capacity- to recognize our own mistakes, to take responsibility for them and to work towards not repeating our mistakes in the future.

Sarina Zaiman Davis teaches English at Paulsboro High School. She is the second child of Rabbi Zaiman.

Lech Lecha
Barbara E. Leibowitz

In the parashah Lech Lecha, which means "go forth," there are several important themes. God tells Abram to leave his native country and enter a land that God will show him. He must go forth from his country, from his father's house. After entering the new land, God promises Abram that he and his offspring will have this land as their own. When God tells Abram to go from his country, Abram obeys. This is one of the first of many trials that Abram endures, proving his faith in God's words.

As Abram, Sarai and Lot enter Canaan, they are faced with famine. They travel on to Egypt where Abram fears that an Egyptian might admire Sarai, kill Abram and take Sarai for a wife. Abram instructs Sarai to say she is his sister, not his wife. Sarai listens to Abram, but the Egyptian, Pharaoh, finds out that Sarai is indeed Abram's wife. God sends plagues upon Egypt and Pharaoh sends Abram, Sarai and Lot from Egypt. It seems that once again, God is there for Abram.

Further into the parashah, Abram and Lot decide to separate their flocks after quarreling. Lot is given the choice of where he would like to settle and he chooses east, which is next to Sodom. Soon after, Lot is taken captive and Abram gathers a troop of fighters and sets out to rescue his nephew. He succeeds and the king of Sodom offers Abram a reward for having saved Lot and the city of Sodom. Abram refuses the reward. It seems that having saved Lot is enough of a reward for Abram.

After rescuing a captive Lot, God speaks to Abram again. God promises Abram that his and Sarai's offspring will inherit the land. Abram thought this would not be possible because at that point, he had no offspring. God did promise offspring and a son, Ishmael is born to Abram. After Ishmael's birth, God changes Abram's name to Abraham meaning, "father of a multitude" and Sarai's to Sarah, meaning "princess." The sign of the covenant that God made with Abraham is the circumcision of all males. Abraham obeys this covenant and circumcises himself, Ishmael and all of his male followers. Once again God speaks to Abraham and Abraham listens. Abraham did not hesitate to listen to God; he always chose to obey God.

Today, as we enter a new century, we also face a choice: whether or not to listen and follow God's commandments. Hopefully, we will choose as Abraham and Sarah: we will keep the mitzvot of God.

Barbara E. Leibowitz is Director of the Arlington Cemetery of Chizuk Amuno Congregation. A longtime member of Chizuk Amuno, Barbara has had the pleasure of working professionally with Rabbi Zaiman for the past 10 years.

Vayyera
Fredelle & Steven Spiegel

Seeing is believing... or is it?

The *sedrah*, *Vayyera*, "and he appeared," is an appellation that itself refers to the capacities of sight. It is a sedrah that is filled with descriptions of seeing. Yet, instead of seeing and then believing, here, believing results in seeing.

The sedrah, one with which we're all familiar because we read so much of it on Rosh Hashanah, if not in the Golden books, begins with the angels' visit to Avraham. It ends with the Akedah. In between are the stories of the destruction of Sodom, the birth of Yitzchak, and the banishment of Ishmael. In all of these stories sight plays a prominent role.

The sedrah begins: *Vayyera alov Hashem b'eilonai mamrei . . . .* The Lord appeared to him by the terebinths of Mamre . . . . *Vayesah ainov vayaar v'henei shloshah anashim nitsavim alov, vayaar vayaratz likratam.* And he lifted up his eyes and looked, and lo, three men stood over against him, and when he saw them, he ran to meet them from the tent door . . . . Franz Rosenzweig interprets this verse by noting Avraham's capacity to see. The text begins by simply saying that God appeared to him, but Avraham "sees" three men. For Rosenzweig, Avraham is the religious man par excellence because he sees God in the human situation.

By verse 16, the capacity for sight switches to the three men. After having told the unbelieving couple that within the year Sarah will give birth to a son, they are ready to proceed to Sodom. *Vayakumu mesham haanashim vayashkifu al p'nai S'dom. . .* The men rose up from thence, and looked out toward Sodom.

In chap. 19, the two angels go down to S'dom and it is Lot's turn to see. *Va'yaar Lot vayakam lekratam.* Lot saw them and rose up to meet them. But when the men of S'dom come to torment Lot and his visitors (verse 11), or perhaps his daughters whom he was ready to offer, they are struck blind. They can no longer see.

And, of course, we all know the story of Lot's nameless wife. This too deals with seeing and looking. Although told not to look back, she did, and turned into a pillar of salt(vs. 26). Undoubtedly not accidentally, Lot's wife's looking back is then mirrored in reverse by Avraham, who (vs. 28) looked out toward S'dom and Amorah, and saw the destruction that neither Lot nor his wife were allowed to observe. *Vayashkaf al p'nai s'dom v'amorah, v'al kol p'nai eretz hakikar va'ya'ar, ...*

Lot's daughters—also nameless—also play with sight. They have sex with their father when he is drunk, so that he does not see what is happening.

After a brief sojourn with Avimelech, Avraham and Sarah finally become parents together. Now it is Sarah who sees. . . *Vaterah Sarah et ben-Hagar hamitsrit . . . m'tshachek.* Sarah sees Hagar's son playing.

With Hagar and Ishmael expulsion Hagar's ability to see becomes paramount. In verse 16, when she runs out of water, she chooses not to see Ishmael die. For she said, "Let me not look upon the death of the child . . . *ki amrah, "al areh b'mot hayeled."* She cried to God, who, in turn, "opened her eyes, and she saw a well of water. *Vayifcach alohim et ainehah, vatereh be'er mayim.*"

Finally in ch. 22, the Akedah. On the third day of their journey to the sacrifice, Avraham lifted up his eyes, and saw the place afar off. He left his men behind and carried on with Isaac. The Midrash teaches that the reason the two went on alone, was that only Avraham and Yitzchak were able to see Mt. Moriah.

When Yitzchak asks Avraham about the sacrifice, Avraham answers in words that evoke the first sentence of the parashah. *Elohim yi'reh lo haseh l'olah b'nee.* God will see to the sheep for the burnt offering.

And finally, when Avraham is about to take the knife to Yitzchak, He lifted his eyes, and looked, and behold behind him a ram caught in the thicket. *Vayisah Avraham et ainav*, mountain of the Lord there is vision."

It's probably not surprising that a parashah named *Vayereh* should have so many incidents where sight is prominent. But what do we learn from these many appearances?

Note the comparative lists. Those of little faith cannot see. Lot's tormentors are struck blind; Lot's wife looks when she's not supposed to and turns into a pillar of salt. The nations of Moav and Ammon, traditionally Israel's enemies, are supposedly created from the children Lot begets with his two daughters when he was drunk and did not see.

In contrast, those who believe, see. Avraham somehow knows that the three men are God's messengers. He is the only one who is allowed to view the destruction of S'dom and Amorah. He knows that God will see to the sacrifice. And he catches sight of the ram to be sacrificed instead of Yitzchak.

Sarah sees that Yitzchak and Ishmael cannot grow up together. Hagar sees the well in the desert.

In a word, for the Torah, seeing does not mean believing . . . but believing enables us to see.

Interestingly, the most recent neuroscience research confirms the point this sedrah makes. Dr. V. S. Ramachandran, in his book *Phantoms of the Brain*, gave convincing neurobiological evidence that what we see is a creation of our own minds, a "reliable—but not always accurate—representation of what exists in the world." Or, as a *New York Times* article put it, scientists "are learning that much of human perception is based not on information flowing into the brain from the outside world but what the brain, based on previous experience, expects to happen next."

An interesting experiment showing how peoples' expectations lead to belief was described last year. Doctors in Texas reported that patients who thought they were given arthroscopic surgery on their knees, because they had been anaesthetized and had three little cuts made in their knee, acknowledged the same amount of pain relief two years after the surgery as those who had

had the real operation. They expected that they were going to be helped, and therefore, they were. Their brains had been programmed to expect results.

So too may we be programmed. May we be blessed by God and have our eyes opened so that we also may be able to see what needs to be seen. May we, like Rabbi Zaiman, see God's work in our daily lives.

Fredelle Zaiman Spiegel is a member of the Jewish Studies faculty at UCLA and a psychoanalyst in private practice. Most important, she is Rabbi Zaiman's sister. Steven L. Spiegel is a professor of political science at UCLA and a well-known scholar on Israel and the Middle East. He considers himself a member of the Zaiman clan.

Chayye Sarah
Robyn Perlin

It's the climactic moment of the story. He has laid out his hopes and dreams. Down to the last detail, he has prayed for a very specific set of events to occur. And, down to the last exact same detail, his prayer has become a reality. All that he wished and hoped for has come true, right before his very eyes. And what, then, is his reaction – glee, joy, gratitude, thanks? None of these. At the very moment that he has seen his prayer realized, he waits, wondering whether, in fact, God has actually made his hopes come true.

"He," in this case, is Avraham's most trusted servant, nameless in this Torah text. The prayer? The very specific chain of events that the servant requested from God as a sign indicating the right woman to choose as a bride for Avraham's son Isaac. The servant has been sent back to the land of Avraham's family to make this all-important choice. Just before he enters the city, the servant offers a detail-laden prayer to God for Divine assistance in his choice:

> "Let it be that the girl to whom I say, Please, tip over your pitcher that I may drink' and she will say 'Drink, and I will also water your camels,' will be the one whom You have determined for your servant, Isaac." (Genesis 24:14)

The servant has asked for an unmistakable sign from Heaven by requesting a specific course of action, accompanied by dialogue, for the chosen woman to complete. The narration builds on the suspense of this unique request by continuing,

> He had not yet finished speaking, and behold Rivkah came out. . . . The servant ran toward her and said, "Please let me sip a little water from your pitcher." She

15

said, "Drink, my master," and she quickly lowered her
pitcher to her hand and let him drink. When she had
finished giving him to drink, she said, "I will also draw
water for your camels, until they will have finished
drinking." (Genesis 24:15-19)

Nothing could be more unmistakable. A sign was requested, with specific details to indicate fulfillment. Immediately, those specifics occurred. That's it, simply put, and should be the end of the story. Yet that one line jumps out: after all of this, the servant is still unsure. As the text next tells us, "the man, wondering at her, remained silent, waiting to determine whether God had made his mission successful or not." (24:21)

How could the servant, most trusted of Avraham, who had presumably learned enough from his master to follow his example of faith in God, still wonder about God's response? Was this what it appears to be on the surface—an utter lack of faith in God? At the very least, the servant should not have ignored the logical sequence of events, as told to us by the text. The immediately sequential placement of the three parts shows the rapidity of events; the servant prays for a sign, that sign occurs even before he has finished speaking, and then he immediately becomes dumbstruck. Why is the servant unable to accept the actualization of the very hope that he just expressed?

Perhaps one possible answer to this question will help explain the servant, not as a doubter of God, but as a doubter of human nature and as a doubter of his own self-worth. Rather than showing his lack of trust in God (despite his obvious hesitancy in the face of overwhelming evidence that, in fact, his mission was clearly successful), the servant's hesitancy can show us something about human nature and our relationship with God. The servant's actions were not an indication of doubt in God, but rather were an indication of doubt in the possibility of utter human kindness and of doubt in his own worthiness to have his prayer answered. The servant trusts God. It is human nature that causes the servant to pause, to hesitate, to express doubt.

We know that the servant has had experience in a land where strangers are not treated kindly. His master's family's experience in Sodom was surely not unknown to him, and now he was traveling to a totally foreign land, not knowing what to expect. His request, that a woman be at the well who would show him and his animals hospitality and kindness, was a request for a prospective bride with her own sense of human compassion. The fact that he was "astonished and shocked" (as Rashi explains the meaning of the word "mishta'eh" or "wondering") shows both the depth of Rivka's kindness, towards man and animal, as well as the depth of the servant's disbelief that such a kind person could actually exist. In fact, Or HaHayim explains that the servant's hesitancy showed that he didn't even believe that Rivka would follow through on her own words.

For Or HaHayim, the servant's silent hesitation was his way of waiting to see if Rivka actually fulfilled her own promise to water the camels "until they will have finished drinking." Since the servant's own prayer only asked for a girl who would give his camels some water to drink, the arrival of a girl offering to bring his camels water until they had their fill, was mind-boggling. Not only was the servant astonished at Rivka's straightforward act of hospitality, but his doubt in humanity was such that he couldn't bring himself to believe that she would honestly fulfill her promise. It is humanity, and its level of compassion, hospitality and trustworthiness, that the servant doubts, not God.

The servant's astonishment and hesitancy can be attributed even further to a natural, human understanding of the world. Despite all of the times that we pray, despite all of the requests we may make of God, something nags away at us when it seems as though our wishes might actually be granted. The servant, just like many of us, needed "just one more sign" that what he was experiencing was not some bizarre coincidence, but was, in fact, a sign from God. Each of us seeks this clarification in life. If we can

17

know that it wasn't simply fate, or coincidence, or luck, that made something occur in our favor, but that somehow it was part of a Divine plan, then we can be more assured of our own personal self-worth. For why would I be part of God's plan if God didn't see some positive purpose to my life and my request? Why would God listen to me if I were unworthy? The servant's hesitation may simply express his own self-doubt, desperately wanting to believe that God heard his prayer and that God chose to answer his prayer definitively. Confirmation of such a conclusion—that God heard what I said and deemed it worthy enough of a response—is something that anyone who prays could only hope for. Avraham's servant, in this case, had the opportunity to receive such a confirmation.

Tradition tells us that every word in Torah has a purpose. How much more so does every person introduced to us by Torah have a purpose. Perhaps the servant's purpose is to be a reflection of ourselves, complete with all of our natural human tendencies towards doubt, disbelief, and self-questioning. Perhaps, however, the servant's acceptance that he was, in fact, worthy of God's hearing his prayer and responding can provide us with a reflection, not of the doubting creatures that we might be, but of the faithful, trusting people that we can become.

Robyn Perlin is assistant director of Rosenbloom Religious School at Chizuk Amuno Congregation. Working and learning with Rabbi Joel Zaiman at Chizuk Amuno is truly a once-in-a-lifetime experience.

Toledot
Rebecca Hoffman

Parashat Toledot introduces a form of brachah, blessing, that does not previously appear in the Torah. In Parashat Bereshit, having created man and woman, God blesses Adam and Eve, giving them a charge to fill the earth. Here, in Parashat Toledot, we find a person blessing another person for the first time.

In this case, Isaac blesses his son Jacob, despite the fact that Jacob was not the first born, and therefore not the son who traditionally would have been entitled to the blessing. Jacob, with the help of his mother, Rebecca, tricks his father by dressing in fur to mimic the hairy skin of Esau. There is much commentary that questions whether or not Isaac knew which son entered his tent for the blessing. The Torah claims that Isaac was blind at the time and was therefore unaware that the wrong son was in the tent. Another explanation suggests that Jacob was the more deserving son, and therefore Isaac knowingly gave the brachah to the more deserving of his two sons.

A more important question, perhaps, may be to ask about the overall importance of this brachah. Could Isaac have offered two of these special blessings? Why was Rebecca so intent on obtaining this brachah for her more favored son? And, of course, is a brachah obtained through deceptive means still a valid brachah? While this essay will not delve into the plot-related questions, a greater understanding of this parashah comes from an explanation of brachot within the context of the Bible and Judaism.

Blessings accompany almost every action of the Jewish people. Jews bless food, nature, our bodies, God, and one another. Blessing is central to nearly all religious rituals and as is found within much of Jewish liturgy. The idea of brachot emerges early in the Bible as God blesses Adam and Eve, saying, "Be fruitful and multiply, fill the earth and master it . . . " (Gen. 1:28). Several types of brachot emerge in the Bible, and then later, in the

Rabbinic writings, eventually taking the form of the contemporary blessing.

Joel Grishaver, in his book, *And You Shall Be a Blessing*, explores blessing according to the model developed by Abravanel, a 15th century Spanish Bible commentator. Abravanel suggests that in the Biblical context, brachot contain three distinct meanings. One form of brachah pertains to God's gifts to people. In other words, God grants a human being a charge or role to fill. The example of God blessing Adam and Eve, as described above, fits into this first form. The second is a reverse of the first, as people bless God. This form is rather rare in the biblical context, but is seen much more often in the structured rabbinic brachot that are common with ritual today. The third form of brachot, explains Abravanel, is of people blessing other people.

A traditional Jewish assumption is that when God says something, it will happen. A notable example is of God's command, "let there be light," and the world lit up. To consider God's blessings of people valid, one must assume that what God says *will* happen, actually *does* happen. When God blesses Adam and Eve saying, "Be fruitful and multiply," God is making a commitment to Adam and Eve. The proliferation of humankind is a fulfillment of God's commitment to the people, and may also be understood as a sign of gratitude from Adam and Eve. They receive their blessings from God and fulfill them, in a way praising God for blessing them. According to Abravanel, this blessing or commitment from God comes with an obligation on the part of the human to show gratitude. Abram is blessed by God, and he builds an altar to show his gratitude. Blessings by God prompt mortals to engage in active relationships with God.

Brachot in which people verbally bless God are rarer in the Biblical text. Most of the biblical characters, when they express gratitude to God, do so in the form of sacrifice. When these individuals do verbally address God it is in the form of a petition, but not blessing. King David, in a rare instance in Chronicles I, publicly blesses God as he hands the kingdom over to Solomon.

This brachah praises God and shows that brachot are spontaneous reactions to gifts that we receive from God.

Brachot can be public or private assertions of gratitude. The Rabbis used the form that David used *("baruch-atah-adonai"* formula) to create the model for brachot that we have today. The brachah that David says is important in showing that although the Rabbis formalized brachot, they were meant to be spontaneous assertions of gratitude towards God.

Some may believe that the formalizing of brachot removes the spontaneity that makes the brachah special. On the other hand, the formal system of brachot makes it easier to have a relationship with God. If there are prescribed words to show appreciation at certain times, then one does not need to have a particularly spiritual moment of thanksgiving in order to say a brachah. In this manner, we are constantly aware of our surroundings and waiting to notice a moment in which a brachah is appropriate. Thus, brachot raise our awareness of our surroundings and force us to recognize that everything around us comes from God. Hamotzi, the familiar blessing for bread, is similar to David's blessing of God. Just as David shows gratitude to God, we show a like gratitude to God for providing us with the food that sustains us. Again, we learn that brachot are a way to maintain an active relationship with God.

Finally, Abravanel explores biblical brachot between people, a form most commonly seen when patriarchs bless their sons. Isn't it slightly presumptuous to assume that people, like God, can bestow a blessing upon others? One of Grishaver's explanations of this final form of blessings is that the "blessor" can only invoke God's help in bringing the blessing to fruition. Therefore, when Isaac blesses Jacob, Isaac is in fact asking God to help his son fulfill the sentiments expressed in the blessing. God's role in human blessing remains pervasive.

The Midrash Tanhuma suggests another interpretation to ease the theological questions that arise when people bless other people. This idea is that God stands or dwells with the people as they offer the blessing, therefore God is a part of the blessing. When human beings bless one another, they are not guaranteed a result, as might be assumed were God to directly bless the individual. Therefore, it is up to the recipient to create an enhanced relationship with God in order for that blessing to be fulfilled. These blessings require the assistance of God.

Grishaver claims that "it is through brachot that ordinary experiences are raised to spiritual encounters." We learn from the biblical models that God is the necessary link in blessings. Each example shows that an enhanced relationship with God is created through the recitation or fulfillment of brachot. But these biblical experiences are hardly "ordinary" in today's terms. While we may believe that God has blessed us with good health, and success, we do not see God using words to bless us. We therefore assume that we are charged with the actualization of God's non-verbal blessing.

Even more ordinary are the experiences of eating, seeing wonders of nature, and the complex workings of our bodies. There are brachot that accompany each of these activities so that the things that we do every day without even thinking become holy. The Talmud teaches that if we do not say a bracha in each appropriate moment, we are stealing from God. To return to the questions posed earlier, perhaps Isaac could have offered a blessing for each of his sons. Perhaps he knew that Esau was incapable of fulfilling the same type of charge as his younger brother, Jacob, and therefore, he only offered one of these blessings. It would have been unfair of Isaac to initiate Esau into a relationship with God that Esau could not handle. Rebecca may have known that her favored son was more deserving of Isaac's blessing and she was therefore willing to be deceptive so that Jacob would be the one to enter into this relationship with God.

Finally, is a brachah obtained through deceptive means still valid? Well, yes. If the recipient takes the responsibility seriously and is able to live up to the expectations laid out in the brachah, then the brachah is valid. The importance is not in the receiving of the blessing, but (the reciter's response to it) in the lifestyle and actions that accompany it. It is our responsibility to maintain a relationship with God by noticing the gifts with which we are blessed. Isaac's blessing to Jacob, a hope for the Kingship of Israel, and a continuation of the covenant with Abraham, is an expression of the third category of blessing. Isaac hopes that God will take an active role in carrying out the brachah. Jacob's initiation into an active relationship with God commences with this blessing.

Rebecca Hoffman is a graduate of the Krieger Schechter Day School of Chizuk Amuno Congregation. She is a senior in the Joint Program with List College of the Jewish Theological Seminary and Columbia University majoring in Modern Jewish Studies and Anthropology, and points to Rabbi Zaiman as a major Jewish influence in her life.

Vayyetze
Drs. Gail Zaiman Dorph & Sheldon Dorph: A Conversation

GZD: This *parashah* has such an elegant literary structure. In studying it this time I noticed that three elements appear at its beginning and end, almost like bookends. You remember the *parashah* begins with Jacob's dream of angels going up and down a ladder. Well, it ends with angels and a dream too. In fact, the same Hebrew roots, *paga* (hit upon or encountered) and *makom* (a place) are used to describe these two meetings (26: 11, 32:1). At the end of the dream, Jacob erects an altar or mound of stones, pours oil on it, and names the place, *Beit El*--the house of God (26:28). At the end of the parashah, he again erects a mound of stones, pours oil on it, declares the place *Beit Elohim*-the house of God, and he names it *Mahanaim*, camp of God (32:2). The third element is making a covenant. At the beginning of the *parashah*, Jacob enters into a covenant with God (26:13-22) and at the end of the *parashah*, he enters into a covenant with Laban (31:44-53). Angels, stone monuments, covenantal agreements.

SD: You know, there are also words that repeat. Two in particular that I think we should look at more carefully are *V'hinei* - And Behold and *Makom*, which means both Place and God. You know how we were taught that repeating words is a signal of something significant. It's as though they say: "follow me for the secret message." Let's start with *V'hinei*.

GZD: At the beginning of the *parashah*, *V'hinei* appears four times in the first twelve verses. The first three are when Jacob's dream begins and the fourth, when God speaks to him.
- *V'hinei sulam mutzav artza*—and behold, a ladder set into the ground (28:12)
- *V'hinei malakhim olim v'yordim*—and behold, angels are going up and coming down (28:12)

- *V'hinei Adonai nitzav alav*—and behold, God standing on it(28:13)

Why do you think it says, *V'hinei* three different times? Wouldn't once have been enough?

SD: Perhaps, each *V'hinei* signifies a stage in Jacob's growing understanding that this dream is something very special and unusual. Maybe, without all three, he actually could not understand that this is God speaking to him.

GZD: Maybe the event was so wondrous that it couldn't be taken in at one time. It's as though each of these perceptions was its own event. Each required its own *V'hinei*.

SD: Maybe *V'hinei* is the text's way of expressing surprise or astonishment, like WOW!

GZD: The fourth time that the word *V'hinei* is used, it doesn't seem to fit any of these explanations, though it doesn't seem to signal surprise or discernment of God's presence. When God says, *V'hinei Anokhi Imakh*-and behold I will be with you and watch over you—this is a statement of promise, not of surprise.

SD: But maybe it is also a statement of surprise, the biggest one. Maybe God is saying: "You deceiver, you tent dweller, afraid of this place. Well surprise, I'm still here. You can't run away."

GZD: That sounds kind of negative. Maybe God makes this promise to Jacob, because through his openness to experiencing the dream, he becomes a person who can experience God and therefore merits God's promise.

SD: Let's look at the word *Makom* and see what it adds to the equation. After all, one of the meanings of the word is God—The Place.

GZD: *Makom* also repeats many times. It is mentioned three times in verse 11: *Vayifga b'makom*—and he came upon the place; *Vayikakh me-avnei hamakom*-and he took from the stones of the place; *Vayishkav bamakom*-and he lay down in the place. And then it is mentioned three more times toward the end of the chapter. In v. 16, *Akhen yesh Adonai bamakom*, surely God is in this place. Then in v. 17, *Mah nora hamakom*-how awesome is this place. And finally, in v. 19, *Vayyikra et shem hamakom Beit-El*—and he called the name of the place the House of God.

SD: *Makom* also reappears at the very end of the parashah, when Jacob encounters angels for the second time. Perhaps one's ability to experience and take in the surprise is one of the ways in which God manifests God's presence in the world. Perhaps the message here is that God is always in the place. But we could miss The Place, miss The Presence!

GZD: I think the way Chapter 29 begins supports your idea. Immediately after the dream and the covenant (and all the *V'hinei*'s and *Makom*s) this chapter picks up the story with the words: *Vayisa raglav Vayelekh. Vayaar V'hinei*—Jacob lifts up his legs, he goes, he sees and again: *V'hinei*-and behold. I am struck by the expression "he lifts up his legs." We say, "pick up your feet" to mean get a move on. But I don't think we find this expression in the Torah. When I looked it up in the Concordance, it seems as though this may be the only time we see the expression "lift up his legs" in the Bible. And then to be followed by "and he saw" is really weird. We read in the Torah about lifting one's eyes and seeing, lifting one's voice and crying, but one does not lift one's legs and see. It is as though his dream has changed the way in which he experiences the world. My sense is that the text is trying to teach us that after experiencing God, Jacob walks differently, experiences differently. He is able to see. And look at what he sees!

SD: Three more *V'hinei's*

- *V'hinei*—and behold, a well in the field. (29:2)
- *V'hinei*—and behold three flocks of sheep are lying around it. (29:2)
- *V'hinei*—Rachel, the daughter of Laban is coming with a flock of sheep. (29:6)

GZD: It is as though this sequence of *V'hinei's* signals the beginning of the fulfillment of God's promise at the end of the dream sequence. He was going to *Haran* to meet his mother's family and already at the well, at the gateway of the city, his path is smoothed. And his success is signalled in the word *V'hinei.*

SD: That's very nice, but do you see where the next *V'hinei* appears?

GZD: Wow! It's where he discovers that he married Leah and not Rachel. *V'hinei*-and behold, she was Leah (29:25). But then . . . that doesn't fit with my theory.

SD: Why do you say that? Maybe it was God's will that he should marry Leah. After all, Rachel was at first barren and then only bore two children. God, after all, needs to fulfill God's promise that Jacob's descendants will be as numerous as the dust of the earth (28:14). This could actually be a good example of how the word *V'hinei* is working to lead us through this account, signaling God's presence and Jacob's growing awareness of It.

GZD: *V'hinei* appears one more time in this *parashah*-at the end when Laban and Jacob make a covenant to live in peace with each other. In this case, there also is a mound of stones upon which oil is poured and a covenant made. Laban says: *Hinei*—the mound, *V'hinei hamatzevah*—the pillar (31:51). The mound and the pillar bear witness to their covenantal agreement to live in peace with each other, each in his own territory.

SD: So, it seems that every *V'hinei* is a symbol of God's promise and presence in the story-and of the unexpected! Here we see *V'hinei* indicate the transformation of Laban from an angry father-in-law into a covenantal ally.

GZD: Every *V'hinei* also seems to represents some combination of God's promise to Jacob and Jacob's vow to God. Think about it: What does Jacob actually need for the covenant to be fulfilled?
- *V'hinei sulam* (the ladder)—representing the ability to experience God's presence in the world
- *V'hinei Rahel*—the love of a woman
- *V'hinei Leah*—many children to carry out God's promise
- *V'hinei matzevah* (the monument)—symbolizing the agreements with people that allow for peaceful coexistence.

This *parashah* uses repeating words and particularly the word *V'hinei* to track Jacob's spiritual journey. We see the process of the transformation of Jacob in his growing awareness of the presence of God in his life. It is probably not obvious to Jacob what is happening. He is caught up in the daily-ness of his lived life. The literary device: *V'hinei* is a signal to the reader. We are to notice that Jacob's life is taking place on two planes, that which is visible to the naked eye and that which is invisible, but only felt. *V'hinei* is Jacob's signal too. For him it is not a literary device, it represents surprise/awareness.

SD: When we started this investigation it seemed to me that *V'hinei* was a very strange word to have as a repeating word. I asked myself, what could the interjection "and behold" signify. I now think that *V'hinei* launches *Hineni*—here I am. When speaking with Rachel and Leah, Jacob uses the word "*Hineni*—here I am!" to describe his response to his encounter with God (31:11). *Hineni* is a combination of *Hinei* and *Ani*—behold and I. It is the special word that the Bible uses to signify one's total presence in the encounter with the Divine. Thus, the awareness represented by *V'hinei* is the necessary precondition for responding *Hineni*.

GZD: That's really nice. This *parashah* holds a message for each of us. *V'hinei*! Notice the things in your life that surprise you! They are important hints. They may signal the presence of God in the world. And if you keep your dreams, your eyes, your footsteps "tuned" in, these surprises may be opportunities to encounter the Divine. And *Hineni*! Noticing is insufficient. Be like Jacob—respond with your whole self.

SD: On a final note, it strikes me that this is a wonderful *parashah* to be commenting about in a volume honoring your brother. In my mind, Joel is a certain kind of Jewish leader and dreamer. First, he is like the ladder in Jacob's dream—firmly rooted on the ground (*V'hinei sulam mutzav artzah*) and yet he possesses a vision that requires real reaching (*v'rosho magia hashamaymah*). Second, he not only has a keen awareness, *V'hinei*, of God's presence in the world, but he responds *Hineni* by sharing it artfully with all of us.

Gail Zaiman Dorph is the senior education officer of the Mandel Foundation in New York and the director of its Teacher Educator Institute. She has a doctorate in Jewish education from JTS. (She is also Rabbi Zaiman's sister).

Sheldon Dorph is the national director of the Ramah Camps. He holds rabbinic ordination from JTS and a doctorate in education from Columbia Teachers College. He has had the privilege of being involved in Chizuk Amuno's mission statement and strategic planning processes.

Vayyishlach
Ellen Friedman

Parashat Vayishlach, Genesis 32:4-36:43, is best known for the passage in which Jacob wrestles by night with a mysterious stranger on the bank of a river, acquiring a limp and a new name, Yisrael. The event that dominates the opening chapters of the parashah, however, is Jacob's reunion with his brother Esau, whose murderous rage had forced Jacob to flee to Haran some 20 years earlier. This reunion is fraught with tension for Jacob, who does not know, even up to the moment of their encounter, if Esau still intends to kill him.

Yet, when the two brothers finally meet, Esau embraces Jacob in tears, and Jacob says to Esau, "To see your face is like seeing the face of God (Genesis 33:10)." What does Jacob mean by this comparison, and upon what knowledge or experience is it based? The answer is contained within the parashah, in which images of faces recur over and over.

The name of the parashah, "Vayishlach," means, "he sent," because Jacob's first action, upon nearing Esau's territory, was to send messengers ahead with humble greetings for Esau. "To my lord Esau, thus says your servant Jacob: with Laban I have sojourned and tarried until now; I have cattle, asses, sheep, and male and female slaves; and I send this message to my lord in order to find favor *in your eyes* (Genesis 32 5-6)." When the messengers return, they inform Jacob that Esau is already en route to meet him, accompanied by 400 men.

Upon hearing this news, Jacob is understandably frightened. He takes three separate actions in response to the perceived threat, employing military strategy, faith in God and human psychology. First, he prepares for the possibility of battle by dividing his people and animals into two camps, so that if Esau attacks one camp, the other may have a chance of escaping.

Second, Jacob prays, reminding God of the promise made

at Beth El that Jacob would become a great nation and inherit the land, and imploring God to deliver him and his children from the hand of Esau. Finally, Jacob selects animals from his flocks, and sends them ahead as gifts for Esau. In a rare moment of omniscient Biblical narrative, we are told what Jacob is thinking: "If I appease him with gifts in advance and then face him, maybe he will show me favor (Genesis 32:21)." Due to the idiosyncrasies of the Hebrew syntax, however, a literal translation of this verse would read, "Let me cover up his *face* with the present that goes before my *face*; afterwards I shall see his *face* and perhaps he will lift up my *face*."

Later that night, on the banks of the river Jabbok, Jacob wrestles the mysterious being, variously interpreted to represent one of the river-demons that populate Middle Eastern folk tales, an angel (Esau's guardian angel, according to Rashi), or Jacob's own alter-ego. After Jacob has withstood the attack and has received a new name in response to his demand for a blessing, he names the spot where he wrestled P'niel, or *"face* of God," because, he says, "I have seen God *face to face*, yet my life has been preserved.(Genesis 32:31)." Jacob's statement acknowledges the danger inherent in seeing God's "face." Compare, for example, Exodus 33:20: "You cannot see My face, for man cannot see Me and live."

According to the 20th century philosopher Emmanuel Levinas, human faces have great significance. "The face is an irreducible mode in which being can present itself in its identity (Emmanuel Levinas, "Ethics and Spirit," in Difficult Freedom: Essays on Judaism, Page 8)." To look at a face is to acknowledge the "otherness" of another being without seeking to possess or to negate it. "In reality," says Levinas, "murder is possible, but it is possible only when one has not looked the Other in the face." Perhaps as a result of confidence gained through his nocturnal struggle, Jacob is enabled to expose his face, his inviolable identity, to Esau in a way that makes murder an impossibility.

Immediately after Jacob's adversary has taken leave, Jacob sees Esau approaching. Jacob has just been renamed Yisrael, "for you have striven with God and with man, and have prevailed," but in this moment of crisis Jacob chooses to rely, not on strength or on strategy, but on his faith in God and in human nature. He arranges his entourage with the concubines and their children in front, Leah and her children next, and Rachel and Joseph behind. He himself goes in front of them all, bowing to the ground seven times as he approaches his brother.

Some commentators criticize Jacob for prostrating himself before Esau, saying that a righteous man such as Jacob should not have shown humility to such a wicked man as Esau, whose descendants are said to include Amalek and Haman, traditional enemies of the Jewish people. Other commentators justify Jacob's behavior on diplomatic grounds. Sforno, the 15th century Italian philosopher, says that Jacob was wise to bend like a reed, instead of trying to stand tall like a cedar and risking being uprooted.

Bowing, however, is more than a token of respect. A bow is a submissive gesture; it puts one in a position of great vulnerability and therefore implies a measure of trust. With his forehead to the ground, Jacob could not see whether Esau was raising his sword or fitting an arrow to the bowstring. Jacob's bowing reveals a degree of faith and trust that is stronger than the natural doubt and fear indicated by his previous actions. To bow before Esau, Jacob had to have faith that God would fulfill His promise of nationhood and blessing, despite the precarious position in which Jacob now found himself.

Jacob also had to have faith in Esau, trusting that that which was God-like and forgiving in Esau's nature would prevail over that which was jealous and vengeful. We do not know what influenced Esau's decision. It may have been the gifts, or the subservient tone of Jacob's messages, but perhaps it was precisely Jacob's display of trust that caused Esau to forego the impulse to seek revenge and to "lift up Jacob's face" with brotherly affection.

In the words of Levinas, when Esau looks into Jacob's face, he must acknowledge the impossibility of murder. For Jacob, surviving the encounter with Esau is tantamount to surviving the danger of an encounter with a divine being, and looking into Esau's face and seeing forgiveness is indeed like seeing the face of God.

Ellen Friedman studies with Rabbi Zaiman and is a candidate for a Masters in Jewish Education at Baltimore Hebrew University. She teaches in the Rosenbloom Religious School of Chizuk Amuno Congregation and at the Krieger Schechter Day School.

Vayyeshev
Harriet Helfand

Alone, abandoned, you have been betrayed by those whom you have trusted. You have been left to rot in a pit, condemned for a crime you cannot comprehend.

Rejected by your patron, you endure, forgotten. Your status in society has evaporated at your feet; you are a nobody, nowhere.

Yet, you cannot remain in this condition. You are too clever, too daring, too desperate, so convinced of the rightness of what you must do that you know that you are directed by God. The risk of failure is immense, the consequences potentially lethal, yet you must act, for the fate of the world depends on what you do.

Parashat Vayeshev presents two stories, seemingly disconnected, one of Joseph and one of Tamar, individuals who, when confronted with hardship, danger and degradation, are able to make the right choices, not only to extract themselves from ruin, but to do it in such a way as to fulfill God's plan for themselves and the people Israel. By navigating the tension between restraint and risk and earning God's redemption through their bold, courageous acts, Joseph and Tamar are forever linked in Torah as mirrors of righteousness.

Twice in the parashah Joseph finds himself thrust into a pit of degradation and ignominy. The first time, it is his jealous brothers who literally fling him into a pit and abandon him in the wilderness, where he is later sold into slavery and brought down to Egypt. Later in the story Joseph again suffers when he is falsely accused of accosting the wife of Potiphar, his Egyptian master. Anguished and angered, Potiphar casts him into prison, another pit, where Joseph will languish for many years until his God given ability to interpret dreams elevates him to a position in Pharaoh's court.

Tamar, too, has been doubly abandoned and banished to the pit of familial displacement and scorn. Left a childless widow by two of Judah's sons, Er and Onan, Tamar is shunted off to her father's house when Judah refuses to give her to his third son, Shelah, out of fear. Failing to uphold his obligation in the institution of Yibbum, or levirate marriage, Judah sentences Tamar to a social netherworld, where she can neither remarry nor honorably bear a child. Tamar's troubles continue when Judah hears of her subsequent pregnancy and cooly orders her to be burned. It is only her discretion and exquisite timing that saves Tamar from this disaster and ensures her role in the unfolding of God's design.

Joseph was no stranger to trouble—between the fury of his brothers and the rage of Potiphar's rejected wife it almost seems as if he couldn't avoid a dangerous situation even if he tried. By the time he is Potiphar's slave, though, Joseph has learned that even in Egypt, he is not alone. In the beginning of the parashah the text is silent as to God's role in the story. However, as Joseph is brought down to Egypt we are told, "the Lord was with Joseph" (Gen.39:2) The Lord is mentioned four more times in rapid succession in the verses that follow (Gen.39:3,5).

It is after the inclusion of God's presence in the story that Joseph faces his greatest challenge, the temptation of Potiphar's wife. Joseph refuses, begging her to understand, "how could I do this most wicked thing, and sin before God" (Gen. 39:9). Day after day, she continues to entreat, but Joseph still resists. Finally, on the fateful day when they are alone, she makes a final reckless move, seizing Joseph by his garment. Alarmed, Joseph flees, leaving his wrap in the hands of Potiphar's wife.

According to Rashi, there is a dispute in the Talmud as to whether the phrase "Laasot melachto," (to do his work) (Gen. 39:11) has the plain meaning of house-work, or whether it connotes an intention of Joseph to accept the offer of Potiphar's wife to have sexual relations. Under this theory, in Sotah 36b, it was a vision of Jacob, his father, that strenghened Joseph's nearly broken resolve. Similarly, in Genesis Rabbah 87:7,8, we are told that upon seeing the image of Jacob, Joseph's desire departed, prompting him to flee.

Perhaps it was the grabbing of the garment that reminded Joseph of Jacob's gift of the ornamented coat in Gen.37: 3, sparking Joseph's vision of his father. Genesis Rabbah cites Gen. 49:24, Jacob's blessing of Joseph, in which Jacob claims, " yet his bow stayed taut " through God's help. R. Samuel plays on this line and on the phrase in our story in Gen.39: 11" v'ayn ish " (there was no man) in the house, to suggest that Joseph intended to sin but that his "bow," was dysfunctional, thus rendering him impotent. R. Isaac refers to the next phrase in Jacob's blessing "and his arms were made supple," changing the word "vayafozu" (made supple) to "vayafutzu"(scattered), and the word "zero'e"(the arms of) to "zar'o" (his seed), to connote an emission by Joseph, and the scattering of his seed through his fingers. This image ironically contrasts with Onan, who is killed for spilling the seed he owes to Tamar, preventing her from perpetuating his brother's name.

Here, the "Rock of Israel," metaphorically the visage of Jacob, has interrupted completion of the deed. Surely the vision of his father, whose reputation has shifted from being a deceiver and conniver to that of a respected elder could have stunned Joseph into outright refusal or the inability to consummate the act, or prompted a willful dispersal of his genetic treasure. However he arrived at this decision, Joseph made the right choice, to reject the wanton wife of Potiphar and to risk his safety and position in the world.

The sages also place great emphasis on the fact that in the passage where Joseph is physically grabbed by Potiphar's wife, the word "fled," "yanas," is used four times. This is equated to Psalm 114, verse 3, "The sea saw them and fled," referring to the bones of Joseph, which the Israelites carried out of Egypt during the Exodus. Here, the implication is that by fleeing, Joseph overcame his nature, thus imparting to his bones the power to suspend the nature of the sea; that in the merit of the one who fled and did not succumb to passion, the sea suspended its nature and split, saving Israel.

Tamar, also driven to desperation, devises her own scheme to pursue justice. Hearing that the newly widowed Judah will be traveling to Timnah, Tamar stations herself at a place mentioned only here in Torah, "Petach Enaim," masquerading as a harlot, waiting for Judah to come and be enticed.

The name, 'Petach Enaim,' literally translated as "opening of eyes," has several connotations. One, in Genesis Rabbah 85:7, describes that at this place, Tamar "lifted up her eyes to the gate (opening) (petach) to which all eyes (enaim) are directed (to God, who is open to receive prayer), and prayed: 'May it be thy will that I do not leave this house with naught.'" It is also ironic that Judah lived with Tamar in his household, yet may have paid her so little attention that he fails, with his eyes, to recognize her.

The midrash goes on to describe God's role in this liaison. Genesis Rabbah continues in 85:8, "He (Judah) wished to go on (past Tamar), but the Holy One, blessed be He, made the angel who is in charge of desire appear before him, and he said to him: 'Whither goest thou, Judah? Whence are kings to arise, whence are redeemers to arise?'," after which "he turned unto her" (Gen.38:16),"despite himself and against his wish."

Tamar is canny, and extracts from Judah a price, and therefore evidences of their encounter. All of the items which she is either promised or receives, the kid, the seal, the cord and the staff, either harken to past events (the brother's deception of Jacob by the blood of a kid), or allude to the future royalty of Judah's descendants. Tamar's boldness succeeds: the life in her womb fulfills the levirate obligation. Now she must save herself and the product of their union from the execution ordered by Judah, who is unaware of his role in her pregnancy.

Summoning all of her courage, Tamar plays her last card, and subtly confronts Judah with his missing goods, "By the man whose these are, I am with child" (Gen.38:25). Tamar implores, "Haker na," echoing the brother's own words to Jacob as they held up Joseph's bloody coat, "examine these, whose seal and cord and staff are these?"

Genesis Rabbah suggests Judah must now lift up his eyes, and although his inclination was to deny responsibility, Tamar demands "acknowledge thy Creator in these, for they are thine and thy Creator's." Thus instructed, Judah swallows his pride and shame, and chastened, confesses his deeds, acknowleging "Tzadekah mimmeni," "She is more in the right (righteous) than I" (Gen.38:26).

This phrase is Tamar's anchor, her affirmation. Genesis Rabbah interprets the phrase, "mimmeni" (than I), as also meaning "through me," as if God, Himself, had finished Judah's proclamation, declaring "Through Me (mimmeni), did these things occur." Rashi confirms this notion, that in His completion of Judah's statement, God revealed that all of the events that had transpired were divinely propelled.

Yet God alone could not ensure that Joseph and Tamar would transcend the sad fate that others had decreed for them. Each had to act decisively, strengthened by their faith in God, undeterred by risk and conquering the impulses and passions that could have kept them from their destiny.

How easy it would have been for Joseph to give in to his desire, to turn his back on the God who had allowed him to be sold as a slave. How understandable it would have been for Tamar to have resigned herself to the cruel fate imposed on her by Judah and their culture. How utterly human it would have been to succumb to the passions and fears that beset their hearts and narrowed their lives.

Yet Joseph and Tamar resisted, Tamar by what she did, and Joseph by what he didn't do. Each refused to submit to the degradation inflicted by others or to the limitation that personal revenge or complacency would have imposed on their lives. Each clearly understood their precarious situations and preserved their own dignity as well as the dignity of their oppressors. Driven by God's inspiration, each acted decisively, mastering their inclinations and risking their lives, for their own sake and for God's.

For these efforts, Joseph and Tamar have been rewarded with the distinction of being remembered as righteous or tzaddik. Genesis Rabbah 34:1 tells us "The wicked- they are under control of their hearts. But the righteous-they have their hearts under their control." The Rabbis call Joseph, who so achingly restrained his passion, Joseph ha Tzaddik, Joseph the righteous one, who not only resisted temptation, but who also later was able to forgive his brothers, acknowledging "it was not you who sent me here, but God" (Gen. 45:8) and "although you intended me harm, God intended it for good (Gen. 50:20)." Tamar is specifically described in Torah as Tzadekah, righteous, for her persistence to pursue that which was commanded by God.

A final link between the paths of righteousness followed by Joseph and Tamar can be found in a vision of the Messianic age. Midrash Tehillim 114:2 teaches" . . . the Holy One sows the doings of the righteous and they bear fruit." Tamar's reward and legacy is that she is destined to become a progenitor of the Messiah ben David. Perez, a son of the union of Judah and Tamar, is listed in the book of Ruth as an ancestor of King David, and thus a link in the chain of the dynasty that will produce the Messiah.

Some midrashic sources, however, describe another Messiah, the Messiah ben Joseph, who will descend from the line of Ephraim, the son of Joseph. The Messiah ben Joseph is described as the precursor to the Messiah ben David, and is the one who who will create the material framework of nationhood for the Jews.after which the final Messiah, the Messiah ben David, will arise to herald God's redemption.

Joseph and Tamar, transcending history, live on as mirrored soul mates, vulnerable people, who, when thrust into untenable positions, sought God's guidance, overcame their human frailities, proceeded boldly, and, looking beyond peril, chose what was right. Their behavior is a model for our own. When challenged by adversity, trust in God and seek His guidance, but understand that God expects us to act in ways which, either by what we do, or choose not to do, exemplify righteousness. We are God's partners in the repair of the world, and in order to bring about redemption, it is our obligation to use the gifts that God has granted us, our vision and ingenuity, to take the risks for tzedek that can change the world. May it be that when God's mirror is held up to us, we will all be reflections of righteousness in that world.

Harriet Helfand is an attorney. She is a member of Rabbi Zaiman's Torah class, studies Biblical Hebrew at the Stulman Center for Adult Learning and is a Trustee of Chizuk Amuno Congregation.

Mikketz
Rabbi Gustav Buchdahl

The Talmud refers to a dream as a "delet naul," a sealed door. The key to that door is speech. Perhaps that is what led Sigmund Freud to comment that "the royal road to the knowledge of the unconscious activities of the mind" is the interpretation of those dreams. It is one thing to unlock a door and quite another to open it. What are dreams made of anyway? Anxiety, memory, elation, fantasy. Beneath it all is the desire for survival. Dreams are places where anxiety and necessity meet.

Jacob knew that when he dreamed of angels ascending and descending that ladder with its feet on the ground and its top approaching heaven. Jacob's dream was personal; he had no need to share it with anybody else. Joseph's dreams of the constellations bowing to him and sheaves of corn bowing to him were personal too. He did, however, feel the need to share those dreams with his brothers and his father. Had he known how to contextualize his dreams he might not have aroused the incredulity of his father and the hostility of his siblings. The dreams of Pharaoh's cupbearer and baker emanated from anxiety over their fates. Ostensibly their dreams also had no repercussions beyond their own personal destinies.

The dreams of Pharaoh that introduce Parashat miketz are different. The biblical commentator Malbim understood the difference. "These were dreams by one who was a king over a whole realm." You cannot treat such dreams as though they belonged to a private individual. That was the error of the Egyptian necromancers. In fact, says Malbim, the dreams were a personification of a universal public figure and hence the concern of all of society. (Malbim on Genesis Rabbah 89:7)

Qohelet tells us that "ba hahalom b'rov inyan" "dreams come into being through a proliferation of concerns." Soncino attributed dreams, Pharaoh's included, to an overactive

imagination but there was reality behind the concerns of the
Egyptian monarch. The Midrash equates Pharaoh's dream with
that of Nebuchadnezzer centuries later. The parallels and the
differences are striking. "In the second year of the reign of
Nebuchadnezzer, Nebuchadnezzer had a dream. His spirit was
agitated, yet he was overcome by sleep. The king ordered the
magicians…to be summoned…" His own people can offer no
interpretation. "The mystery was revealed to Daniel in a night
vision; then Daniel blessed the God of heaven." (Daniel II: 19)
An alien Hebrew does for Nebuchadnezzer what Joseph did for
Pharaoh. It is the wisdom of the outsider who can see and
interpret what the natives cannot grasp.

Freud was right. Dreams explore the unconscious and have
their own reality. Elihu puts it distinctly to Job: "God speaks time
and again though man does not perceive it; in a dream, a night
vision, when deep sleep falls on men, while they slumber on their
beds, then He opens men's understanding." (Job: XXXIII: 14, 15,
16a) God never addresses Joseph directly. That does not imply a
failure of communication. It does mean that Joseph had to intuit
the will of God, right and wrong, the nature of the world in which
he lived and what his subconscious was trying to convey through
the medium of his dreams. If that was true of Joseph, it is true of
the rest of us as well. How one processes such information is a
matter of maturity, life experience and learned wisdom.

There is in the whole Joseph narrative and in the whole
Parashat Miketz in particular a fascinating choreography in which
power passes from one character to another. There is a tension
between those who have it, those who need it and those who
exercise it. The protagonists are Pharaoh and Joseph. Pharaoh
possesses the might of Egypt. Joseph possesses Divine intuition.
The usually omnipotent Pharaoh is made vulnerable by his dreams
which he correctly surmises bode ill for Egypt. The debased
foreigner, Joseph, is brought from prison. Eric Lowenthal, in his
book, *The Joseph Narrative in Genesis*, opines: "The Torah is
about to contrast Egyptian wisdom with the true wisdom inspired

by God." An incredulous Pharaoh tries to keep control. "About you I have heard" he tells Joseph, "You listen to a dream and make it interpret itself." (Genesis XLI: 15) Joseph responds: "It is not I. May God answer for Pharaoh's welfare." (Genesis XLI: 16) The shift in power is subtle but potent. The Hebrew God will make Pharaoh dependent on Joseph. Shakespeare would have understood Pharaoh. Does not Hamlet echo the tormented monarch when he says: "I could count myself a king of infinite space where it not that I have had bad dreams." (Hamlet. Act II. Scene III)

Joseph interprets Pharaoh's dream implying that the monarch already had a handle on it. Ibn Ezra recognized Joseph's trump card. "The dream's duplication indicated the irrevocability of the events to come. The immanence of the events is shown by the two dreams taking place in one night." These two factors, irrevocability and immanence, Lowenthal points out, embolden Joseph to instruct Pharaoh to set a ruler over Egypt to facilitate the draconian measures needed to control waste in abundance and discipline in austerity. Rambam on the other hand, comments: "It must not be understood as Joseph's suggestion but rather what God intends." Either way, the plan restores the perception that Pharaoh is still in control. His dream is interpreted. His mind is relieved. The solution to the dilemma is assured.

An alien attaining power in another's land is a mixed blessing. The very appointment of Joseph evokes jealousy and hatred by the passed-over natives. "Could we find another man like this, endowed with the spirit of God?" asks Pharaoh. (Genesis XLI: 38) The text indicates that Pharaoh's servants were in agreement. Is there a contradiction here? Certainly! They were pleased that taxation, privation, storage and redistribution of food would not be their responsibility. Let the alien be the instrument of such a policy. Pharaoh himself has not abdicated at all. To all appearances, however, Joseph has taken the helm regarding the economic and agricultural fate of Egypt.

There is another dimension to the choreography of power in Miketz. For all intents and purposes Joseph is an orphan. He may still have a father back in Canaan but that does him no good in Egypt. Joseph does what any orphan would do. He ingratiates himself to power. He finds a father substitute. He did it with Potiphar and does it now with Pharaoh. A strange transformation takes place. The father becomes dependent on the son. There are echoes from the past. As Jacob asked: "Will I indeed bow before you?" so Potiphar says: "All I have is in your hands." and Pharaoh will say: "I herewith install you over the whole land of Egypt." Pharaoh will call Joseph ABREKH. The Targum renders it: "Father of Pharaoh." Quite a switch for an orphan. All this prefigures Moses – also ostensibly an orphan – who will become another Pharaoh's stepson and ultimately his nemesis as he saves his family of origin. Joseph will do the same.

One tangible symbol that appears again and again in the Joseph narrative is clothing. In Miketz Pharaoh gives Joseph a ring and then: "vayalbesh oto bigdey shesh" "he clothed him with garments of fine linen." Rashi says: "Material much valued in Egypt." It is hard to avoid recalling the long ago gift of that "k'tonet pasim" that technicolor dreamcoat. Jacob's gesture of love for his "special" son infuriated Joseph's brothers, almost compelling them to drive him from home. It was the same coat, drenched in blood, which was returned to Jacob. Then there was the coat with which Potiphar's wife convinced her husband of Joseph's attempt to seduce her. Now Pharaoh's gift is on Joseph's back and not, I suggest, only physically.

Now there are the good times. Joseph is 37 years old. Twenty years have passed since his adolescent dreams and his exile from home. These were twenty years of adventure that saw him in a pit and a prison, that saw him in charge of a household and now in charge of a kingdom. That kid, who suffered homelessness, privation and injustice, now stores up corn as numerous as the sand of the sea, beyond his capacity to count it. He has Asenath, his wife, and two children, whose very names are redolent with a past he barely remembered, but could neither forget. He calls his first son Manasseh. "God has caused me to forget all my hardships and parental home." He calls his second son Ephraim: "God has made me fruitful in the land of my affliction." Both names reflect the ambivalence Joseph feels about Egypt. There are some holes in the human psyche that all the wealth, power and success in the world cannot fill.

Miketz is profound for what it does not say. It leaves the reader to guess what must have transpired in the intervening years back in Canaan. That includes the guilt and sorrow of Jacob and the guilt and fear of the siblings after their sale of Joseph to the Ishmaelites. Hanging over the whole parashah are the unfulfilled dreams of Joseph and the silence of God in the face of travesty and tragedy. We are kept in suspense even when we know the end of the story. Just as Pharaoh's dreams come to fruition, so, too, must Joseph's dreams find fulfillment. Theirs were dreams in tandem. The players are unaware that they are actors in a Divinely ordained drama. There resides the tension between their apparent freedom and the predestination to which they are all subject. "Hakol zafui v'har'shut n'tunah." "All is foreseen yet free will is given." It is an enigma.

Finally, the text does segue back to Canaan. Jacob sends his sons to Egypt even as he sent Joseph to his brothers and his fate. The denouement is chilling. The brothers lay prostrate before Joseph. The historian van Rad says that the juxtaposition of the words "vayakeerem" and "vayitnakker" is a pun. "He recognized them even as he estranged himself." (Genesis: XLII: 7) Not quite! Alienation and recognition vie in Joseph's consciousness. The past and the present mesh. The dreams and the reality abut each other. Joseph accuses his brothers of being spies. They have come to reveal the nakedness of the land. He repeats "nakedness" twice. This tonsured, royally garbed ruler is as naked emotionally as the kid who was stripped of his tunic. Now he stands face to face with those who left him naked years before.

The brothers will now weave an emotional garment in which they will attempt to re-dress their reluctant sibling. "We are one man's sons. We are twelve brothers. The youngest is with his father and one is no more." The Midrash captures the panic of the brothers as they scour the city for evidence of Joseph's survival. It is that self same panic that Joseph uses to call their intentions into question. He is trying to maintain his equilibrium as well. Rage and longing coexist in Joseph's mind as he demands that Benjamin be brought down to Egypt. For three days Joseph quarantines his brothers. On the third day he reiterates his demands. "Do this that you may live for I fear God." Again Joseph evokes God's name at a crucial moment of confrontation. It is this evocation that provides Joseph with the valance he needs to extract his brothers' subservience, to punish his father for the latter's inability to protect him, and to connect with the only biological link he has with his deceased mother.

This demand also causes the brothers to interpret their predicament as a punishment for having sold Joseph in the first place. Reuben tells his siblings that they deserve their fate. Joseph turns his head and weeps. Lowenthal reminds us that this is the first time Joseph cries. His facade is beginning to crack. This is the first time the author lets us glimpse the internal life of Joseph. The exterior remains hard even as the heart begins to melt. A premature reconciliation would not suffice. He has waited too long for this moment. Simeon is held hostage as the other brothers return to Canaan. In their bags are not only the provisions needed to feed the family. The money too is restored. This gesture will also keep the brothers off balance. It has also succeeded in putting the fear of God into their hearts. "What is this that God has done to us?" they ask. That question reverberates as they tell their father what transpired in Egypt. They refer to "that man, the lord of Egypt." "Me you have bereaved of children" Jacob cries. "Joseph is no more. Simeon is gone and now you will take Benjamin." Reuben tries to intervene but Jacob does not relent. "His brother is dead and he alone remains."

In the meantime food is becoming scarce. Jacob is forced to reconsider. Judah promises that he will be the ransom instead of Benjamin if anything goes wrong. Jacob is asked to consider the little ones, his grandchildren. Too much time has already elapsed. Jacob sends Benjamin to "the man" in Egypt. "V'el shadai yiten lakhem rachamim lifney haish." "May Almighty God give you compassion before the man so that he may send away your other brother and Benjamin." Two things! First, Jacob broadens the arena of his compassion to include Simeon. Second, he now seems to accept this situation as punishment for his acquiescence in the fate of his children. "If I am bereaved, let me be bereaved." The Targum makes it poignant. "...and they led Benjamin away."

The segue is breathtaking. The brothers, Benjamin included, stand before Joseph. Their fear is palpable. The grain! The money! The elapsed time! Simeon is brought back. Joseph again evokes God as the source of their good fortune. They cannot comprehend what is happening. They join Joseph for lunch. He asks about their family, their father. Is he still alive? Joseph addresses Benjamin: "elohim yachn'cha b'ni," "May God be gracious to you, my boy." God again! Joseph cannot admit to his own compassion, his own longing. Joseph retreats. Lunch is served. The tension subsides. There is laughter. There is, however, one ominous note. Joseph must eat alone. For Egyptians to eat with Hebrews in an abomination. The brothers receive gifts from "the man." Benjamin's gifts are five times greater. De ja vu all over again.

Joseph has not exacted his due. The brothers are sent back to Canaan laden with gifts. Joseph's cup finds it way into Benjamin's sack. The brothers are returned. Whoever has taken the goblet will remain in Egypt as Joseph's servant. Judah speaks. They cannot justify themselves. God has found out their iniquity. They are now at the mercy of the man who stares them down.

Bereshit Rabbah extrapolates. The brothers have spent a lifetime trying to repent, to make amends, to search for their missing brother. Joseph asks: "What happened to the other brother?" "We sold him for five selas." Only their death, implies the midrash, would be an equitable execution of justice. Jacob too reaches a new level of understanding. "R. Levi said in the name of

R. Tanhum bar R. Hanilai: "Jacob said: 'Is it possible that the trembling that I caused my father (Genesis XXVII: 32) has now come down to me?" That is the underlying motif of Miketz. There is retribution. There is justice. There are unforeseen consequences to all human behavior. All the modern psychological principles come into play: family patterns, unconscious motivations, sibling rivalry, the potency of dreams. All these are encased in this parashah that straddles between the patriarchs and the exodus.

Gustav Buchdahl is the rabbi of Temple Emanuel in Baltimore and a friend of Joel Zaiman.

Vayyigash
Leslie Smith Rosen

"I am Joseph your brother . . ." One statement, yet heard eleven ways, spoken once yet heard throughout time. A revelation that brought redemption. A response before the question, answering the question that had received no response: "Am I my brother's keeper?" An acknowledgment that goes beyond the denial which came before: Ishmael too is the son of my great-grandfather; indeed it was his children who redeemed me for twenty pieces of silver from the depth of your hate, so that I could redeem you from the height of my father's love with one cup of silver in a bag of grain. I have done this for you, and for the sake of Esav, my father's brother: let us make peace.

"I am Joseph your brother . . . " This is what Reuven, the first born of Jacob, heard with anguish. Anguish for the reckoning of the blood that he predicted to his brothers. Anguish as he felt that long-ago day when his brothers resolved to kill the interloper, and he had pled for his life. Anguish he knew when he had returned and found the pit empty. Reuven's spirit had never quite climbed out of that darkness, and in darkness he had gone to Bilhah, his father's concubine, and consorted with her, desperate for distraction. Indeed Reuven knew the anguish that comes with dark and desperate secrets that corrode a family's soul. And so the children of Reuven would pray for the day that would end all anguish born of darkness, a rebirth into light and clarity.

"I am Joseph your brother . . ." This is what Simeon, the butcher of Shechem, heard with fear. Fear that he would be bound as he had once bound the boy who became the vizier of Mitzrayim. Fear of the final triumph of the younger, the dispossession of the wicked. Behind Simeon were the ruses of the past; ahead of him lay the curse of his father's diaspora; around him now the power of Pharaoh. And so for the children of Simeon would there always be the ultimate punishment of the wicked: the fear of living in unending fear of warranted retribution.

"I am Joseph your brother . . . " This is what Levi, the murderer of Hamor, heard with anger. Anger that he had again been trumped. Anger that he would forever be in debt to the favored son of his father's favored wife. Anger that his brother forgave him for outrageous jealousy and yet his father would not forgive him for the judgment he pronounced in defense of his sister. Levi's wrath was kindled anew in the dark brooding of the mind, and yet smoldered in the face of starvation. And so for the children of Levi the decisions of the closest often seemed distant and confused, shrouded in mystery and fettered by injustice.

"I am Joseph your brother . . ." This is what Judah, the orator for his father's old age, heard with awe. Awe of yet another life-changing revelation for Judah, who learned again the hidden intimacy of the apparently foreign. He recalled Tamar: daughter-in-law and "whore," the one he had pronounced "prostitute" and who he later declared was "more right than I." She, whom he declared worthy to die by fire and for whom he had burned with lust, had lived to give life to his seed. Now the one whom he had sold to passing Ishmaelites was buying them hope. And so it would be that the children of Judah would learn to find the familiar at the deepest core of the stranger.

"I am Joseph your brother . . . " This is what Dan, the first son born for Joseph's mother by her handmaid Bilhah, heard with confusion. Indeed his life had been confusion: the first of four who were not sons of his father's wife nor credited as sons of their mothers, whose own mother would sleep with his half-brother. Named for his step-mother's vindication, blessed as one who would govern, his life struggles were for admission to the inner circle and the governing of his own impulses. He was the first fruit of Rachel's infertility, her own solution for her own problem. And now, the once-dead first fruit of Rachel's fertility, God's solution to her problem, stands before him, revealed living. And so Dan's children learn that merely human solutions unravel with time, that the simple perplexes upon closer examination, that the paradigm in God's world is the paradox.

"I am Joseph your brother . . . " This is what Naphtali, the simple shepherd, heard with bewilderment. Long ago, Naphtali tended their flocks while Joseph dreamt dreams and foretold the future. Who would have guessed the one who was too busy to watch the sheep would one day feed all of Egypt? And so the children of Naphtali learned to expect the unlikely, account for the mutability of human possibility.

"I am Joseph your brother . . . " This is what Gad, the unlucky one named luck, heard with doubt. What were the odds, after all, of Joseph going from slave of passing Ishmaelites to becoming celebrated in the land of Pharaohs? And so the children of Gad learned the invincibility of the will of the Eternal even in the face of rational human supposition.

"I am Joseph your brother . . . " This is what Asher, the second son of the less favored's wife's handmaiden, heard with resignation. Asher's name evoked his mother's mistress's hope that all women would call her fortunate for his birth, desire dashed by circumstances greater than he. And so the children of Asher learned that seeing the world as it really exists is the first step to envisioning its potential.

"I am Joseph your brother . . . " This is what Issachar, the son whose conception Leah purchased with mandrakes, heard with empathy. Issachar, who knew the indignity of being bought and sold, who had seen his brothers sell his father's son, and yet realized the real worth of pieces of fruit and pieces of silver: a human soul. And so the children of Issachar learned to use every means to save a life.

"I am Joseph your brother . . . " This is what Zebulun, the last of Leah's sons, heard with relief. Zebulun had seen long ago in Laban's tent a child not so very much younger than he was, who, like him, would be the last boy to nurse at his mother's breasts, a youth whose dreams threatened the grown men who were his brothers, men who had used their strength in age and number to overpower the weak and young. With these words, Zebulun, the younger and weaker, and Zebulun's children had been reassured: the victory is not always to the swift or the strong, but to the one on the side of the Almighty.

"I am Joseph your brother . . . " This is what Dinah, Jacob's only daughter, did not hear because she was not there. Joseph was the little boy she had nurtured, in age her closest playmate, her half-brother and full cousin, the one who because of his gender and mother was the most favored of all, while she — because of her gender and mother - was the most neglected of all. This little brother once thrown into a pit, had predicted the Nile's future, the river that gave life, and thus saved Egypt. Dinah was not there. But one descendant of Dinah's family would be there one day, by the side of the Nile, now a symbol of death, protecting a baby brother who would defeat Egypt. And so all of the children of the tribe would come to wonder at what might have happened if all the daughters of Israel had been allowed to hear, if all sisters as well as brothers had been present at each moment of every revelation.

"I am Joseph your brother . . . " This is what Benjamin, the only full brother of Joseph, the only child named by his father, whose life itself had brought death, the last remaining cherished one of Jacob, heard with love, the love of his brother and toward his brother, the love that his mother's son had for their aged and widowed father. At last he, too, had a brother again; Joseph, whom he could barely remember and who knew him the least, had become his champion. This was the existential commitment of a brother beyond experience, beyond all expectation, beyond all probability, hineni: here I am. Hineni: here I am crying beside you in Babylon; camouflaging you in a cave; hiding you from an Inquisition; redeeming you from captivity and pogroms; clothing you and feeding you and teaching you in a golden land when you had no gold; burning a ghetto with you; holding you while you watched our beloved ones curl into smoke over our heads; smuggling you behind enemy lines; rebuilding with blood and sweat a promised land with you; snatching you from the oppressor's claw on eagle's wings back to a home we barely knew but fiercely loved.

"I am Joseph your brother . . . " This is what Joseph heard himself say. Brothers, beneath the hated robe of your memory, bereft of the revered title of the Egyptian, beyond the gift of visions you did not see and the dreams that kept you awake, sleepless with hate. This is who I am: Joseph, your brother. Look into my eyes and see yourselves. We are children of one father, different founders of the same future. I am the familiar face of the other you denied; I am the other who shares your blood. Look and discover what you have already seen. Know that life is always more clear through a veil of tears, tears which will wash away the pretenses of the past, tears which will quench the drought of hate, reverse the hunger of jealousy. The bag of grain that we open together and over which we cry will be seed for our children, all our children, to become a nation in a strange land, to be family beyond blood and transcending time; and our harvest shall reap life from death.

Leslie Smith Rosen is a Ph.D. candidate in modern Jewish philosophy at Baltimore Hebrew University, teaches and develops curriculum for Chizuk Amuno's Krieger Schechter Day School and Rosenbloom Religious School. Prior to coming to Baltimore, she founded the Aleph Bet Jewish Day School in Annapolis, MD.

Vayyechi
Dr. Moshe D. Shualy

> *"When the boys grew up . . . Jacob was an innocent man living in tents* (Gen. 25:27). *The portion which I wrested from the Amorites with my sword and bow." (Gen. 48:22)*

> *"'Sword and bow.'"—these are wisdom and hope." (Rashi)*

> *"Do no judge your fellow until you have reached his place." (Avot 2:5)*

Jacob utters that very phrase, *"I know,"* when he flees his brother Esau's lethal rage after the deception for Isaac's blessings. On his way to Haran, Jacob is alone and vulnerable. That first night away from home he sleeps in the open with a rock for a pillow. Jacob dreams that he meets his fathers' God Who says,

> *Remember, I am with you*
> *I will protect you wherever you go*
> *and will bring you back to this land.*
> *I will not leave you*
> *until I have done what I have promised you.* (Gen. 28:15)

Parashat Vayehi is the closing portion in Genesis. Here we find Jacob at the end of a long and dramatic life, a very different man than when we first meet him. Jacob's personal transformation is stunning: he begins as a simple, innocent man of the tents and becomes a warrior, sage, the towering Patriarch of Israel.

Our tradition tells us that we can get insight into another if we strive to be "in his place." What elements in Jacob's life shed light on his transformation? How can we learn to grow in our own spiritual journeys as did Jacob? Two key events in Jacob's life are examined: his first direct encounter with God in a dream as he flees to Haran, and twenty years later on his return to Canaan, Jacob's name is changed to Israel. Moreover, we will show that these events are direct links to Isaac's transformation by the hands of Abraham and Sarah. It will take the combined efforts of three generations for Jacob to attain his spiritual magnitude. The thread weaving our interpretive tapestry opens with Jacob's utterance in *Vayehi*, "I know my son I know." (Gen. 48:19) Jacob tells Joseph after reversing the order of blessings for his grandchildren that he knows the order is inverted. The verb *"know" (yada)* is pivotal both in Genesis and the Bible. Man can acquire Divine knowledge; this is the foundation of Torah. Awareness is the instrument of transformation and salvation. Knowledge of Torah is the manifestation of God; it is to be mastered by man. Torah is the bridge uniting man with God.

Upon waking Jacob says, "Indeed there is God in this place and I did not know it!"(Gen. 28:16) Jacob discovers a new spiritual reality within. *"In this place,"* is not geography; it is the spiritual center of Jacob. He will carry this Power and Presence with him; it will protect him until he returns safely. Jacob's new self-awareness of God within emerges only after a series of crises, "a head-on collision" with reality. The crises are numerous: conspiring with his mother against his father and brother, betraying and deceiving both father and brother, invoking a death contract from master-hunter Esau, and fleeing to a hostile land hundreds of miles away without skills or experience. Jacob is at "rock-bottom" when he makes his stunning self-discovery of God within. He seals this vision of God in a legal and binding covenant. (Gen. 28:20) We too are on a similar journey "away from home," sleeping with a "rock under our head." We need to ask, "What is here in this place?" If we are fortunate we too will say, Indeed there is God in this place and I did not know it!

Jacob continues his transformation as he attains another spiritual peak, again while in the throes of an extraordinary crisis. After twenty years of "basic training" with Laban, Jacob sets out to his father's home. This time he is not alone and poor. Jacob returns with four wives, twelve sons, a daughter, many servants, flocks, herds and other property. But now he is facing a far greater test than when he left home. Jacob is terrified by the prospect of total destruction. His brother Esau is coming to meet him with four hundred armed men.

> *"Jacob was greatly frightened; in his anxiety, he divided the people with him... into two camps, thinking, 'If Esau comes to the one camp and attacks it, the other camp may yet escape.' Then Jacob said, 'O God of my father Abraham and God of my father Isaac... Deliver me, I pray, from the hand of my brother, from the hand of Esau; else, I fear, he may come and strike me down, mothers and children alike.'"*
> (Gen. 32:8-12)

On the night before the fateful meeting with Esau, Jacob has transferred all his family and property across the river Yabboq. Jacob returns alone across the riverbank, aware that by the following night his entire family may be extinct. The Torah tells us pointedly, Jacob was left alone. And a man wrestled with him until the break of dawn. (Gen. 32:25) Most scholars, based on a variety of Midrashim, speak of Jacob wrestling with an "angel." This is simply not so! Jacob is wrestling with himself. The wrestling is a spiritual—and psychological self-encounter. Jacob reaches deeply within to find the Divine Presence that will assist him to survive yet another test. He finds this power and is renamed Israel—"for you have striven with beings divine and human, and have prevailed." (Gen. 32:29) Jacob the man secures the name for the people Israel. Jacob is not fully aware of the magnitude of this event. Ironically Jacob asks for "the other's" name, yet he actually knows it already—it is Israel for he is wrestling with himself. (Gen. 32:30)

He views the previous night's experience, as a struggle for survival and spiritual growth. So Jacob named the place *Peniel*, meaning, "I have seen God face-to-face, yet my life has been preserved." (Gen. 32:31)

Jacob identifies this place as *Peniel;* place is not a geographic place but instead is a spiritual region within. The name *Peniel* denotes that he saw God "face to face"(*panim el panim*). In Hebrew *panim* also denotes "interior." Jacob experiences his interiority as a spiritual domain within that is also the place of God Himself. *Peniel* denotes "my interior is God." Jacob needed this experience before meeting his brother Esau. Jacob knows that he must project power; Esau must not perceive him as a victim. In this context Jacob defines the encounter with his brother in spiritual terms, "For I have seen your face as if I had seen the face of God and you have accepted me." (Gen. 33:10) Jacob incorporates the Divine into his personal affairs. *Panim el panim*: just as the two different faces make up a single coin so do the two faces of Jacob, one face is man and the other is God, make up one being.

Jacob did not launch his twenty-year odyssey of self-discovery; Rebecca did. But why? Why did Rebecca, who loves Jacob, "set him up" in a scheme of deception that guaranteed the deadly wrath of Esau? Rebecca is the "prime-mover" in the deception of Isaac. Surely she anticipated Esau's murderous reaction. Jacob was a reluctant conspirator; he wanted no part of the deception of Isaac; he protested to no avail. Rebecca commanded Jacob and forced him to conspire with her. She instigated, designed and executed the complex, split-second timing of the deception. Jacob's innocence is painfully pathetic. His sole objection, "if my father touches me I shall appear to him as a trickster and bring upon myself a curse not a blessing." (Gen. 27:12) Jacob is clueless. His real problem will arise if he succeeds in fooling Isaac. Esau's homicidal reaction is a far greater danger. Why would Rebecca place Jacob in harm's way? Regarding "the blessings," these "precious" blessings are not "money in the bank." The blessings are ideals that need to be actualized after much hard work. By themselves they are meaningless; there is no supernatural are conditional. They depend on moral and ethical living.

Isaac and Rebecca are debating as to who will be the next Patriarch. This debate is framed in terms of "who loves whom."

Isaac believes Esau is far more capable and powerful and that Jacob is naive and inexperienced. Rebecca perceives Jacob to be the best next Patriarch: though innocent he is idealistic and moral; Jacob can yet learn to be practical and flexible. Esau, however, is murderous and concerned with immediate gratification; he will never have the idealism and vision to be a Patriarch. The character difference is clear. Had Esau stolen the blessings, Jacob would never threaten to kill him. Had Esau chosen a moral and virtuous life he too would be blessed regardless of Isaac's actions.

Rebecca's "blessing deception" teaches Jacob to be practical rather than naively truthful. Moreover, Rebecca's exercise proves to Isaac that Jacob can change and be practical but Esau's homicidal streak makes him unsuitable as a Patriarch. Isaac is aware of Jacob's attempt to deceive him; seven times Isaac inquires and tests Jacob's honesty and identity. (Gen. 27:18-26) In the end, Isaac agrees with Rebecca, Jacob is to be the next Patriarch. Rebecca's deception is necessary to initiate Jacob to self-discovery and spiritual growth. Jacob needs to change from an innocent man, into a powerful Patriarch. He must be steeled by adversity in a hostile, deceptive and carnivorous world. Rebecca is correct; Jacob's twenty years in Haran prepared him well for his destiny, to be the Patriarch who established the people Israel spiritually and biologically.

Where did Rebecca learn to be the master architect of Jacob's fate? This she learned from Isaac, her loving soul mate. Isaac was the only Patriarch who lived with only one woman and with whom he found epic mutual fulfillment. "Isaac then brought her into the tent of his mother Sarah, and he took Rebecca as his wife. Isaac loved her, and thus found comfort after his mother's death. ."(Gen. 24:67) Rebecca understood that Isaac the Patriarch is the spiritual product of Sarah and Abraham's labor of transforming Isaac the child.

Isaac too started as a quiet, simple and loved child at the center of a family storm. Sarah wages mortal battle against Hagar and Ishmael. Isaac is protected from fateful life and death decisions while Sarah secures Isaac as the next Patriarch. She is prepared to deal death to mother and child to protect her Isaac. However, Abraham will need to take Isaac to the next level before he will become the second Patriarch. Isaac will find that level on top of mount Moriah bound upon an altar at the Akedah.

The Akedah is a mystery. Why does Father Abraham, who loves Isaac, commit such a repulsive and terrifying act? It is not acceptable to simply say God ordered it. We firmly believe that Abraham does the right thing and that we too would do exactly the same in a similar setting. But why? What could compel us to do the same? The angel's command to Abraham, "Do not raise your hand against the boy, or do anything to him" (Gen. 22:12) is ironic and absurd. True, there is not a scratch on Isaac's body but the pure terror and trauma cut deep into his psyche will never heal.

Even as the Akedah continues to inspire faith, selflessness and martyrdom among the people Israel for millennia, there is no satisfying explanation as to its meaning provided by scholars over the centuries. We suggest a new insight into the Akedah that draws its inspiration from the narrative itself. The very first words that Isaac utters in the Torah are, "Father, here are the fire and wood. Where is the lamb for slaughter?" (Gen. 22:7) Isaac's innocence is heartrending. Can he possibly be the next Patriarch? Isaac will not survive the least of his enemies. Ishmael, his foremost adversary, master archer of the desert, will utterly crush him. Isaac does not stand a chance!

Abraham himself is a practical man and a seasoned warrior. Escaping severe famine in Canaan, he pleads with Sarah to say she is his sister lest the Egyptians kill him. Later, Abraham successfully routs four kings on a night raid to rescue his nephew Lot. But Abraham now is too old to teach Isaac about the brutal facts of life.

His young son needs a "crash-course" in survival. Isaac needs to learn that reality flows from the edge of a knife. Father Abraham takes Isaac up the mountain to make sure that NEVER AGAIN will Isaac ask, "Where is the lamb for slaughter?" On Mount Moriah, Isaac's innocence was slaughtered. This enables Isaac to become whole. His virtue is now strengthened with power. Isaac emerges ready to become a Patriarch. Rebecca follows perfect suit. Just as Abraham took Isaac and bound him as an Akedah on Moriah to liberate him, so does Rebecca "bind" Jacob in the "deception" for Isaac's blessings to liberate him.

Thus the journey of our faith's founding fathers and mothers is a spiritual journey of self-discovery, *"indeed there is God is in this place."* Each reaches within to experience the *"Image of God"* within, providing them with strength and ethics, courage and vision, innocence and experience. They are a living inspiration within their children to this day.

AS A DEER & MIGHTY AS A LION TO

DO THE WILL OF YOUR FATHER WHO IS IN HEAVEN.

BE BOLD AS A LEOPARD & LIGHT AS AN EAGLE, AS SWIFT

EXODUS · שמות

ANGELA MUNITZ, 2000

Shemot
Stanley I. Minch

> *"And it came to pass, in the course of those many days, that the king of Egypt died, and the children of Israel sighed from the bondage, and they cried, and their cry for help went up unto God from the bondage. And God heard their groaning, and God remembered His covenant with Abraham with Isaac and with Jacob. And God saw the children of Israel, and God took cognizance of them." (Exodus, 2:23)*

Why did God suddenly hear the cry of the Hebrews and remember his covenant with Abraham? Is it possible that He had forgotten this covenant? Is it possible that He was so busy and occupied that He was not aware of the problems of the people? Did God lose sight of the children of Israel and pay no attention to them before he heard their cry this time? And, on the other hand, should we believe that until this time, the people has no need to ask God to intervene and help them? Was this the only time that the Hebrews had cries to God?

W. Gunther Plaut, in his commentaries in *The Torah, A Modern Commentary*, offers the opinion that the Hebrews perhaps knew of God whom their ancestors worshipped, but they did not deem Him capable of ending their distress. He goes on to cite midrash that speculates that perhaps they had forgotten God and that this led to their enslavement. The Torah does not deal with the subject of God's "absence from Israel's history of four hundred years" other than to infer that it was a mysterious plan of God. Thus, we are left to speculate why there was this unexplained gulf of years in which there was the absence of contact between God and the Hebrews. However, the oppression sets the stage for the confrontation between the Pharaoh and the "savior of Israel." Plaut goes on to say that at the time of the oppression the people may not have known of God, but "they will come to know Him as the drama of salvation unfolds."

Ramban explains, that in the beginning, "God hid His face and they had been devoured. Now, God heard their cry and 'saw' them." In other words he no longer hid His face from them but "took cognizance" of their suffering and their needs. The question still remains . . . why? Why did God hide His face?

Nehama Leibowitz comments that there is a discussion of the thornbush and how God "called out to him(Moses)in the midst of the bush." Why the thornbush? Why didn't God merely call out to Moses? Midrash suggests that the bush symbolizes another attribute of God , in which God says "I also am suffering," but, He has hidden his face from the Hebrews in order to "chastise His children for their own good."

Perhaps the children of Israel, as they multiplied and grew in number, began to mingle and dwell among the Egyptians. Maybe they wanted to be like the Egyptians and forgot Jacob's wish that they live apart. Because of their behavior God punished them by allowing the Egyptians to enslave and oppress them.

This is not unlike a parent who loves his children but also understands that they must be punished if they have done something wrong and have disobeyed. The punishment handed out may deprive the children and penalize them in different ways, but, at the same time that the children suffer, so, to a degree, does the parent suffer. Parents punish only to impress and teach children the right or proper way. In this way we can understand that as God allowed the Hebrews to suffer, so He suffered as well, much like the parent of a disobeying child.

In the explanatory notes in the Rabbinical Assembly Mahzor for Rosh Hashanah and Yom Kippur we find the following. "As tender as a father with his children, the Lord is compassionate with His worshippers (Psalm 102:13)." But sometimes a father must reprimand his child for a lapse in behavior. A father feels both love and a sense of responsibility.

If we were to carry this forward, would it then explain why, in the course of Jewish history, the Jewish people have suffered from time to time down through the ages? The destruction of the Temple, the dispersement of the people, the Crusades, the pogroms, the Holocaust, are these are evidence of God's way of punishing the Jewish people for not observing the laws and commandments they are expected to follow? Perhaps this is why Judaism has survived despite all that it has suffered, because, after sufficient punishment, God has, "heard their cry and remembered his covenant with Abraham, Isaac and Jacob."

Recently, we were saddened to learn of the very untimely death of an eighteen year-old woman as a result of an airplane crash. The grandmother of the young woman was heard to say, "I don't believe there is a God above or else he would not have allowed this to happen." Is this another manifestation of God allowing something to happen as punishment for something this family did or did not do? Can we explain every tragedy with the same logic?

The answer, of course, is no. When God speaks or when God "hides His face to chastise," God does this toward "the people," and not toward an individual. God's judgement is corporate—it is toward the whole, not a single part. Thus when tragedy strikes an individual or a group of people, fate, and not a God hiding His face, is the cause. We must believe that one-day we will find the answers to all of those things in life that happen.

If God's judgement is corporate, why then, during the High Holy Days do we, pray "Be-rosh ha-Shanah yika-teivu," "on Rosh Hashanah it is written And on Yom Kippur it is sealed how many shall leave this world and how many shall be born into it, who shall live and who shall die, who shall live out the limit of his days and who shall not, etc." If punishment is corporate, why do we pray that penitence, prayer, and good deeds can annul the severity of the decree?

Of course we may never know why certain things happen. There are events that no one can explain. We must believe in God's judgement—that there is a purpose and a reason. Yes, God's judgement is corporate. It is toward the whole and not a single entity. But there also is the one-to-one relationship of each human being to God. It is in this sense that we pray, as individuals, for forgiveness for sins that we have committed during the year.

The Book Of Ecclesiastes closes with the following: "The sum of the matter, when all is said and done: Revere God and observe His commandments: For this applies to all mankind: that God will call every creature to account for everything unknown, be it good or bad."

Stanley I. Minch is Director of the Chizuk Amuno Foundation, Inc. For three decades he served as Executive Director of Chizuk Amuno Congregation and has enjoyed a close relationship with Rabbi Zaiman, both professionally and personally, since he first arrived in Baltimore.

Vayyera
Dr. Carol K. Ingall

The highlight of our Seder is, and has always been, the recitation of the plagues, most of which can be found in *Parashat* Va'era. As they say in Hollywood, this is a story "with legs." The riveting drama captivates both our young and old. Kieran Egan's recent book, *The Educated Mind: How Cognitive Tools Shape Our Understanding*, has helped me to understand that appeal.

Egan, a psychologist interested in cognitive development, contends that we go through various stages in the way we make meaning of the world. Before we know how to read, we learn about the world through the senses, through what Egan calls *"somatic understanding."* "Our body is where we start from in our exploration of the world and experience. We begin, as it were, by our minds expanding through our bodies and then from our bodies out into the world." (p. 244). In early elementary school, Egan argues, children learn through "mythic understanding." Mythic understanding is characterized by a binary motif: good battles evil. According to Egan, "the human brain is innately 'hardwired' to build understanding on the basis of binary distinctions." (p. 39)

At about the age of ten, we are ready for "romantic understanding," a fascination with the exotic, with that which stands on the margins of reality, and the fantastic. (Watch what middle schoolers are reading: Harry Potter *and The Guinness Book of Records*.) The next stage is "philosophic understanding." Egan notes, "The philosophic mind focuses on connections among things, constructing theories, laws, ideologies, and metaphysical schemes to tie together the facts available to the student." (p. 121) Any of us who have come into contact with teenagers knows how wedded they can be to an ideological stance. A single world view can explain everything. ("Because my parents hate me" comes immediately to mind.)

For Egan the goal of the educated mind is *ironic*

understanding, the sum total of the earlier understandings, the ability to juggle many interpretations of the same event. Ironic understanding demands texture instead of flatness, ambiguity instead of simplicity. "Multiple perspectives disclose multiple meanings—one might look at that stand of trees with esthetic delight, or with calculations of what its timber would fetch in current markets, or with religious awe as the sacred resting place of an ancestor's spirit, or with determination to preserve it as the last sustaining habitat of an endangered species of moth, and so on . . . . The fluent ironist can slip from perspective to perspective." (p. 145)

I suggest that what we find so compelling about the plague narrative that begins in *Parashat Va'era* is the pleasure derived from all these understandings. For those who have arrived at an ironic understanding, that pleasure is the most intense. Think about the Seder and the dramatic recitation of the *Makkot*, the plagues. The youngest child at the Seder table is captivated by the recitation of the plagues which begins in our *parashah. Dam, tz'fardea, kinim...* There is rhythm, counting, and repeated physical movements: dipping our spoons or fingers into our cups of wine. This is somatic understanding at its purest. Yet even adults rely on the somatic mode to derive meaning from a piece of text. It is our love for patterns, our residual somatic understanding, which can make rabbinic commentaries on the order of the plagues so appealing. The Maharal of Prague, the Great Rabbi Judah Loewe, teaches that the plagues may be understood in three groups. Blood, frogs, & lice all attacked the Egyptians from below. The second group, beasts, pestilence, and boils, attacked the Egyptians on their own level. The third group, hail, locusts, and darkness, attacked the Egyptians from the heavens above. Thus, continues the Maharal, all Creation was turned against the Egyptians, while in the slaying of the first-born, listed alone, it is God alone who seals the destruction of *Mitzrayim.*

In the contest between God and Pharaoh, we see the mythic understanding writ large. This is the battle of Titans. Pharaoh has thrown down the gauntlet in Exodus 5:2: "Who is God that I should listen to God's voice?" The plague narrative is God's rejoinder to that impertinent question, increasing the dramatic tension until we see God and Pharaoh going at it, "mano a mano," at the Sea of Reeds. In Chapter 15: 3 Pharaoh gets the answer to his arrogant question. "The Lord, the Warrior—Lord is His name!" We adults, along with the five-year olds who first learn this narrative, delight in the triumph of redemption over slavery.

Egan claims that the romantic understanding develops as children come to grips with their vulnerability. God protects the underdog, the children of Israel. "I have now heard the moaning of the Israelites because the Egyptians are holding them in bondage, and I have remembered My covenant." (Exodus 6: 5) Out of love for *B'nai Yisrael* and for their forbears' merit (*z'khut avot*), God will perform miracles and suspend the natural order. God will turn water to blood, cover Egypt with frogs, lice, wild beasts, plagues, boils, hail, locusts, and darkness, and finally slaughter the first-born of all the Egyptians. In his brilliant analysis of fairy tales, *The Uses of Enchantment*, Bettelheim noted that this literature, as grim (no pun intended) as it is, provides children with a sense of security. They know enough about the world to comprehend that it is a scary place. In reading about fairy godmothers and wizards who protect the weak and helpless, they derive courage to deal with their own monsters. The plague narrative serves this same function, not only for seven to twelve-year olds, but for all of us.

Teenagers, according to Egan, are ready for philosophic understanding. One of the questions they always raise, as do the adults who study this text, is how can we reconcile the idea of free will with God's intervention in human affairs? How can Pharaoh be responsible, if it is God who hardens his heart? Beginning with Exodus 4:21, the Torah tells us ten times that God does this, using verbs like *ahazek/va'yehezak* (strengthen), *aksheh* (harden), and *va'yakhbed/va'yikhbad* (made heavy). Most of these instances occur in our *parashah*. For those of us with a philosophical bent, there is no ducking the issue. Is Pharaoh a helpless pawn in God's cosmic drama of redemption? If so, how then can he be culpable?

In *Hilkhot Teshuva*, Chapter 7, *Hilkhot* 1-3, Maimonides offers an explanation:

> But it may sometimes happen that man's offense is so grave that he is penalized by not being granted the opportunity to turn from his wickedness, so that he dies with the sin that he committed. To this the Almighty referred in Isaiah: 'Make the heart of this people fat, and make their ears heavy and shut their eyes' (6, 10). Cf. too (II Chronicles 36, 16): 'but they mocked the messengers of God, and despised His words, and scoffed at His prophets, until the wrath of the Lord arose against His people and there was no remedy.' In other words, they sinned of their own free will, till they forfeited the opportunity of repentance, which is the classic remedy. To this end, Scripture states too: 'And I shall harden Pharaoh's heart.' He sinned, first of his own free will... until he forfeited the opportunity to repent.

According to Maimonides, Pharaoh is trapped, not by God, but by his own patterns of callousness: patterns that he chose and cannot break. He is too inured to evil.

The ironic understanding avoids the univocal interpretation, calling forth echoes of all the previous understandings, asking us to savor them all, singly and in juxtaposition to each other. Yesterday I saw a performance of *Aida*, another story of slaves ground down by Egyptian oppressors. For me, the high point of the opera was the second act, when Verdi weaves together eight voices: the heroine, Aida; her rival, Amneris, the princess of Egypt; Amneris's father, the King of Egypt; his prisoners, the Ethiopian captives; their king and Aida's father, Amonasro; the high priest of Egypt, Ramfis; the corps of Egyptian priests; and the triumphant Egyptian general, Radames, beloved by both Aida and Amneris. Each of the principals relates to the action from his or her point of view; the audience is overcome by the glorious layering of the voices and the poignancy of multiple interpretations.

I am advocating that we embrace irony, not only for its esthetic implications, but because irony is the dominant mode of modernity. To live with irony is to live with paradox, to "slip from perspective to perspective." We are Jews, trying valiantly to live in a secular culture with all of its "isms" that we cannot reject, such as individualism, feminism, and pluralism. At the same time, we are Jews wedded to community, duty, and our unique destiny. We are Conservative Jews who are bound by both Tradition and Change. Egan's lesson, so vividly made manifest by this *parashah*, is that we can find meaning in this narrative through the somatic, the mythic, the romantic, and the philosophical, but the richest meaning of all is in the ironic understanding, in accepting the fact that the truth can never be fully known. The lesson of ironic understanding is the rationale of Jewish study—and Jewish life in our time—to live with ambiguity, to reject simple solutions to complex problems, and to embrace that challenge with passion and intensity.

Carol K. Ingall, Ed.D., is an associate professor of Jewish Education at the Jewish Theological Seminary and is the grateful recipient of Rabbi Joel Zaiman's scholarship, mentoring, and friendship.

Bo
Eric Beser

I have always been troubled by tefillin. In the Reform synagogue where I grew up, tefillin was a custom that had been removed by the quest for modernity. I never fully understood the rhyme or reason behind the custom. The only time I had ever worn them was as a summer graduate student in Israel when a Lubavitcher grabbed me at the Kotel, asking first if I was Jewish and then asking if I would perform the mitzvah of tefillin. When my father died I started to attend minyan regularly, and wore the tefillin from the bottom drawer in the chapel for the morning service. The borrowed tefillin were always too stiff, too short, too uncomfortable to wear. I wore them without truly understanding their full meaning, surrendering to the fact that, among Conservative Jews, tefillin were worn during weekday morning minyan. One day I asked why do we wear tefillin and was told "tefillin was the price of our independence out of Egypt."

In Parashah Bo, Moses said to the people, "Remember this day on which you departed from Egypt." The word Zachor is the imperative form of the word "remember" implying that the Exodus should be remembered constantly. The 12th century commentator Samuel b. Meir takes this command as a figurative and literal one. In his commentary on Exodus 13:9 he says: "according to the essence of its literal meaning it means 'it shall ever be as a memorial as though it were written upon thy hand.' It was accepted that the verse was to be taken literally and that the words of the scripture had to be bound on the hand and placed (on the forehead) between the eyes."

"Tefillin, by virtue of where they are worn, parallel the heart and the mind, the organs through which the neshamah and the intellect reveal their powers. However, the heart and the mind, being physical, are subject to man's will, and the powers of the neshamah and the intellect can be lessened by the choices man makes. Therefore, **God** commanded that we wear tefillin, a crown which is separate from the body and which therefore will be unaffected by man's will. To the contrary, the holiness of the tefillin causes rays of "light" to spread out over the entire body and reach the heart and the mind. As a result, the power of the intellect predominates over the power of the will." R' Avraham Yitzchak Hakohen Kook z"l

Tefillin is probably the most Jewish of all symbols, and I am troubled by Parashat Bo's choice of words to introduce them. The Parashah commands the children of Israel to wear tefillin by saying "(The tefillin (phylacteries) shall be worn) as a sign on your arm and as "Totafot" between your eyes." (Exodus 13:16) The word 'Totafot' usually translated as "frontlets" was understood by the Rabbis simply to mean tefillin.

There is a discussion in the gemara Sanhedrin 4b: "letotafot occurs thrice in the Torah, twice defective and once plene, four in all, to indicate (that four sections are to be inserted in the phylacteries). Such is the opinion of R. Ishmael. But R. Akiba maintains that there is no need of that interpretation, for the word totafot itself implies four, (it being composed of) tot which means two in Katpi and fot which means two in Afriki. Sanhedrin 4b

The Talmud in Sanhedrin is concerned with the origins of the word totafot. Clearly it has no Jewish origin. The Talmud declares that totafot is a compound word that combines two foreign words. The tefillin on the head has four compartments. Thus, tot-fot or totafot, means four. But there is a second difficulty with calling the tefillin "totafot."

Why did the Torah teach us to make four sections by adding two and two? Why didn't the Torah just use a word meaning "four?" Rabbi David Cohen (Cong. Gevul Ya'avetz, of Brooklyn, N.Y., author of Ohel David, 4 vol., Aidi d'Zutar, 2 vol., etc.) suggests an original approach to this question.

Presumably they did so immediately, making themselves

their first pairs of tefillin. Our Parashah tells us that the Jews were commanded in Egypt to place two passages from the Torah "as signs on our arms and tefillin on our foreheads." However, doing so would be somewhat problematic, since tefillin include more than just those two passages. They include two additional passages, "Shema Yisrael" and "v'Haya Im Shamo'a," which Moshe only told the Jews 40 years later, when they were about to enter the Land of Israel.

We must conclude, suggests Rabbi Cohen that the Jews were only required to put two of the traditional four passages in their tefillin for the first forty years. This, explains Rabbi Cohen, is why the Torah split the total number of passages into two sets of two. This was meant to show that the original installation of the passages in the tefillin was done in two stages: the first two of the four were installed upon leaving Egypt, while the other two had to wait until some 40 years later!

But this is a good explanation for why the word for tefillin implies two plus two - why would the Torah use a compound of two very foreign words to describe a Jewish - perhaps the most Jewish— symbol?

We must first determine what exactly these two languages are. The first, Katpi, is Coptic, an Egyptian language. As for the latter, the Targum often substitutes the word 'Africa' for Tarshish (I Melachim 10:22 etc.). The prophets tells us in a number of places that when the Mashiach will come, 'Tarshish' and 'the far-away Isles' will learn the glory of **God**, and they will come out to greet the Messiah (Yeshayah 66:19; Tehillim 72:10). Apparently, these distant locales have not even heard of the Jews' worship, and still staunchly serve their idols; however the time will come when they, too, will join us in the service of **God**. This is why these particular languages were chosen to develop the theme of the omnipotence of **God**.

The theme of tefillin is that **God** is One, and His nation is one. No other nation serves the God that is One, to the exclusion of all other deities. This is the hidden message of "'Tot' in the

Coptic language means '2,' and 'Fot' in African means '2'." The highest praise that any foreign nation can sing to its deity is "Two." That is, any object of Avodah Zarah is but one of the many powers that God created in the world; not the exclusive Power of Powers that controls and decides all that happens in the universe. The Coptic and African idolaters can but say "two."

Furthermore, no one nation can lay claim to being unique in serving their deity. Although different nations serve different Gods (or ideals), they are all out to accomplish the same goal. They are attempting to effect their own financial and political success by appealing to the deity of their choice. They are serving themselves, not their Gods. Also, each of their Gods represents but one element in the whole of creation, and why should one element be ranked higher than another? Figuratively, for every "two" that the Katfi nation cries, a corresponding "two" is shouted by the Africans. The Jewish people, on the other hand, are willing to sacrifice all their worldly possessions—even their very lives—for the service of God. They are unique among the nations of the world in their selfless devotion to the Creator of all.

Our parashah described the tefillin using two foreign terms for the word "two" to emphasize that other nations cannot put on tefillin—i.e., they do not serve a God that is one—and for that reason they do not receive the reciprocal praise of "Who is like Your nation, Israel, *unique* on earth!"

Just a few verses prior our Parashah refers to the tefillin boxes as a zikaron (remembrance) between the eyes (Exodus 13:9). If the Torah calls tefillin a remembrance than why does it refer to them as totafot? Moreover, if they are totafot then why call them a remembrance?

I was first told that tefillin was the "price of our independence out of Egypt." That description was not accurate. Wearing borrowed tefillin, stiff and ill-fitting, did not help me connect the true meaning of why we wear them. Parashah Bo connects tefillin with the Exodus, but strongly reminds us to teach our children as well.

For my daughter's Bat Mitzvah (a Rosh Hodesh service), I wore tefillin that felt as if I had worn them since I was age thirteen. My mother gave me my father's tefillin that had sat in a drawer for as long as I can remember. I cannot remember a single time seeing my father ever wear them. I can picture him wearing them at his Bar Mitzvah, and perhaps other times because the tefillin had signs of wear. Perhaps it was the familiar smell or that the leather seemed to fit my arm and head perfectly, I found another connection to wearing tefillin that I didn't know existed. The "Totafot" and "zikaron" blended together. I finally got it!

I was connected together, generation to generation, even if I couldn't see the link. My father's tefillin connected me to a part of my father I never saw while he was alive, but I knew existed. My father at some point connected to his father in the same way. And so on. Tefillin was not the "price of our independence out of Egypt," but our "connection" to our independence. It is a very basic and systematic way of reiterating the message of the Exodus "With a strong hand did God removed us from Egypt."

Eric Beser has been a member of Chizuk Amuno for 13 years. He was in the 2nd graduating class of the Baltimore Institute for Jewish Communal Studies (now in its 25th year) and is an active participant in the Saturday Shahirit Rotation, alternate Minyan and the Tikkun Olam Advocacy Group.

Beshallach
Debby Hellman

"To sing your praises"—it is a colloquialism that is familiar to us. But why do we speak of "singing" praises? Why not proclaiming or shouting? Where did this idea originate, that praises are to be sung?

In Parashat Beshallach, we encounter the first biblical example of singing praises. Subsequent biblical writings, commentaries and midrashim, and the development of liturgical practice reveal that this ancient antecedent has had far-reaching influence beyond its first historical chanting.

The parashah includes the miracle of the parting of the Reed Sea. After successfully crossing the sea, the Israelites, inspired by God's redeeming hand and their subsequent joy in escaping from the pursuing Egyptians, erupt into a spontaneous song exalting God. This song has become known as Shirat Ha-yam, Song of the Sea, or simply, Shirah. So significant is this song that when we read Parashat Beshallach on its appointed Saturday in the regular weekly cycle of Torah readings, we give the day a special name, Shabbat Shirah, the Sabbath of Song.

Shirat Ha-yam (Exodus 15:1-18) is often seen in connection with another biblical triumphal ode, the Song of Deborah (Judges 5:2-31). In fact, when portions from the Prophets became a fixed part of our Shabbat readings, the sages selected the story of Deborah and her song as the Haftarah for Shabbat Shirah. These two songs are the oldest examples of sustained poetry in the Bible.

The ancient scribes had their own method of drawing attention to these songs. When you see these two songs in Torah as well as in many Humashim, you will notice a writing pattern that differentiates these verses from the rest of the written text. The visual format is a blank space above and below each phrase, imitating a bricklayer's pattern: "a half brick over a whole brick and a whole brick over a half brick" ("ariah al gabbei levenah u-levenah al gabbei ariah"). This scribal form became the halahically approved tradition. (*The JPS Torah Commentary, Exodus*, Nahum M. Sarna, p.76)

Both the Song of Deborah and the Song of the Sea are exaltations of God, acknowledging His hand in the affairs of mankind. In the book of Judges, Deborah's song is chanted by the prophetess herself and Barak, her champion. The uniqueness of Shirat Ha-yam is in the phrase "Az yashir Moshe uv'nay Yisrael," "Then sang Moshe and the children of Israel." (Ex.15:1) Through these opening words we are told that an entire nation - not merely its prophets, scholars and leaders - all rose to a state of prophecy. Rashi says that so clear was the manifestation of Godliness that even the humblest Jew could point with his finger and say "This is my God and I will glorify Him." (Ex. 15:2) The midrash teaches that at the Sea of Reeds, even the suckling child stopped nursing in order to join in the singing. The chanting multitude extended to include the unborn child in the womb, and the angels as well.

Because the Israelites had faith in God and in His servant Moses, they were found worthy to sing the Song of the Sea. The two verses preceding the song read:

> "And when Israel saw the wondrous power which the Lord had wielded against the Egyptians, the people feared the Lord; they had faith in the Lord and His servant Moses." (Ex.14:31)
> "Then sang Moses and the Children of Israel this song to the Lord." (Ex. 15:1)

In other words, because of their faith, az yashir, then they sang.

The implication drawn by commentators is not just that the Israelites were moved to sing because of their faith, but that God created the Children of Israel for the specific purpose of extolling Him. The Mechilta (the Shirta) teaches that God loves all the peoples of the earth and all may sing His praises. Yet His favorite songs are those sung by Israel, for they are the ones He chose to redeem and be His people ("am-zu ga-alta," "this people You redeemed," Ex. 15:13). The proof-text is in Isaiah 43:21, "This people (am-zu) I formed for Myself that they might declare My praise (teheelati)."

Shirat Ha-Yam as Precedent

As the first of its kind, Shirat Ha-yam set the precedent. It became the form, the methodology, by which future generations would praise God. "Az yashir Moshe uv'nay Yisrael" (Ch 15:1), is the biblical basis for our tradition of Hallel and possibly even the nusach for prayer.

In the Tikkune Zohar (p. 45a), we read, "There is a Temple in Heaven that is opened only through song." Is it any wonder that so much of our tefilah is put to song? And in the Arakin, 11, "What is service with joy? Song." In the Zohar we read, "Why were the Levites selected to sing in the Temple? Because the name Levi means cleaving. The soul of him who heard their singing at once cleaved to God." (Zohar, ii, 19a)

The Song of the Sea established a formula for thanksgiving. It was the precursor of our Hallel, psalms of joy and thanksgiving for God's redemption, recited on all major biblical festivals except for Rosh Hashanah and Yom Kippur. In the Talmud, R. Eleazar asserts that Moses and the Children of Israel chanted the first Hallel; and Rabbi Akiva said, "The Holy Spirit rested upon them, and they uttered it in the manner that people recite Hallel."

It is generally accepted by the sages that Shirah was originally sung antiphonally. The song's use of parallel clauses supports this view. Philo, as early as the first century B.C.E. supposed the use of a male chorus led by Moses and a female chorus led by Miriam. Later rabbinic perspective proposes that Moses sang a phrase and the people responded. The exact form is unclear. However there is evidence of Levitical choirs in the temple and professional Levitical singers.

By the Second Temple times, Shirat Ha-yam had already become part of the liturgy. The Levitical choir would sing it during the tamid offering on Shabbat afternoons. Following the destruction of the Temple and the dissolution of the sacrificial cult, the tradition of chanting Shirah persevered. Eventually, the Jews of Rome incorporated this song into the daily Shaharit service, a custom that gradually spread to Jewish communities throughout the world. (*The JPS Torah Commentary, Exodus*, Nahum M. Sarna, p.76)

Prototype for the Future

For the Tannaim, the events in Torah were not perceived as simply a chronicling of an historical past. Perhaps even more important was the pattern they provided for understanding contemporary experiences as well as previewing the future. Therefore, many of our sages understood "az yashir Moshe uv'nay Yisrael," "then sang Moses and the Children of Israel" (Ex. 15:1) to be prophetic in nature. The word "yashir," translated here in this context as "sang," is in the imperfect or future tense, "will sing." The sages of the Mechilta saw "yashir," "will sing" as the basis in Torah for the doctrine of Resurrection of the Dead and Messianic Redemption. Shirat Ha-yam, the song of praise memorializing our first redemption from Mitzrayim, then is also the prototype for the celebration of our future redemption.

In *The Legends of the Jews* by Louis Ginsberg we read:

"As Moses and the race that wandered from Egypt with him sang a song to the Lord by the Red Sea, so shall they sing again in the world to come. In the world to come, all generations will pass before the Lord and will ask Him who should first intone the song of praise, whereupon He will reply: 'In the past it was the generation of Moses that offered up to me a song of praise. Let them do it now once more, and as

Moses conducted the song by the Red Sea, so shall he do in the world of the hereafter'" (Vol. III, p. 35)

The poetry of Judah Ha-Levi (ca. 1075-1141), perhaps the greatest Jewish poet of the Middle Ages, expressed the yearning for the ultimate redemption as a reflection of that initial song at the Sea of Reeds:

> *"Ah, take her as of yore.*
> *And cast her forth no more;*
> *Let sunlight crown her day*
> *And shadows flee away.*
> *Then a new song*
> *Sang Thy redeemed throng.*
>
> *For Thy beloved throng*
> *Still come to Thee with song,*
> *Singing with one accord:*
> *Now who is like Thee 'mid the gods, O Lord!*
> *Still Thy redeemed throng*
> *Sing a new song."*
>
> from *Selected Poems of Jehudah Halevi*, by
> Nina Salamon. Philadelphia, 1928, p. 171)

This theme of a new song heralding our messianic redemption was picked up in our prophetic literature, "Sing to the Lord a new song, His praise from the ends of the earth." (Isaiah 42:10)

In the Psalms, as well, we have obvious references to the original Song of the Sea as a prototype for the future:

> *"Sing to the Lord a new song,*
> *His praises in the congregation of the faithful.*
> *Let Israel rejoice in its maker;*
> *Let the children of Zion exult in their king.*

> *Let them praise His name in dance;*
> *With timbrel and lyre let them chant His*
> *praises." (Psalm 149:1-3)*

The Power of Shirah in our Liturgy Today

In modern times, Shirah continues as an integral part of our liturgy. According to the account in Exodus, Moses and the children of Israel sang the song on the seventh day after leaving Mitzrayim, and so, in keeping with the historical chronology, it is traditionally sung as part of the special holiday Torah reading each year on the seventh day of Pesah, as well as in the weekly sequence of Torah readings on Shabbat Shirah.

Since Roman times Shirat Ha-yam has also been part of Pesukei De-Zimra, recited daily by Jews all over the world. In the Zohar we read: "Whoever recites this song daily with devotion, shall be privileged to recite it in the (Messianic) future. For it alludes to the past and to the future, it is an expression of faith, and contains allusions to the royal Messiah; it also (mystically) embraces praise-songs...to tell it to all future generations, that it might never be forgotten...they were to sing it then (at the Exodus), in the Holy Land when they dwelt therein, in Exile, in freedom, and in the World to Come." (Zohar 2, 54b) Thus, Shirat Ha-yam has become a song for all time.

While we continue to chant the ancient ode, it serves, by example, as an inspiration for new ways to give voice to our adoration and glorification of God. As such, song is not just a vehicle to exalt God for the miracles of the past or the future, but for those miracles performed in every generation. "Sing to the Lord a new song . . . . Proclaim His victory day after day." (Psalm 96:1-2)

The ancients understood the potential of song to give form to our feelings, to raise them to a level of understanding and awareness. One midrash asks why the Children of Israel were given the honor of beginning the singing of Shirah before the angels.

The reason is that "the angels are eternally and at a moment's notice prepared to offer songs of praise, but not so the children of Israel. They are only capable of song when the desire and the feeling are spontaneously awakened within them. God feared that unless they were permitted to sing immediately, their desire would pass." (*Sparks Beneath the Surface*, Lawrence S. Kushner and Kerry M. Olitzky, p.81)

Song is our human response to the glory of God. It also enables us to keep His glory in our consciousness. The Zohar underscores the value of daily recitation of Shirat Ha-yam, "to tell it to all future generations, that it might never be forgotten." A case in point is the miracle of the splitting of the Jordan River that is chronicled in Joshua 3:16-17. How many remember that miracle? Rabbi A. Chein taught, "The miracle of the splitting of the Red Sea endures in the memory of the people on account of the song that they sang at the sea. The miracle of the splitting of the Jordan has not survived in our memory. There was no song." (*Sparks Beneath the Surface*, Lawrence S. Kushner and Kerry M. Olitzky, p.81)

Because of the all-inclusiveness of the phrase "az yashir," past, future and present meld into one. In chanting Shirat Ha-yam we have the potential to connect with Klal Yisrael, with our People, past and future, and beyond the confines of time. In our siddur, Shirah is a daily reminder of how we can offer thanksgiving to God, but encouragement is given throughout Tanakh and rabbinic commentary to use that example to write a new song. "Az yashir" can be seen as the biblical injunction to respond to our faith and give shape to the loftiest thoughts of the human spirit. It is not enough for us to experience God; we need to give form to our experience, to heighten our awareness of it, to capture it so we can relive it and keep it with us in our consciousness. Our ability to sing of God's marvelous ways is in itself a gift from God.

Whenever we raise our voices in songs of praise—whether to chant Shirat Ha-yam, or Hallel, or the nusach of our tefillah—we pay homage to the legacy of our people and leader, Moshe, at the

81

Sea of Reeds. They have endowed us with the tradition that has ever since enriched and informed our method of glorifying, adoring and thanking our Lord.

Debby Hellman coordinates the Bar/Bat Mitzvah program at Chizuk Amuno Congregation. She has been a student of Rabbi Zaiman's Adult Bat Mitzvah Class and his Women's Torah Study Group.

Yitro
Hazzan Emanuel C. Perlman

In this parashah, Yitro is described in the biblical narrative as a wise, sagacious and spiritual being. He is intensely interested in the details of Israel's struggles in their journey from slavery to freedom, both physical and spiritual. Yitro is practical and efficient. He has deep insight into social structures and the ability to implement institutional changes. Yitro's direct, blunt and insightful advice is instrumental in shaping the legal system of early Israel.

Moreover, Yitro is keenly involved with theology and spirituality. Both the biblical narrative and rabbinic commentary attest to Yitro's religious active involvement. The Bible tells us that Yitro is "Priest of Midyan" and the midrash informs us, Rashi (Ex 18:11) also picks up on this, that Yitro sought to understand all forms of religion known to mankind in antiquity seeking the "True God."

In fact, the phrase, "Now I have known that God is greater than all other gods" becomes the phrase which informs the reader of Yitro's seriousness and commitment to spiritual discovery. It is instructive that the rabbis named the Torah portion, where the Ten Commandments are given, after this man Yitro. The opening narrative in the parashah is indeed instructive to the extraordinary spiritual world of Yitro especially as he is so close to the greatest prophet, his son-in-law, Moshe.

Our examination begins with two accounts that Yitro receives about the Exodus from Egypt. The portion begins, "Yitro, priest of Midyan, Moshe's father-in-law, heard all that God had for Moshe and for Israel His people, how the Lord had brought Israel out of Egypt." (Ex18:1) After meeting Moshe, Yitro hears again the tale, "Moshe then recounted to his father-in-law everything that the Lord had done to Pharaoh and to the Egyptians for Israel's sake, all the hardships that had befallen them on the way, and how the Lord had delivered them." (Ex 18:8) After the second account Yitro attains an extraordinary enlightenment into the nature of God, His role in history, and man's relation especially regarding the possibility of human insight and experience of God.

The second account is Moshe's personal and subjective account; let's follow it. Before Moshe receives his mission to go to Pharaoh, he is a humble shepherd at the edge of the desert. (Ex 3:1-4:17) One can hear Moshe think. "This is it. Me and these dumb sheep. We both will be buried in the desert sand without a trace." The emptiness, the nothingness had to be crushing and devastating. Moshe especially feels hopeless and helpless because his people are still in the grip of the Egyptian Empire. There is no chance that they will ever be liberated. At this point, the rock bottom pit of despair, Moshe has a revelation of "God in the Burning Bush." The epiphany is carefully wrought in the Torah.

Moshe is the source of revelation. It is not God who calls out to Moshe, as He does throughout Genesis to the Patriarchs. Moshe beholds a vision and asks WHY? Only after Moshe is intent on examining the Burning Bush, does God address Moshe. The Torah pointedly notes that God speaks to Moshe only after Moshe approaches closer to examine this "Great Sight." What is this Great Sight? What is the Burning Bush, which burns but is not consumed? We suggest that Moshe is aware once more, in a most moving way, of his own thought process, which he understands as possessing the Image of God. Moshe experiences the vision within. There is no greater sight to behold, there is no greater direct experience felt, than this Presence. A living, thinking human being who is aware of the Divine potential and power that is man and God.

Moshe is made aware that the Exodus can be made real by using this very power, the power of speech and spirit. He needs to go to Pharaoh and simply tell him, "Thus said the Lord God of Israel, 'Let My people go!'" (Ex 5:1) Moshe's awareness and spirituality, his direct accessibility to God is stunningly described in the Torah. "The Lord would speak to Moshe face to face, as one man speaks to another." (Ex 33:11) This description is poignant and achingly elusive, yet so close to all who read this verse. We all speak to a friend sometimes, even if it is only ourselves! In Hebrew, "face-to-face" is *"panim el panim,"* which denotes "within." Moshe experiences his interior consciousness as place, *"maqom"* where God is Experienced. It is singularly instructive that the Torah frames Moshe's knowledge and experience of God in the ordinary state of being. The supreme knowledge of God is not experienced in ecstasy or in an altered heightened state of consciousness. Supreme revelation and manifestation of God is to be attained in direct simple human conversation with a friend, with oneself.

Yitro's comment, "Now I know" is all the more striking because it informs us that this knowledge is available and accessible to man. Elsewhere, we also find the experience of epiphany, of experiencing God described in terms of place and knowledge. Jacob on his first night away from home has a dream where God speaks to him directly. When Jacob awakens he exclaims, "Indeed there is God in this place (maqom) and I did not know." (Gen 28:16) Jacob experienced God within; place is not geography, it is the conscious sacred Image of God that every thinking aware human being owns. In order to discover It, one needs only to behold this extraordinary vision and ask: Why? Soon he or she will hear a Voice calling on him/her. Inevitably they will exclaim, "Indeed there is God in this place; Now I know that God is greater than all gods!"

Emanuel C. Perlman's relationship to Rabbi Zaiman has been enduring and endearing. Their families have been spiritually connected for over 35 years. Hazzan Perlman's father, Hazzan Ivan Perlman, served with Rabbi Zaiman at Temple Emanu-El in Providence, Rhode Island. Hazzan Perlman currently serves with Rabbi Zaiman at Chizuk Amuno Congregation

Mishpatim
Rabbi Steven Schwartz

When *Time Magazine* named Albert Einstein as its "Person of the Century," it explained that the choice was based on the overarching impact Einstein had made in the field of science. As Frederic Golden wrote in his article about the great scientist, "The touchstones of the era—the Bomb, the Big Bang, quantum physics, and electronics—all bear his imprint." And so the greatest scientist from the century that will be remembered for scientific and technological advancement deserved *Time*'s Person of the Century honor.

Einstein, however, gave us more than just descriptive physics equations about the relationship between time and space. He actually gave us new ways to think about, or to conceive of, time and space. He helped us to understand that time and space are not absolute—instead, they depend upon gravity, matter, and perception. In his theory of general relativity, Einstein showed that gravity actually warps space and time, potentially changing the size of an object or the length of a unit of time, measurements that had long been considered constant. In short, even something like time, long perceived as unchanging and irrevocable, can be manipulated. Time itself is changing and changeable—not the straight line of progression we had always imagined.

The medieval exegetes whose work appears on the pages of the *Mikraot Gedolot* were not strangers to the idea that time is malleable. It is not uncommon to discover within their comments on the Torah's text ideas like *ain mukdam u'mechar batorah*—there is no set chronology in the Torah. And the rabbinical commentators were not afraid to suggest that certain sections of the Torah were out of place chronologically. That is to say, that certain events in the Torah are presented in the wrong order—either earlier or later than they actually might have happened. One such instance of rabbinic commentary occurs in

Parashat Mishpatim, the sixth Torah portion found in the Book of Exodus.

Parashat Mishpatim deals primarily with a series of laws or judgements (*mishpatim*) which God gives to Moses to give to the Israelites. Most of the laws are presented in a straightforward manner— "these are things you will do and these are things you will not do"—and fall under the category of civil law. The series of laws begins as the *sedra* itself begins, and it takes up almost the entire *parashah*.

However, just as the *parashah* is ready to end, a strange and unexpected story appears in the text at the beginning of the twenty-fourth chapter of Exodus (verses 1-11). God tells Moses and Aaron, Nadav and Abihu (Aaron's sons), and the seventy elders of Israel, *alei el adonai*—to "Rise towards God." What ensues is a surreal encounter between this exclusive group of Israel's leaders and Israel's God. According to the Torah, the group sees God and eats a meal in God's presence. The normal danger associated with close contact with the Divine seems to be momentarily suspended for the group, almost as if they have entered another world, where different laws and expectations apply.

Rashi, perhaps picking up on the out-of-context feel of this story (and also following the *midrash* and the *gemara*), suggests in his commentary that this encounter with God actually occurred *before* the giving of the Ten Commandments, a full four chapters earlier in Exodus. The other major commentators on the text, including the Ramban, the Ibn Ezra, and the Rashbam, all disagree with Rashi. They are not prepared to suggest, such a radical warping in the Torah's time chronology, based on the evidence before them, and so prefer to leave the story of the encounter with God in its original "time slot."

Lurking beneath this disagreement between Rashi and the other commentators are perhaps two different understandings of the way we arrive at spiritual experiences in our lives. It seems that Rashi, by placing the story of the encounter with God before the Ten Commandments are given, is implying that the experience of God can be independent of the experience of Sinai. That is to say, we human beings are open to the mystical, intimate experience of the Divine, regardless of the system of law that God gave at Sinai. We do not need that system of law to mediate the Divine for us.

The other commentators, disagreeing with Rashi, are uncomfortable with this idea. They believe that the Ten Commandments and the laws given later in *Parashat Mishpatim* are the very means through which Jews can approach God. Therefore, it is the actual giving of the law that opens up the possibility of the intimate encounter between the Israelite leaders and the Divine.

I would suggest that both factors are at play in our own religious lives. We need to remain open to the possibility of encounter with God – if we close that off we will lose our ability to sense the Divine Presence in this world. At the same time, we need a system that regulates our spiritual quest. In Judaism, the *halakhah*—the Jewish legal corpus—has become that system.

Joel Zaiman, throughout his career in the rabbinate, has exemplified this idea. He has led his congregation forward in a spiritual quest, always reminding them to keep their minds open to the Divine experience. All the while he has framed that quest in the context of the tradition, ever mindful of its legal foundation.

May he continue to do so for many years to come.

Steven Schwartz is Assistant Rabbi of Beth El Congregation in Baltimore, Maryland.

Terumah
Dr. Paul D. Schneider

When moderns ask the question, "Where is God?" they are either engaging in a theological exercise or crying *gevalt* at God's apparent disinterest in a human tragedy. When ancients asked the same question, they were reaching for a lifeline. Confronted by the capricious forces of nature, over which they had neither control nor understanding, ancient people sought divine intervention to preserve their lives.

But, to beseech their gods with their requests, ancients needed an address. Where do the gods dwell? Perhaps it is where heaven and earth were joined together, and what could be a more appropriate "connector" than a holy mountain. Or, in the flat plains of Mesopotamia, a man-made mountain, a *ziggurat*, whose bottom is fully anchored in the earth, and whose top reaches into the clouds. For pagans, the mountain was the "navel of the earth," the very center of life's coordinates.

When viewed in this perspective, Mt. Sinai was the Jewish holy mountain par excellence. It was at this very place that God revealed Godself to the new nation of Israel. It was at this very place that masses of former slaves, with the words *na-asah v'nishmah*, "we shall do and we shall listen," were transformed into a covenental people.

But the people of Israel were on the move, and could not take the mountain with them. Thus in *Parashat Terumah*, we find the imperative *va-asu li mikdash v'shokhanti b'tokhom*, "let them build me a sanctuary, that I may dwell among them." (Deut. 25:8)

The tabernacle was to be constructed according to the intricate plans presented to Moses by God while on the mountain. A major part of the book of Exodus describes in detail the construction of the tabernacle.

Rambam and others show in their commentaries that the tabernacle was symbolic of the historic experience at Mt. Sinai.

The tabernacle was to function as did the holy mountain, as a place to communicate with God, and to elevate the people spiritually and morally.

What were the characteristics of this sanctuary, the prototype of all subsequent sanctuaries? What needed to be done in order to merit God's presence among the people, to fulfill the mandate, "that I may dwell among them?"

First, the building of the tabernacle was a true community project reflecting the generosity and skill of the masses. The gifts for the tabernacle's construction were to be voluntary, at different levels of giving—bronze, silver and gold, depending on the ability of the donor and the wishes of his heart. Secondly, the half *shekel* contributed in the census by each man of military age went toward the daily sacrificial offering, thus serving also to elevate them spiritually. And thirdly, the treasure contained in the holy ark was not an image of God, as found among all other peoples in the innermost shrine of their temples, but rather the word of God, the Decalogue. The Decalogue was a symbol of the covenant, and of God's social and moral demands upon the people. Through the observance of these *mitzvot*, indeed all *mitzvot*, all Israelites could bring themselves closer to God. As it is written, *kodshenu b'mitzvotekha*, make us holy through your commandments."

Thus, it was no longer necessary to climb a mountain to find God: God's Torah was easily accessible. As we read later in Deuteronomy, "*Lo bashamayim he . . . Velo me-ever layam he . . . Ki qarov elekha hadavar m'od b'fikha u-vilvavekha la-asoto.*" (Deut. 30: 12 - 14) The Torah is not in the heavens . . . Nor is it across the sea . . . But rather it is within your mouth and heart to observe it." God could be found close by among the community, in the sanctuary, and in the performance of the *mitzvot*.

Dr. Paul D. Schneider is headmaster of Krieger Schechter Day School of Chizuk Amuno Congregation.

Tetzaveh
Alan N. Kanter

The first section of Parashat Tetzaveh deals with the meaning of the Ner Tamid or Eternal Light.

When one enters the sanctuary of a synagogue, one cannot help but notice the Ner Tamid hanging above the ark. In modern times it is lit by an electric light although in the past the light remained glowing, fueled by oil. Aaron and his sons Nadab, Abihu, Eleazar and Ithamar were commanded by God to bring clear oil of beaten olives to the sanctuary in order to fuel the eternal flame.

There is tremendous symbolism in this passage. In *A Torah Commentary For Our Times* (Page 72): "What, the rabbis ask, does Israel have in common with an olive tree, or with the clear oil of beaten olives? The answer is not a happy comparison. The life of the olive, the rabbis explain, is a hard one. It dries and shrivels while on the tree. Then it is cut down, crushed, ground, impressed until it yields oil. So it is, the rabbis claim, with the history of the people of Israel. They have been beaten, chained, imprisoned, and surrounded by those threatening to crush them. Enemies constantly endanger them. Yet they have survived because they were loyal to God, asked God's forgiveness for their errors, and repented their wrongdoings. In this interpretation, the Ner Tamid with its beaten olive oil, symbolizes the cruel oppression Jews have endured and their constant faith in God. Like the Ner Tamid that burns forever, the Jewish people will survive forever despite their persecutors."

Every year at the Passover Seder, Jews are reminded of the suffering that they endured and their exodus from bondage. It is important for us to always repeat the story so that we will never forget all that we endured to survive and achieve the freedom that we now have. However, today we Jews, especially in America, do not endure the type of persecution and suffering that we did in previous times. There are enemies that we face on a daily basis, but there are other races and religions that are confronted with the same type of hatred and bigotry. We have remained loyal to God as a people through all our encounters of bigotry, cruelty and attempts to exterminate us. We cannot forget the lessons of the past but as a people we must not constantly dwell in the past and have a singular view of ourselves as victims. Rather, we must work to reverse the evil that fosters intolerance, hatred or bigotry towards any individual, race or creed.

If the eternal light symbolizes the fact that the Jewish people will survive forever, it is incumbent upon Israel to become a light of all nations. The commentaries in the Hertz Humash state that "the rabbis interpreted the lamp as a symbol of Israel whose mission was to become a light of nations (Isa. Chapter XLII, 6). In Genesis, Rabbah Chapter 36, Verse 2, Prophet Isaiah said God has chosen Israel to be "a light to all the nations." Light helps one to see the path that they must follow. A light can brighten the world and if Israel is to be the light among the nations, it has the obligation to make sure that the Ner Tamid is always lit.

If the State of Israel is the "light to all the nations," then its citizens and Jews throughout the world help to create that eternal glow. It is through study that one becomes enlightened, and then educated. Torah provides us with the answers but also poses many questions.

At Chizuk Amuno, our mission statement is based on Torah, Avodah and Gemult Hassadim. By adhering to these three ideals, we, as Jews, become a light not only to other nations but also to individuals. When one studies Torah, prayer and acts of loving-kindness are sure to follow.

For a Congregation to commit itself to learning just does not occur without a light to help it see the path it must follow. From the time he arrived at Chizuk Amuno twenty years ago, Rabbi Joel Zaiman has been our continual light. He has emphasized the need to study Torah and become educated Jewishly so that we can fulfill our obligations as Jews to help repair the world. When performing the mitzvahs expected of us, we become a light to all the nations and individuals.

Chizuk Amuno Congregation takes education very seriously. Our emphasis is not just on the education of our children but on all members of the community regardless of their age. Each person through educational programs has the opportunity to be a light unto others and just like a candle, which when it is first lit, continues to glow, provide light, and even as it burns down, it still emanates the same type of bright light. Just as the shofar awakens us at Rosh Hoshana, adult learners have experienced a constant awakening to Judaism and all that it has to offer.

More members of Chizuk Amuno are leading their life in a more Jewish fashion than ever before. Little steps are being taken by a large number of people. They have become a light unto others and become role models for young adults and children. An atmosphere for learning has been created which expands and transcends the educational horizons as we had previously known them. Becoming involved leads to attendance at Shabbat services and Holidays throughout the entire year and support for synagogue activities such as a special day (Tikun Olam) where our members provide services to the Baltimore community.

Members of Chizuk Amuno Congregation would have never experienced, to the degree that we have, the ability to partake in educational programs and become guiding lights to others if it were not for Rabbi Joel Zaiman. It has been through Rabbi Zaiman's vision and leadership that this has been accomplished and it is continuing to grow. Education has created an awareness of the world and how we can apply our Jewish values to everyday situations in our lives.

Alan N. Kanter was President of Chizuk Amuno Congregation from June 1996 until June 1998. During this time, he and Rabbi Zaiman worked together and forged a bond of mutual respect and friendship.

Ki Thissa
Rabbi Elana Zaiman

According to the biblical text, there are reasons, good reasons, why Moses broke the first set of tablets. He was angry at the Israelites for making the golden calf, for not awaiting his return from Mt. Sinai, for not believing in the God of Israel. According to the Tanhuma, there is another reason. If Moses hadn't broken the tablets, the people would have been responsible for observing the third commandment inscribed on the tablet, *"lo yehyeh lecha elohim acherim al panai."* ("You shall have no other gods beside Me.") Moses, therefore, broke the tablets in order to protect the people Israel from transgression. (*Tanhuma Yelamden*u Chapter 9:30)

Shortly after Moses broke this first set of tablets, God commanded him: *"Pesal lecha shnai luchot avanim."* ("Hew yourself two tablets of stone.") (Exodus 34:1) This command concerns the second set of tablets. Unlike the first set of tablets, which God gave to Moses, the second set of tablets were to be fashioned by Moses himself. After all, he did smash the first set. He should be held accountable. Rashi comments: "You (Moses) broke the first tablets, you hew the others." (based on *Tanhuma Yelamdenu* Chapter 9:28)

What interests me most in God's command to Moses to "hew two tablets" is the use of the word *"pesal."* Why is the word *"pesal"* used? The verb *"pesal"* means "to hew," and the noun *"pesel"* means "idol." Why associate the word "idol," in any of its forms, with the building of the holy tablets, tablets on which God's word was to be inscribed, especially since Moses had broken the tablets in response to the building of an idol, the golden calf? Wouldn't another word make more sense? A word having no association with the theme of idolatry? What about the word, *"chatzov"* which also means "to hew"?

What about the word, *"asah"*(to make), as in "Make yourself two tablets of stone?" What about the word, *"banah"* (to build), as in "Build yourself two tablets of stone?" Surely these words would be more fitting. Or would they?

With these words in mind, I closely reread the story of the golden calf. It is interesting, ironic even, that the words used in the story of the golden calf are *"asah"* (to make), as in *"aseh lanu elohim"* ("make us a god") and *"banah"* (to build) as *in "vayiven mizbeach"* ("and he (Aaron) built an altar"). Also interesting is that, in the story of the golden calf, the words *"pesal/pesel/pesalim"* (hew, idol, idols) are never used. Perhaps, then, the choice of the word *"pesal"* ("to hew") in reference to the tablets was purposeful, in that the words used to describe the golden calf were rejected for this holy activity of rebuilding the tablets. It makes sense to use a different verb to distinguish between the building of the golden calf and the hewing of the two tablets of stone for the second set of commandments. But, I still come back to the question, why the word *"pesal?"* Why not the word *"chatzov?"* Even though the word *"pesal"* is not directly used in the description of the golden calf, it certainly brings that episode to mind.

Rabbi Yehoshua's comment on "hew yourself two tablets of stone" offers insight, for he is very much attuned to the literary connection between the verb "pesal" and the noun "pesel" (idol). He states, *"shehu mevaer **pesilai** eloheyhem"* ("that it removes the idols (*pesilai*) of their gods."). (Tanhuma Ekev 9) According to Rabbi Yehoshua, the use of the verb *"pesal"* in God's command to Moses to hew two tablets of stone, serves, in a sense, to cancel the Israelites' previous idolatrous acts. The Ten commandments were to become the words embraced and fulfilled by the people Israel. The Ten commandments were to take the place of idolatry.

Another interesting point. The scene that directly precedes God's command to Moses to hew two tablets of stone is the scene where Moses requests to see God's Presence. Though God did not allow Moses to see God's face, since human beings may not see God and live, God somehow understood that Moses needed to experience more. So God allowed Moses to see God's back and God's qualities of goodness and compassion. Moses, too, desired what the Israelites desired. Moses wanted some kind of physical sign of God's presence before he could lead the Israelites forward on their journey. Although he did not need an idol to supplant the gods of Egypt, as did the Israelites, he did need to see some physical attribute of God.

Perhaps, then, the use of the word *"pesal"* is a subtle warning to Moses. "Be careful Moses, these tablets, like the idols of Egypt, like the golden calf, can also be used for idolatrous purposes. People can worship the stone on which the commandments are written. People can follow the commandments with such fervor and passion that the fervor and passion become more meaningful than the commandments themselves. And then there is the subtle message, Moses. Anything human beings create—art, music, poetry, children—can become the source of idolatry. People need to work hard not to let their creations turn into idols."

Of course, we need to enjoy our creations, to fully appreciate our works, but we also need to remember that our creations are not just our creations. We do not create by ourselves alone. We create with God's help. Moses hewed the stone for the tablets. But God inscribed the tablets with meaning. This set of tablets was a joint venture. Our creations are about this joint venture, this divine-human partnership, this understanding that when we create we are involved in a sacred process.

Elana Zaiman, rabbi, social worker, educator, writer, wife and mother, decided to enter the rabbinate as a result of growing up in her parents' home.

Vayyekel
Rabbi Deborah Wechsler

The Scene: Parashat Vayyekel begins with Moses gathering the people together. "Moses then convoked the whole Israelite community and said to them: These are the things that the Lord has commanded you to do: On six days work may be done, but on the seventh day you shall have a sabbath of complete rest." (Exodus 35:1-2)

The Curiosity: Out of all the possible mitzvot in the Torah, the first one Moses describes is the commandment to keep Shabbat. It is Shabbat that will transform the group of Israelites into a whole community. Not the belief in one God, or the sanctity of the Tabernacle, nor the drive for holiness, but the week-to-week observance of Shabbat is the most important element of the new covenant between God and the Jewish people.

The command to keep Shabbat is forever tied up in the command to build the Tabernacle that immediately follows it. Rashi's famous explanation is that these two are brought in the same parashah to teach that the work of building the Tabernacle should not take place on Shabbat. But we devoted readers of Torah find that the two concepts of Shabbat and the Tabernacle are interwoven in many ways that alter our ideas of physical space and space in time.

Why, one might ask, does the command concerning space in time precede the command concerning physical space? "Rabbi Samuel Bar Nahmani said in the name of Rabbi Jonathan: Betzalel (the builder of the Tabernacle) was so called on account of his wisdom. When the Holy One said to Moses: Go and tell Betzalel to make me the Tabernacle, Ark and vessels, Moses went

97

and reversed the order saying, 'Make an Ark, vessels, and Tabernacle.' Betzalel countered, 'Moses our teacher, as a rule a man first builds a house and then brings his vessels into it; but you say, 'Make me an Ark, vessels, and the Tabernacle?' The vessels I make—where am I to put them? Perhaps the Holy One said to you, 'Make the Tabernacle, Ark and vessels?' Moses replied, 'You may well have been in the shadow of God (betzel-el) and so you know!'"(Babylonian Talmud, Berahot 55a) The command to keep Shabbat must come before that of building the Tabernacle because Shabbat is the home in which we dwell. It is Heschel's "sanctuary in time," and the ark and the Tabernacle are the physical vessels which serve us in the holy house of time. They would be homeless and useless without the structure to contain them.

Twice in the Torah, the commands of Shabbat and the Tabernacle are linked in one verse. "You shall keep my Sabbaths and venerate My sanctuary: I am the Lord." (Leviticus 19:30, 26:2) Nahum Sarna, in *Exploring Exodus,* explains the connection between the two concepts: "It would seem that the sequence here conveys a statement about a scale of values, a judgement about the relative importance of sacred time and sacred space . . . in the biblical value system the concept of holiness of time takes precedence over that of the holiness of space." (page 214) The locale of the Tabernacle is only sacred while the Tabernacle is resting there, at other times it loses its inherent holiness. Shabbat is the only permanent Tabernacle because it dwells in our hearts.

Parashat Vayyekel is about artistry, the artistry involved in constructing the Tabernacle. So one would think that this parashah, in focusing on a body part, would focus on the hands, the instrument of the artist, but it does not. The physical focus in this parashah is on the heart. The evidence for this is found immediately after the instruction to keep the Sabbath, when we are commanded, "Take from among you gifts to the Lord; everyone whose heart so moves him shall bring them." (Exodus 35:5) What gifts could we possibly give God that would be meaningful to Him?

Shabbat is one of the few gifts that we can give to God. There is a Midrash that says that when the Torah speaks of the construction of the Tabernacle and the Temple, the structures that are built here on earth are a mirror of the structures in heaven above.

If we are to understand Shabbat as the "portable Tabernacle" that we carry with us through time and space, then the Shabbat we observe here on earth must be a mirror of the Shabbat that is celebrated in heaven above. In keeping Shabbat we fulfill the command of *imitatio dei*, to imitate the divine.

When we give a gift to a loved one, we want it to be an honest expression of our heart's desire. A free donation demonstrates our devotion, our commitment and willingness to sacrifice for a larger ideal. Each Shabbat is an offering to God, *nidvat lev*, an offering of the heart and purely received. The root *n.d.v.* is one that is repeated many times in this parashah. It is a leitwort of the building of the Tabernacle and, by association, of Shabbat.

When called upon by Moses to provide furnishings for the Tabernacle, the people responded overwhelmingly. With generosity of material resources and spiritual resources, the Israelite people responded to the call with offerings of gold and silver as well as their skilled workmanship. This is the artistry of the Tabernacle and there is a similar artistry to Shabbat. While an "amateur" Shabbat can have a certain excitement and raw, natural beauty, Shabbat is a craft that needs to be honed.

Shabbat is best learned with a master craftsman, someone who has been engaged in the art of Shabbat for many years, someone who knows how to take the raw material of Shabbat observance and turn it into a work of art: each Shabbat unique, yet embossed with the original stamp of the artist. Each person needs a Betzalel and Oholiab to guide them and supervise them with the divine qualities of skill, ability and knowledge.

Betzalel and Oholiab were no ordinary craftsmen. About them the Torah says, "And God has put in his heart that he may teach." (Exodus 35:34) One might ask why the Torah found it necessary to add the idea that the artists would also teach the people. Ibn Ezra, the twelfth-century Spanish Bible commentator, explains that some scholars have a great deal of wisdom, but they keep it to themselves because they are unwilling or unable to share it with others. Thus the Torah felt it necessary to stress that Betzalel and Oholiab had been endowed with both the artistic ability and the desire to teach and communicate their skill and knowledge to those willing to learn. Ibn Ezra indicates that the true artisans of Torah are those who are not only masters of their crafts, but also are able to communicate their Torah knowledge to others in a way that makes them grow in their ability to relate to the Holy One.

There is a traditional Jewish song whose author is unknown. Its words, beginning *Bilevavi Mishkan Evneh*, speak to the Tabernacle that each of us carries within us.

> *"In my heart I will build a Tabernacle to glorify God's honor, and in the Tabernacle I will place an altar to the glory of God's splendor. And for the Ner Tamid I will take the fire of the Akeidah, and for a sacrifice I will offer my one, unique soul."*

We say that the Ner Tamid, the Eternal Light, is the permanent light of yiddishkeit that was lit when the Tabernacle was constructed and continues to burn in each modern synagogue. But the reality is that synagogues get torn down or burned down, they become churches and bulbs burn out. The only Ner Tamid in Judaism is the Shabbat candle.

In every country Jews have lived, in every time of persecution or great prosperity, Jews have lit Shabbat candles. As candles are lit each Friday night, we step into the work of art that is the Shabbat. Before we begin to build for ourselves magnificent Tabernacles in space, Parashat Vayyekel reminds us to build a magnificent Tabernacle in our hearts and offer as a sacrifice that gift that is most meaningful to God, the Shabbat.

Pekudey
Rabbi Stuart Seltzer

When the children of Israel left Egypt, they were physically free. When they received the 10 Commandments at Sinai, they became a free people with laws. But they still lacked something.

These wanderers needed a place, so the Divine Presence could dwell among them, as it had among their patriarchs. So at the end of the book of Shemot, we have the building of the Tabernacle as commanded by God through Moses, and a detailed recounting of all the work and materials that went into the building.

"These are the records of the Tabernacle..."

They hammered out sheets of gold and cut threads to be worked into designs.

"We are free, but tired of wandering."

Carnelian, chrysolite, emerald, turquoise, sapphire, amethyst, jacinth, agate, crystal, beryl, lapis lazuli, and a jasper.

"For the first time in our lives we are working on something together, as a free people."

The stones correspond to the names of the 12 Tribes of Israel.

"Now the same hands that built the Golden Calf are doing a different kind of work."

The ephod was made of gold, purple and crimson yarns, and fine twisted linen.

"We need a sign that God is not angry anymore."

As the Lord had commanded Moses, "We will be different when we go in there."

As the Lord had commanded Moses,

"This work is an expression of our longing for God."

As the Lord had commanded Moses,

"We want a permanent home."

As the Lord had commanded Moses,

"Any place we set it down is sanctified."

As the Lord had commanded Moses,

"We hope that God will dwell among us."

As the Lord had commanded Moses,

"We thank you for giving us this new work."

They made the frontlets for the holy diadem of pure gold, and incised upon it the seal inscription: "Holy to the Lord."

"In slavery we built temples of our masters. Now as a free people, and servants of God, we are building our own Temple."

The opening of the robe, in the middle of it, was like the opening of a coat of mail with the binding around the opening, so that it would not tear.

"We will always place the Tabernacle in the center of our camp."

They also made bells of pure gold, and attached the bells between the pomegranates, all around the hem of the robe, between the pomegranates: a bell and a pomegranate, a bell and a pomegranate, all around the hem of the robe for officiating in—as the Lord had commanded Moses.

> *"Every stitch, every bang of the hammer, every swing of the logs sanctifies God's name."*

Thus was completed all the work of the Tabernacle of the Tent of Meeting. The Israelites did so; just as the Lord had commanded Moses, so they did.

> *"As great as it is, let it be as a sketch of the Temple that our children will one day build in the Promised Land."*

And when Moses saw that they had performed all the tasks—as the Lord had commanded, so they had done—Moses blessed them.

> *"May it be God's will, that the Divine Presence abide in the work of your hands and let the graciousness of the Lord our God be upon us and the work of our hands."*

You shall bring Aaron and his sons forward to the entrance of the Tent of Meeting and wash them with water.

> *"We wash as a sign that this work has purified us and made us ready for you, Oh Lord."*

When Moses finished the work, the cloud covered the tent of meeting, and the glory of the Lord filled the Tabernacle.

> *"How beautiful are your tents, O Jacob, your dwelling places O Israel."*

For over the Tabernacle, a cloud of the Lord rested by day, and fire would appear in it by night, in the view of all the house of Israel throughout their journey.

> "We will carry this Tabernacle to the Promised Land. This Tabernacle will carry us to the Promised Land."

Rabbi Stuart Seltzer is Director of Rosenbloom Religious School of Chizuk Amuno Congregation.

LEVITICUS • ויקרא

BE BOLD AS A LEOPARD AND LIGHT AS AN EAGLE, SWIFT AS A DEER AND MIGHTY AS A LION TO DO THE WILL OF YOUR FATHER WHO IS IN HEAVEN.

ANGELA MUNITZ '99

Vayyikra
Michelle Sullum

The wrongs that we commit unintentionally are the ones for which we find it most difficult to apologize. Not having set out to cause harm, we are not prepared for the consequences of wrongdoing. We do all sorts of mental gymnastics to absolve ourselves of responsibility. We find it nearly impossible to say, "I'm sorry," without immediately continuing, "but I didn't know..." We feel compelled to make excuses—to point out that, had our knowledge been more extensive, our choices or actions would have been different. We would not have chosen to do wrong in this situation.

Our compulsion to excuse ourselves for our accidental sins stems from anger and frustration. These unintentional sins highlight for us the tension that permeates our lives: our power to choose our actions and affect the world around us does not negate our helplessness before the whims of circumstance. The Torah, with its remarkable sensitivity to the paradoxes of human existence, gives us *Parashat Vayyikra* as a bandage for the spiritual wounds we incur and the estrangement from God we feel when we are confronted with our limited nature.

Parashat Vayyikra is a text that deals with the minutiae of animal sacrifice. Though it begins with the instructions for sacrifices of homage and well-being, the majority of the *parashah* deals with the sacrifices to bring if one sins unintentionally. On its surface, the practice seems absurd. How can the act of slaughtering and burning an animal repair the wrongs we have done in the world? The notion only makes sense if the wrongs we do have an effect beyond their immediate, physical outcome. According to Rabbi Samson Raphael Hirsch, they do: they weaken the fire in our souls that allows us to connect with God.

Rabbi Hirsch's commentary focuses on the language the Biblical text uses to describe the person who commits an inadvertent transgression. The text reads: "*Nefesh ki techeta*

107

bishgaga—a soul that sins unintentionally" (Vayyikra, 4:2). According to Hirsch, the use of the word "nefesh"—soul —instead of "adam"—"person"—is significant. The soul, says Hirsch, is where the seat of our humanity lies, the source of our free will. That free will allows us to make choices that result in sin, but it becomes corrupted if we do so. The purpose of the free will residing in our souls is to allow us to make choices that will bring us closer to God. When our choices result in sin, the result is estrangement from God rather than keruv, closeness.

By bringing a sacrifice, a korban, our ancestors were able to regain that sense of closeness to God, that *keruv*, that is the soul's ultimate desire. When they burned an animal at God's altar, they were symbolically taking the physical aspect of life that tempted them to choose wrongly and transmuting it into the fire they wished to strengthen in their souls. To bring a korban was to engage in an act of sympathetic magic. By bringing a korban our Israelite ancestors could strengthen the aspect of their souls that was divine. A korban did not repair the damage they had done in the world, it repaired the damage they had done to their souls and to their relationship with God.

We modern Jews, living in the era of rabbinic Judaism, do not have recourse to the sympathetic magic of the Temple Cult. What do we do, then, when we commit an inadvertent wrong and feel ourselves estranged from our Creator as a result? The rabbis, sensitive to the human need for physical action to express what is essentially an emotional and spiritual process, provided us with a different ritual. Instead of sacrificing animals, we now sacrifice ourselves. How do we do this? In the Babylonian Talmud, Berachot 17a, we find the following account of the process:

When Rav Sheshet kept a fast, on concluding his prayer he added the following: "Sovereign of the Universe, You know full well that in the time when the Temple was standing, if a man sinned he used to bring a sacrifice, and though all that was offered of it was its fat and blood, atonement was made for him therewith. Now I have kept a fast and my fat and blood have diminished. May it be

Your will to account my fat and blood which have been diminished as if I had offered them before You on the altar, and do You favor me."

In Temple times, the Israelites would convert the fat and blood of animals to fire. Through this act of sympathetic magic they would strengthen their souls and feel themselves closer to God. In modern times, we use our own bodies as the offering. Every Yom Kippur, we deprive ourselves of food and water for twenty-five hours, so as to diminish the fat and blood in our bodies. Six times over the course of that twenty-five hour period, we chant a list of sins that we may have committed, either intentionally or unintentionally. At the conclusion of each recitation of the confessional we add, "Forgive us too, for the sins for which, in the days of the Temple, the law would have required a burnt offering, a sin offering, an offering varying according to our means, and an offering for certain or for doubtful trespass." These are precisely the sins detailed in Parashat Vayyikra.

Though the Temple is gone, our spiritual and emotional need for its rituals remains. The paradox of power and powerlessness that is God's gift of free will can never be resolved. It is the essence of the human condition, simultaneously drawing us near to our Creator and keeping us forever distant.

According to Rabbi Hirsch, the sacrificial system offered the Israelites comfort in the face of this paradox. Though God was distant, we could still draw near. The very words used for sacrifices, "korban," bringing near, and "olah," rising up, conveyed the possibility of closeness with God. We modern Jews, lacking as we do the symbolic language of the Temple cult in our forms of worship, are less sanguine about this possibility. Parashat Vayyikra reminds us that we humans always have the ability within our souls to reach out and connect with our Creator.

Michelle Sullum is Education Director for the Society for the Advancement of Judaism in Manhattan. Rabbi Zaiman is her uncle.

Marci Dickman
Tzav

What a relief this parashah was to those with authority! Imagine being responsible for the most important functions of the sacred sanctuary and having only sketchy details about the *korbanot* (sacrifices) from the book of *Shemot* and *Parashat Vayyikra*. In fact, *Parashat Tzav* does come to the rescue of the priests (Aaron and his sons) by fleshing out many of the instructions of the *korbanot*, which were previously explained in lay terms for the common Israelite.

Once *Parashat Tzav* is understood as a "cookbook" for the priests, it is also understandable why the emphasis and the order of the sacrifices are slightly different than in *Parashat Vayyikra*. In *Parashat Vayyikra*, the audience is *b'nei Yisrael*, "*Daber el b'nei Yisrael,*" and the sacrificial offerings are arranged in order according to the need to bring them; those that are voluntary precede those which are obligatory. In *Parashat Tzav*, the primary audience is the priests, and therefore, the description of the offerings is arranged in order of holiness, with those that are very holy *(kodesh kadoshim)* preceding those which are holy *(kadosh)*. Inherent in the structure of these paragraphs is the emphasis on *kedusha*, holiness. Underlying the rites of the sacrificial offerings is the desire and the commandment to make the ordinary holy.

In our "cookbook," we might expect to find a recipe for that which we are making followed by serving instructions, and finally, perhaps instructions on storing and cleaning after our cooking. In fact, we find the opposite, and we need to ask why. The first precept commanded to the priests in *Parashat Tzav* regards the removal of the ashes after the sacrifice of the *oleh* (burnt offering). (*Vayyikra 6:2-5*)

> *"And the priest shall put on his linen garment, and his linen breeches shall he put on his flesh, and take up the ashes which the fire has consumed with the burnt*

offering on the altar, and he shall put them beside the altar. And he shall put off his garments, and put on other garments, and carry the ashes outside the camp to a clean place." (Vayyikra 6:3-4)

Why the specific instructions about how to clean off the altar after sacrifices? Why the change of clothing? And, why must the priests clean off the area? Have they not done enough already? Recall that the text is not referring to a small amount of ashes. For a fire to be kept burning day and night, (another imperative which we are given several times in this *parashah*), a large amount of wood is required resulting in heaps of ashes. One response to our question can be found precisely in recalling that these instructions are given in the **beginning** of the detailed directions on the *korbanot*. The cleaning of the altar is not to be thought of as something to be done after sacrifices but is in fact the preparation for the next day's sacrifices. The preparation for mitzvot is known as *heksher mitzvah*. The concept of *hidur mitzvah*, beautification of the mitzvah, is also applicable here as the priests clean and beautify the altar in order to enhance the sanctity of the *mitzvah* of the *korbanot*. Even the work to prepare for a mitzvah is sacred.

Lest the priests become too haughty as they fulfill their responsibilities in the *Ohel Moed*, Tent of Meeting, it is they who will also remove the ashes and prepare the altar for the next day. And, they must wear their sacred garments while cleaning the ashes at the altar, remembering that cleaning the ashes is itself a *mitzvah* to be preformed in a sacred, and not mundane, manner. The priests are then instructed to put on old clothing before removing the ashes outside the camp, a potentially humbling act after fulfilling their sacrificial responsibilities. The ashes are not simply to be placed in the most convenient place, but rather in a "clean place" (Beth Jacob, the Rabbi of Isbicze, compared the ashes to people. Just as a lonely spark may ignite within the ashes, so too can a person who has gone astray rekindle oneself. Just as God endeavors

111

not to put aside an outcast, we must not discard the ashes in despair but put them in a clean place. (Alexander Zusiz Friedman. *Wellsprings of Torah*, The Judaica Press, New York, 1969.)) This is the end of the day's sacrifices, but still the ashes themselves carry sacredness with them. The next day, the priests don fresh linen clothing to administer the sacrifices of the new day. Even though the routine is the same, the zest for each day's *mitzvot* must be strong. Tomorrow's mitzvah is a fresh mitzvah to be fulfilled in fresh clothing.

Aaron and his sons were making the profane "sacred." In fact, the word "sacrifice" in Latin means to "make sacred," to change objects from common (hol) to holy (kadosh). The Hebrew word *korban* has it's root in "to come close," as in to come closer to God. It is clear that objects, clothing and people can become sacred. Jacob Milgrom, in *Leviticus 1–16, The Anchor Bible*, discusses the role which sacrifices played in ancient peoples, including the Israelites. He concludes that we have to assume that *b'nei Yisrael* believed that the sacrifices had intrinsic value, they were not simply a means to an end. Sacrifices, according to Milgrom, served as a gift to God when making a request or expressing thanksgiving. 2 Samuel 24:24 supports this notion of a gift by stating that "neither will I offer burnt offerings to the Lord my God of that which cost me nothing." Here, a gift is not a gift if it did not cost the giver anything.

Parashat Tzav describes five sacrificial offerings with specific instructions regarding the priests' responsibilities as well as the beneficiaries of the various parts of the offerings. Several insights are offered.

The description of the first offering mentioned, the *Olah*, burnt offering, includes the prescription that the fire on the altar must be kept burning all night. The repetitive nature of this instruction demands our attention. Clearly there was the knowledge that this was a very ambitious task, requiring a great deal of material (wood) and human energy. The primacy of service to God is clear. *"Aish tamid tukad al ha-mizbeach lo tikneh."* "The eternal fire shall burn on the altar shall not be go out. Many traditional commentators point out that the repetition of this instruction emphasizes its importance even in times of economic hardship. Others note that this *"aish tamid"* can be seen as a metaphor for the Jewish people. The Jews require careful tending, not an easy responsibility. Even when there are other pressing needs, the fire must not be allowed to go out. The role of the leaders of the Jewish people is great to assure that the fire burns bright and clear continuously.

Because *HaMinhah*, the meal offering, is composed from grain (as opposed to animals that are always offered in their entirety), it must be apportioned before it is offered. The amount, which is to be burned in an offering, is separated from the remainder of the portion that is given to Aaron and his sons to eat.

Before we are told that the priests and all their male relatives are to eat from *Hahatat*, the sin offering, we are told that the sin offering is to be burned in the same place as the burnt offering. Both the Jerusalem Talmud and the Babylonian Talmud make reference to this as a way of sparing embarrassment. (Jerusalem Talmud Yebamot ch. 8, h. 3 and Sota 32b) If the offerings are burned in the same place on the altar, no one will know if one brought a sin offering or a burnt offering. This interpretation underscores both the public nature of making atonement as well as the warning to remember that the offerings are brought before God and not before other Israelites. In public, one took responsibility for one's actions and in public one approached God. However, the rabbis felt strongly that embarrassment *(busha)* of others should be avoided when possible.

The reasons for *Zevach Hashlamim*, the peace offering, are unclear. Nehama Leibowitz views the peace offering as motivated by much joy and gratitude to God. Perhaps it signifies harmony between worshipper and God. Perhaps it is recognition and appreciation that one's inner peace and contentment was achieved by cleaving to God, or it can be an offering with a wish to attain such a state of well-being. In all three types of peace offerings, thanksgiving, vow and free will, the sense of gratitude to God is central. When the peace offering is brought as a way of thanksgiving, the owners eat of it (with specific parts given to the priests) on the day it is offered and none shall remain until the following day. If the peace offering is a manner of a vow or a voluntary offering, it is eaten by the owners (with specific parts given to the priests) on that day and the remainder may be eaten the day after. However, that which remains of the offering on the third day must be burned and not eaten. These laws were not to be taken lightly; if one ate the offering on the third day, the offering itself was not valid and the person who ate of it was cut off from his people (*karet,* usually understood as excommunication).

Following these instructions for the sacrificial offerings, Aaron and his sons are officially and publicly ordained to fulfill their responsibilities as priests. The initial directions for this ceremony are given in *Shemot* 29:1-37 where the purpose for the consecration is stated as *"l'kadesh otam l'kahan li,"* "to make them holy to administer to Me (God)." Thus, we know that the importance of this moment is great. The presence of the entire congregation of Israel at the door of the Tent of Meeting made this a most public event. (It was also a miraculous event in that over 600,000 males were present in a very small area.) All must know that not only the sacrifices, but also those who offer them, must be pure and holy. During this initiation, Aaron and his sons were washed and dressed in fine and specific clothing. Blood was sprinkled on the horns of the altar and next to the bottom of the altar. Oil was sprinkled on the altar and on its vessels. Blood was put on the right ears, the right thumbs and the right large toes of Aaron and his sons. (Traditional commentators suggest that the ear, thumb and toe are extremities of the body, representing a ritual purification of the entire body. A second interpretation is that one who is fully consecrated is pure in words (ear), actions (hand) and entire life (foot , journey of life). Philo notes that the priest is consecrated at his ear to hear the word of God, at the hand to perform duties of priesthood, and at the foot to walk in the path of righteousness.) Blood and oil were sprinkled on their garments. Like the utensils and the altar, Aaron and his sons, became sacred vessels. During their consecration, the only action of Aaron and his sons is to place their hands on the heads of the bullock of the sin offering and the ram of the burnt offering. Aaron and his sons are passive during the entire ceremony as Moshe not only prepares and anoints them, but also prepares and offers the bullock and the ram. The question arises, what is the meaning of this unique action, placing their hands on the sacred animals? What is in the act of placing one's hands on an object, which signifies responsibility, and authority?

> *"And he brought the bullock for the sin offering; and he placed (leaned) Aaron and his sons their hands on the head of the bullock of the sin offering." (Vayyikra 8:14)*

> *"And he brought the ram for the burnt offering; and Aaron and his sons laid (leaned) their hands upon the head of the ram." (Vayyikra 8:14)*

The first time their hands are on the bullock for the sin offering, the text can be read as ambiguous as to who placed their hands on the bullock. The verb used *"vayismoch"* (verse 14) is in the singular while the presumed subject, Aaron and his sons, is plural. It is possible that this time, Moses, who just brought the bullock, is the subject of the second clause as well, and he placed the hands of Aaron and his sons on the ram. Even this remains ambiguous because of the lack of construct form in the hands of Aaron and his sons. The second time however, it is clear that Aaron and his sons are now taking responsibility for themselves and for the offerings as it is written *"vayismichu,"* a plural verb which makes it clear that Aaron and his sons are the subject and the ram is the object. Several commentators note Aaron's reluctance to accept the awesome responsibility inherent in priesthood. Their reluctance and then acceptance emphasizes the seriousness of the challenge to administer the sacrificial offerings.

Moshe also took an unleavened cake and a cake of oiled bread, and one wafer and the fat of the ram, and the right shoulder of the ram, and he placed all this upon the hands of Aaron and his sons. Only after the offering was in the hands of Aaron and his sons was it burned. The priests relied heavily on their hands to fulfill the precepts surrounding the sacrificial offerings. Their hands must be pure, and equally important, the priests must understand the significance of the weight of their role for the people of Israel in service to God. In placing their hands on the ram, Aaron and his sons accept the charge which Moshe gives them. The image that their hands are sacred and that they create sanctity is powerful. Hands, which God created, are able to fulfill the prescripts and *mitzvot* of God or to deviate from them. In a very physical manner, placing their hands on the animals to be offered, Aaron and his sons accept the responsibilities of acting as intermediaries.

In *Shemot*, Moshe is commanded to consecrate Aaron and his sons for seven days and to anoint the altar for atonement for seven days. In *Parashat Tzav* this ceremony is fulfilled. For seven days Aaron and his sons do not leave the Tent of Meeting and they are consecrated. *Vayyikra* adds that the process is to make atonement for Aaron and his sons so that they do not die. Immediately following the seven days of consecration, Aaron and his sons begin to administer the sacrificial offerings.

This *parashah* began with the word "*tzav*." It is quite a strong Hebrew word meaning "command" in the imperative. Rashi understands this as being "*lashon ziruz*," language of urgency, carrying the connotation of a very important commandment, one which must begin immediately and remain for generations to come. The emphasis on details is critical; special care and a certain meticulous nature are needed to administer the sacrificial offerings to prevent impurity. Sometimes, no matter how specific, the details simply are not sufficient. Immediately following this *parashah*, with its carefully crafted instructions, two sons of Aaron die as a result of in correct actions in fulfilling the duties of priests. The fate of Nadav and Abihu underscore the need to perform the rituals strictly according to the prescribed rules. Priests must faithfully discharge their duties. Aaron is pushed to go forward, and God responds with even additional specifications for carrying out the sacrificial offerings. The *parashah* emphasizes that it is through the meticulous attention to the details given by God (*mitzvot*) that the profane, the usual, can become sacred, holy.

Parashat Tzav ends with two key words, "*tzav*" and "*yad*," "command" and "hand." *Vayyikra* 8:36 states that "Aaron and his sons did all the things which the Lord had commanded by the hand of Moshe." Again, the emphasis of the word hand indicates a sincere acceptance of one's responsibilities as *mitzvot*. The chain of command is clear. The directions come from God to Moshe and are given to Aaron and his sons to fulfill. The "*hol*," the ordinary, becomes "*kadosh*," sacred, only when this connection is clear and the precepts carefully fulfilled.

Marci Dickman is Head of Judaic Studies of Krieger Schechter Middle School of Chizuk Amuno Congregation. Currently, she is studying in Israel as a Jerusalem Fellow.

Shemini
Ronald N. Millen

Shemini is the third Parashah in the book of Leviticus, Sefer Vayyikra. There are 27 Chapters and Shemini contains 9,10 and 11. The oldest name for the third book of the Torah is "Torat Kohanim" or "The Law of the Priests" i.e. "The Book which describes the functions of the Priesthood and the duties of the Priestly Nation."

From the *Hertz Humash* we learn that Vayyikra has 5 sections. Chapters 8-10 (of which 9 and 10 are found in Shemini) "describe the inauguration of worship in the completed sanctuary." Chapters 11-17 (of which 11 is found in Shemini) "deal with the laws of clean and unclean, of purity and purification, culminating in the institution of Yom Kippur."

In Parashat Shemini itself there are three main topics.
1. The priesthood is formed (chapter 9).
2. The death of Nadav and Avihu (chapter 10)
3. The laws of kashrut (chapter 11).

The first two topics are related. The third, however, appears to be a separate, stand-alone subject. As noted before, chapter 10 concludes those ten chapters that concentrate on the laws of the sanctuary. Chapter 11 begins what might be described as the law of Daily Life. Hermann Cohen states "the law of God embraces the whole of life with all its action; and as none of these actions can be withdrawn for the unity of life, so can the law be excluded for none of them."

Of these main topics in this sidra, the most confusing is the second—the death of Nadav and Avihu. In the immediately preceding passages Moshe instructs Aaron and his sons on the duties of the newly installed High Priest. Although it may be difficult for us to comprehend the relationship between the different animals and the associated offerings, e.g. a bull calf for sin offering, a ram for a burnt offering, an ox for peace offering, we understand that there are different types of prayer and therefore can accept the different types of animal sacrifice. Aaron and his sons are attending to these sacrifices, commanded by God and instructed by Moses. A sin offering is made on behalf of the priests. Then a Burnt Offering is made and finally a peace offering. Enter Nadav and Avihu "acting independently, without a command from God, Nadav and Avihu take pans, place fire and incense upon them, and offer them upon the altar. God sends a fire and destroys Nadav and Avihu."

Why? Why did Aaron's sons do what they did? Why was the punishment so severe? The answers have been the subject of much discussion. One explanation is that the priests were intoxicated when they entered the sanctuary. Early Rabbinical commentators claim that the two brothers were not punished for offering the wrong kind if incense or fire, they were condemned for the evil intent that motivated them. The thought was that the two were planning to usurp the authority of Moses and Aaron. A Midrash as to why they died explained that it was because they had not married. According to *Wellspring of Torah* "These two reasons given in the Midrash for the death of Nadav and Avihu are closely interrelated with each serving to explain the other. Their failure to marry would not in itself have made them liable to death by the hand of Heaven." It could have been assumed that Nadav and Avihu also had been so utterly devoted to the study of the law that they did not want to assume the added responsibility of starting a family.

But the second statement clearly indicates that their failure to marry was not motivated by such noble ideals. The position of leadership which Nadav and Avihu coveted would have left them little time for the study of the law.

Therefore, if we know that Nadav and Avihu aspired to become leaders of the children of Israel, we know too that their devotion to study could not have been so all absorbing that it would have explained the unwillingness to marry, which, unless motivated by a passion for the study of Torah, is considered a grave sin."

Rashi points out that, "rather than following the carefully detailed direction of offering sacrifice or bringing fire to the sanctuary, they took upon themselves the power of deciding what to offer, how to bring the offering, and when. For disregarding the process and failure to consult with Aaron and Moses about what they planned to do, they were punished. Their arrogance led them to believe that they were accountable to no one."

Rashbam, Rashi's grandson explains "that they offered a kind of fire that had not been commanded. That is why the Torah calls it esh zarah, an alien or foreign fire. In other words, Nadav and Avihu took the law into their own hands."

Naphtali Hertz Wessely argues "that the two sons were deeply moved by the beauty and meaning of the ritual sacrifice offered by Moses and Aaron. In their enthusiasm and joy they lost their heads and entered the Holy of Holies to burn incense, something they had not been instructed to do by Moses. Their wrongdoing was not the deliberate breaking of the law but rather their failure to control their religious enthusiasm. They should have been more humble instead of blindly assuming that whatever they did in the sanctuary would be acceptable. They were punished because they occupied a position of importance, which they misused in their misguided excitement and zeal."

So why were they punished? Rabbi Samson R. Hirsch asks, " Was it ruthless ambition, arrogance, insensitivity, or the failure to consult others and to honor elders? Was it youthful zeal, blind faith or a failure to realize the dangers of changing rituals and practices of a community?"

Personally, I do not think there is **one** answer to the question – so why were they punished. However, I also see a relationship between the reason given by Rashi—arrogance; Rashbam—taking the law into their our hands; and Wessley—abuse of position. Arrogance is a trait that I do not respect and that I have always tried to avoid. I do not like it; I do not see any redeeming value in it. Arrogance, I believe, can lead people into taking the law into their own hands, which in itself is abuse of position.

Could the answer be that simple? I would like to think so but my aversion to arrogance warns me that others may have equally compelling arguments. As a matter of fact, Jewish commentators see in this sad tale, significant ethical and social lessons that continue to challenge Torah interpreters today.

Ronald N. Millen is Executive Director of Chizuk Amuno Congregation. He has the unique distinction of being the first person (at Chizuk Amuno) to work with Rabbi Zaiman. Rabbi Zaiman was USY advisor for Temple Emanu-El in Providence, Rhode Island when Ron served as Treasurer there in 1963.

Lee M. Hendler
Tazria

The *halacha* of menstruation, conception, pregnancy, and childbirth is complex and sometimes baffling. As Jacob Neusner observes, in *A History of the Mishnaic Law of Women*, "The goal and purpose of Mishnah's division of Women is to bring under control, and force into stasis, all the wild and unruly potentialities of female sexuality. . . ." Discussion of these four physiological states immediately leads to deeply entangled debates about sin and redemption, desire and restraint, life and death, refracted through the lens of gender. In *The Enchantments of Judaism*, Neusner observes, "The notion that Midrash exegesis rests on allegory in the deepest sense—finding in Scripture something that is not explicitly stated but is in the profound layers of Scripture's meaning—is illustrated time and again." A woman encountering the halachic and aggadic discussions on female sexuality cannot help but be moved, angered, surprised, confused and saddened.

The plain meaning of Leviticus 12:1-8 is that the mother is impure, as in her *niddah*, for seven days after the birth of a male infant. *Niddah*, a legal status meaning "excluded," pertains to the menstruant woman. Contact with her or with things she has touched during menstruation automatically contaminates; the defiled must bathe to become pure again by evening. During normal *niddah*, on the eighth day, the woman takes two pigeons or turtle doves-one each for a *hataa't* (sin offering) and an *olah* (holocaust/burnt offering)-to the Temple. *Hataa't*, which the priest partially consumes, restores the right of the *niddah* to reenter the sanctuary. *Olah*, totally consumed in fire on the sacrificial altar, is meant to please the Lord. Its consumption represents the supplicant's first completed act of worship after readmission to the Temple. *Tazria* adds a 33-day purification period after *niddah* before a proper sacrifice can take place. The period of *niddah* and the purification period are doubled in the case of a female infant.

Though sources pay scant attention to this restriction, some speculate that it relates to the future procreative capacity of the female offspring. The impurity for which the woman now atones is embodied in the baby girl, so that the mother is doubly impure. Others connect it to the newborn female's potential bloody discharge that ends a week after birth and contaminates the mother. Privately, the new mother and her husband may resume intimate relations after *niddah*, but she cannot reinstate her public relationship with God until her blood purification period, *dam tohar*, ends.

How wondrous a system that works this well for the worshiper and the worshiped! And how impoverished our modern religious experience is for its loss! The God/worshiper relationship sits at the system's epicenter. Both parties have a stake in a relationship that a major life-changing and life-threatening event disrupts. However, since the relationship is essential and the disruption is anticipated, provisions are made in advance for its restoration. The steps are clear. The process is straightforward. Satisfaction is guaranteed.

Our understanding of *Tazria* deepens further when we consider the following: dread and terror accompanied the prospect of childbirth in ancient Israel. Infant mortality rates were extremely high; the average life expectancy was 30 years for a woman, 40 for a man. Legends abound in the ancient Near East of female demons who steal (and murder) unprotected newborns. The myth of Lilith, a she-devil rabbinic creation, illustrates Neusner's allegorical proposition. It links rabbinic understanding of the ordeal of childbirth and the danger and mystery surrounding this life passage event with their ever present concern about female sexual power and autonomy. The story of this female creature who precedes Eve (and mirrors Eve's subsequent independence, disobedience and punishments) comes to us from Ben Sira, an eighth or ninth century BCE sage in the court of King Nebuchadnezzar. (Alphabet of Ben Sira, 23a-b, 33a-b) God, seeing Adam's loneliness, creates Lilith from earth, like Adam, and brings her to him. They immediately argue, for she refuses to lie beneath him during intercourse. She demands equal rights, since they were created in the same way. Understanding that they will never agree, she pronounces the ineffable divine name (she—not Adam—has that power) and flies away. God responds to Adam's complaint by sending three angels to pursue her, with the admonition that they may not force her to return against her will. When they find her at the Sea of Reeds (where, of course, Egypt will later perish and Israel will be born), she refuses to return. They threaten her with the death of 100 of her children every day, but she prefers that punishment to returning to Adam. In retaliation, she claims that she has been expressly created to injure newborn infants. They depart only after she swears that whenever she sees their images or names on an amulet she will forfeit her power to harm the baby the amulet protects. A rich tradition of Jewish birth amulets, carefully researched and chronicled by Tikva Frymer-Kensky in her book *Motherprayer,* depicts this tradition and other conception, pregnancy and childbirth folk practices.

The Temple cult provides the orientation for most of these contemporaneous and later rituals and anchors them as symbols within the sacred rather than the magical realm. They express the specific Jewish desire for what the cult assures: a reliable way to maintain an intimate relationship with God. In *tazria* we find a striking ritual that allows the new mother to reaffirm, at the same time, her relationship with God and her role in the life of community. She emerges from the all-consuming care of a newborn, having safely navigated the dangerous childbirth, post-partum and early infancy passages, to reassert her connectedness to the Divine and her right to participate in the communal Temple cult. When seen this way, the rite of *tazria* seems less a bizarre punishment and more a remarkable privilege: a special, public way for women to celebrate the triumph of life over death.

Our problem is to figure out what to do with this understanding after the destruction of the Temple. Should it remain a quaint but irrelevant artifact from the Temple cult, or does it contain a compelling message that we would do well to acknowledge? How can Torah—God's constant revelation—ever be irrelevant to us? Rachel Biale argues, in *Women and Jewish Law*, that discrepancies in Leviticus already indicate a shift from the public, Temple-based cult to the private home-based community. While acts of lovingkindness or prayer substitute for many Levitical sacrifices after 70 C.E., the laws of *niddah* are transmuted and purposefully transferred to the home. According to Leviticus 18, intimate contact with a *niddah* makes the transgressor sinful, rather than impure, with the devastating possibility of *karet*-being cut off from his people. In Ezekiel and Ezra, *niddah* is directly linked to moral corruption: the land that the Israelites will inherit has been made *niddah* by pagans practicing abominations. Sinning Israelites are themselves referred to as *niddah*. The *halacha* is made even more stringent, with *niddah* extended to 14 days. In stark contrast to the attention and weight given to *niddah* as a private rite, the rabbis make no effort to salvage or perpetuate *tazria*—the public restrictions and offerings after childbirth. Instead, there is an active effort to sever any connection between Temple sacrificial offerings and public practice in synagogue: "All persons who are impure read the Torah and recite the Shema and pray in the synagogue," directs the Shulkhan Arukh. (Orah Hayyim 84:1)

From the post-Temple period onward, despite *halacha*, there is ample documentation of the persistence of *niddah* restrictions in the public realm. Scholars sensibly conclude that these practices, which at minimum prohibit all three of the sanctions permitted in the Shulkan Arukh, are vestiges of the symbolic connection between the synagogue and the Temple, devised to maintain the historic tension between *niddah* impurity and Temple sanctity. We know of one example of a *tazria*-inspired practice–an eighteenth century Italian set of prayers recited upon the woman's return to synagogue after the birth of her child. *(Out of the Depths I Call to You)* Leviticus 12:1-8 is the centerpiece of this *tkhine*–a sixteenth to mid-nineteenth-century European tradition of prayers, created outside of the formal *siddur*, especially for women. If these behaviors were not required, why do they persist as *minhag*, even in our time? And why would the rabbis fail to create a substitute for *tazria* that includes such a powerful public act of restitution, one of the few positive *mitzvot* women possess, when they take such pains to conserve *niddah* as a cornerstone of private life?

First we must understand *tazria* as many of the sages did. Noting the *hataa't*, some insist that the atypical order of the offerings (*olah* precedes *hataa't*) indicates that *hataa't* is only a purgation offering. (Sifre) Others struggle with the conundrum of sin in the context of childbirth. The commandment to be fruitful and multiply (*p'ru ur'vu*) is interpreted as commanded to man alone (Yevamot 65 b) Obviously, woman cannot sin by helping man to fulfill it. Contemporary commentators avoid the problem altogether by treating *tazria hataa't* as a variation on *niddah*-not having to do with sin, but with the status of impurity related to bleeding—for in the ancient mind impurity leads to sin but is not necessarily equivalent to it. This approach comforts those who resist associating sin with childbirth and menstruation but ignores a parallel tradition that views menstruation as one of the ten curses women bear for Eve's sin. (Erubin 100b) It also denies us a potentially richer understanding of the *pasuk*.

What of the other *hataa't* applications in Leviticus? In the preceding *pesukim*, they are necessary to compensate for inadvertent sins. For the remainder of *Tazria*, they are needed after recovery from a variety of skin diseases, traditionally viewed as God's punishment for gossip. The special requirement that the woman after childbirth offer a lamb as her *olah* seems to highlight her singular condition. But given the deliberate organization of Leviticus, it is illogical to conclude that her *hataa't* differs significantly from the others with which *tazria* is grouped. What connects her to these other categories of sin? Perhaps it is the concept of unavoidable transgression. The transgression in each case seems to be one that the individual, by the very nature of his or her humanity, is bound to commit. All of us will, at one time or another, inadvertently subvert commandments; all of us are likely to gossip; men are bound to have nocturnal emissions; women are bound to bear children and, as our sages understood it, bound to experience pain and distress in that process. That is because women cannot escape the curse of Eve. For the sin of having led Adam to disobedience and death, Eve will bear children in pain. (Genesis 3:16) But this understanding only provides the context for *tazria*, which suggests that there is a unique, though unspecified sin, related to the act of childbearing. What sin can a woman in childbirth possibly commit? Rabbinic logic dictates that the answer lies in Eve's original curse. In her unavoidable pain, they conclude, a woman may vow never to again have sexual relations with her husband. (Niddah 31b) *Hataa't* is necessary to atone for a vow she cannot keep because, according to 3:16, her desire is toward her husband (the original Catch-22). If *hataa't* is required, then *olah,* as atonement for the resentful thoughts that led to the vow against her husband or God (Ibn Ezra), begins the sacrificial process.

The problem is that these explanations do not satisfy women. An informal, unscientific poll of over 30 mothers confirmed that not one had committed either of these "sins" during labor. In fact, the explanations seem to skirt the real issues of childbirth and procreation which seem to have more to do with freedom and deliverance than with pain and sin. Men need women to fulfill *p'ru ur'vu* but women are free moral agents who can choose (like Lilith and Eve at their mythic best) to help men fulfill the commandment or not. On the one hand, the sages acknowledge this with their rather unconvincing rationale for *hataa't*. On the other, they don't even consider it an issue. They rule that women are destined to desire children (Ketubot 62 a-b), whereas men come to the desire only by harnessing their sexual drive, paradoxically characterized as the *yetzer hara*. (Rabbi Nachman ben Samuel) Since Genesis 3:16 insures that women's desire shall be toward their husbands, women's power and freedom appears to be properly contained. Ironically, the counterweight for the woman's wish to be free of childbearing pain is desire for her husband, while serving her desire is what countermands his lack of desire for children! Desire is the center around which this view of procreation holds. But, as Tikva Frymer-Kensky reminds us, "Pregnancy may be a holy task, but only free human beings can perform a holy task. One cannot be forced to devote oneself to a service, no matter how sacred." (*Motherprayer*) Or to quote R. Hanina: "Everything is in the hand of heaven except the fear of heaven. . . ."

Women, endowed with the power to carry and bear children, can choose when and how to exercise that power. With regard to procreation, women are, despite their desire for their husbands, free, not obligated, and uniquely capable, because they alone can carry the child, as men can never be. In blood that mystifies and terrifies men, women bring forth life and engage in an intimate, monthly dance of life and death. Men need women to bear their children, but after insemination women no longer need men. Perhaps the real fear is that men may become, in modern vernacular, "sperm donors."

The ancillary role of men in conception is captured in a set of extra-canonical sources that eventually find their way into midrashic texts. They relate to Eve's statement on the birth of Cain: "I have got myself (acquired) a man with the (help of the) Lord!" The rabbis wonder at "man" and determine that Cain is unnaturally precocious (he walks off and returns with a reed *qaneh*-hence his name *qayin*). (Life of Adam and Eve (Vita) 21:3) He could therefore only have been conceived with the help of the Lord. Others consider the preceding phrase, "Adam knew his wife," and conclude that he knew something *about* her, in this case that the wicked angel Samael has impregnated her with a child who will become the first recorded murderer. (Targum Pseudo-Jonathan) In these readings, Adam, the first husband, is cuckolded by either God or Satan! These *aggadot* skillfully play on a number of rabbinic themes: the freedom of women to choose their mates, their strong but inarticulate sexual appetites, their fertility, the secondary role of men in conception and birth, and the depiction of Eve as the first human progenitor of evil in the world rather than the originator of disobedience. Perhaps we should return to this story, rather than to Eve's curse, for the context in which to place the potential sin related to childbirth. This is, after all, the first birth in Torah after God's curse on Eve takes effect.

Isn't the real danger of transgression in childbirth the possibility that, after birth, women will behave like Eve? All mothers have experienced the profound transformation that overtakes them at the moment of birth. Excruciating pain instantly vanishes as they joyfully greet the life they have just delivered. In blood, pain, confusion, and fear, women labor, but in the end, no matter how many are in attendance or assisting, by themselves they have triumphantly gotten themselves a child. Their toil alone produces the infant. "I have got myself a man with the Lord!" Eve exclaims and, almost as if to reassure herself that this power of hers is no fluke, she conceives again and bears Abel. Rashi interprets *et Adonai* "with the Lord" to mean *im Adonai* "like the Lord" and suggests that the sub-text is, "When He created me and my husband He created us by Himself. In this one, however, we are co-partners with Him." This supports the commentary, "Three partners create a child-the Holy one, the father and the mother." (BT Niddah 31A) But what happens if we take the plain meaning of the text? Then, "It takes three partners. . . ." is transformed from a definitive declaration into a significant caution.

The rites of *tazria* teach us that the exercise of our inherent design and purpose can, unfettered and unconsidered, undermine our holy design and purpose. The ability to carry, nurture and deliver a human being, a power unique to women, may be the closest that humans ever come to experiencing God's creative and redemptive force. Significant powers become dangerous when unbounded. Consequently, we most respect and fear those human powers that are hardest to contain and regulate. Eve got it right and wrong at the same time. Her delight in the miracle of birth is palpable. Every woman who has birthed thrills at the spontaneous joy contained in these words. But *tazria* reminds us of the danger the moment contains. We hover precariously between life and death, but when life prevails we are in jeopardy of overreaching our bounds. At that moment, we may confuse our gift with God's gifts and forget that, though we may be free agents, we are not solo agents. Eve puts herself first and God second, and she neglects Adam altogether.

Perhaps women observed *tazria*-related practices after the destruction of the Temple because they understood and needed to acknowledge that female sexuality was key to their continuing relationship with God and an essential source of their power. How sad that the rabbis could not transcend their fears of female sexuality to bring a different set of questions to the first female conception and birth. If they had chosen to locate the *hataa't* of childbirth in the first childbirth (Eve's peak moment, her first act as *Hava*, "mother of all life") rather than in Eve's expulsion (her nadir as *Isha*), we might have both reason and means to preserve the rites of *tazria*, just as alternatives were created for other significant Temple sacrifices. Then women might have retained the distinctive role in public communal worship they once enjoyed—feared and revered for the profound personal sacrifices they alone were willing and able to make in the service of God and our people. And who knows? Perhaps female rabbinic voices might have joined our tradition far earlier, enriching and expanding Judaism for generations to come.

Lee M. Hendler, author of **The Year Mom Got Religion**, *is currently President of Chizuk Amuno Congregation. She is a graduate of the Florence Melton Adult Mini-School and a regular attendee at Chizuk Amuno's Stulman Center for Adult Learning programs. She has studied with Rabbi Zaiman in his Women's Torah Study Group since 1993.*

Metzora
Dr. Andrew J. Miller

The text of this *Parashah*, like that of the preceding one, *Tazria*, reflects a keen concern for the state of ritual purity among the people Israel. This is expressed by means of an exhaustive discussion of *nega tsara'at*—translated variously as "scaly affliction," "plague," or "leprosy"—occurring in people, in fabrics, and on the walls of buildings; and of the terms and conditions for quarantine and purification. Other forms of ritual impurity addressed in the second part of *Metzora* (Leviticus 15:1-33), include emissions from sexual organs, namely seminal emissions by men and menstruation by women.

The language here reads very much like a clinical manual for diagnosis and treatment of an affliction, with almost no discussion of root causes or of the connection between the physical and the spiritual or religious dimension of the affliction. To a modern reader not steeped in traditional readings of the text, it may seem almost paradoxical that the mere mention of *Tazria* or *Metzora* leads almost immediately to the conclusion that the natural topic for a sermon or a *D'var Torah* will be the perils of gossip or evil talk—"*lashon hara.*"

The assumption that the physical ailment in question can be attributed to God's punishment for a specific category of sin certainly appears to be at odds with the assumptions of modern secular society and the underlying basis of medical science. Yet it is inescapable that the text does in fact assume a direct and powerful connection between the spiritual trespass and the physical ailment, and this theme is emphasized by rabbinic commentators.

If we refer back to the text of *Tazria*, which introduces the topic of *nega tsara'at* in chapter 13 of Leviticus, there is no specific explanation of the cause for the onset of the condition. Yet the word *nega*, literally translated as "touch," may be interpreted as an expression of the belief that disease resulted from the "touch" of

God and was therefore the direct result of God's punishment. (JPS Leviticus commentary, p.76)

In Leviticus 14:34 there is an explicit statement that *nega tsara'at* may be inflicted on a house by an act of God:

> *"When you enter the land of Canaan that I give you as a possession, and I inflict an eruptive plague upon a house in the land you possess..."*

While clearly indicating divine intention, the tone of this verse seems curiously matter-of-fact, as though the *tsara'at* might be viewed as a routine and predictable consequence of expected behavior. The behavior itself is not deemed worthy of comment.

More direct evidence linking cause and effect may be found by looking for additional descriptions of *tsara'at* in Torah or elsewhere in Tanakh. In almost every case they are ascribed to divine action or invoked as a curse. The two best-known examples occur in Exodus 4:6, wherein God causes Moses' hand to be encrusted with leprous scales—*"m'tsora'at kashaleg"*—and in Numbers 12:10, where Miriam is stricken with scales—also *"m'tsora'at kashaleg."* The first is a sign to Moses, after Moses suggests that the Israelites will not believe that God has spoken to him. The second occurs immediately after Miriam speaks ill of Moses and incurs God's wrath. This incident is recalled also in Deuteronomy 24:8-9:

> *"In cases of a skin affection be most careful to do exactly as the levitical priests instruct you. Take care to do as I have commanded them. Remember what the Lord your God did to Miriam on the journey after you left Egypt."*

The same fate befalls Gehazi, Elisha's servant, when he acts dishonestly and then lies about it (II Kings, 5:27); King Azariah, who fails to remove forbidden shrines (II Kings 15:5); and King

Uzziah, who trespasses against God by entering the Temple to offer incense against the warnings of the priests. (II Chronicles 26:19-21) In II Samuel 3:29, King David curses Joab for an act of treachery with the statement, "May the house of Joab never be without someone suffering from a discharge or an eruption."

The etymological connection between *"metzora"* or "leper" and *"motzi ra"* or evil talk is drawn in the Talmud (Arakhin 15b), as noted by Leibowitz. (1980, p. 128) Rashi's commentary on the purification ritual described in Leviticus 14:4, which makes use of two live birds, makes a similar connection:

> *"Since plagues come from evil talk, which is the act of babbling words, consequently there were required for his purification birds which babble continually with chirping sounds."*

Leviticus Rabbah XVI:I (Neusner, 1986, p.327) cites a variety of sources to draw connections between *tsara'at* and the seven abominations of Proverbs 6:17-19: "A haughty bearing, a lying tongue, hands that shed innocent blood, a mind that hatches evil plots, feet quick to run to evil, a false witness testifying lies, and one who incites brothers to quarrel." Leviticus Rabbah XVII:III extends the list by citing ten reasons for *tsara'at* (idolatry, promiscuity, murder, profanation of God's name, blasphemy of God's name, robbing from the community, stealing what does not belong to a person, arrogance, gossiping, and grudging), all drawn from biblical texts. (Neusner, 1986, p.343)

With all of this as backdrop, it is interesting to return to the text of Leviticus for instruction on how we are to understand this connection between the physical and the spiritual. Given the emphasis placed by subsequent commentators on the moral condition associated with *tsara'at*, one might expect to find some pronouncement of guilt and recitation of the need to repent and to expiate the sin. After all, the next Parashah after *Metzora*, *Acharei Mot*, deals not only with the purification rituals of *Yom Kippur* but also is explicit about the need of the Israelites to make atonement for their sins. The remainder of *Acharei Mot* is concerned almost entirely with sin and with prohibited ritual and dietary practices as well as sexual offenses.

As noted above, however, we find no explicit commentary about the causes of *tsara'at* in either *Tazria or Metzora*, and the only mention of a connection between sin and punishment is reserved for those who defile the Tabernacle by coming into contact with it while in an unclean condition. (Leviticus 15:31) Instead we find an accumulation of details on how to identify *tsara'at*, which variants of the visible symptoms require isolation for seven days, what kinds of changes in those symptoms call for a change in diagnosis, and what the diagnosis of impurity means for the afflicted person.

A similar level of detail is provided in the discussions of *tsara'at* of garments and of houses, and in the description of the purification ritual for both persons and houses after a priest has declared that the affliction is cured. Although the consequences of being diagnosed unclean are serious—separation from the community for a person, potential destruction for garments and for houses—the text might easily be read as though it were a manual for physicians.

However, the quarantine imposed on the afflicted is not a medical quarantine and the motivation is not medical isolation. This is reiterated in the Mishnah, Purities, *Negaim* 3:1:

> 3:1 A. *"All are made unclean by plagues- 1. Except for the gentiles and a resident alien. B. All are suitable to examine the plagues. C. But the (actual declaration of) uncleanness and cleanness is in the hands of a priest."* (Neusner, 1988, p.984)

Furthermore there are other considerations that take precedence over what we would see as norms of medical quarantine in the declaration of uncleanness:

3:2 A. *"A bridegroom on whom a plague appeared-they give him the seven days of the marriage feast (before inspecting him) B. him, and his house, and his garment. C. And so with respect to the festival: they give him all the days of the festival."* (Neusner, 1988, p.984-985)

Similar accommodations are made with respect to the declaration of uncleanness in the case of a house. The contents of the house are removed prior to inspection so as to avoid the possibility of having the owner lose all of his possessions. (Leviticus 14:35-36) In this instance, *Negaim* 12:5 states:

H. *"For what has the Torah shown concern? I. "For his (clay) utensils, his cruse, and his ewer. J. "If thus the Torah has shown concern for his humble possessions, all the more so for cherished possessions. K. "If thus for his property, all the more so for the soul of his sons and his daughters. L. "If thus for the evil person, how much the more so for the righteous person."* (Neusner, 1988, p.1005)

Leibowitz (1980) cites David Hoffman in making this point clear:

"Hoffman in his commentary to Leviticus opposes the medical interpretation of the leper regulations. He points out that the very nature of the rulings runs counter to this explanation. In the case of the leprosy of dwellings, the Torah prescribes that the house affected be cleared of all its utensils before the arrival of the priest to examine the place and pronounce it unclean, so that all the contents of the house should not similarly be defiled. Had the Torah been concerned with

the sanitary measures to prevent contagion, the contents of the house which had actually come in contact with the disease should have been declared unclean. Hoffman further cites other examples of rulings governing diseases which show an even greater disregard for the principles of medical isolation. According to oral tradition, the diseases mentioned in the Torah are to be disregarded during the time of the festival pilgrimage in Jerusalem and the priest is not to be called upon to investigate. Had there existed here any intention of safeguarding public health, these quarantine regulations should have been enforced even more strictly with regard to the pilgrims, when masses of people were congregated in one place." (p.116-117)

The religious calendar and the spiritual realm clearly take precedence over any concern about the medical condition in question, for the simple reason that we are talking about a world in which it is meaningless to try to separate the physical from the spiritual. There is no such thing as a medical condition independent of God's will; if the appearance of *tsara'at*, a disease of the skin, is a sign of an unclean condition, it is still within God's purview (and that of the rabbis, expounding the Oral Torah) to make allowances for festivals and marriage feasts, as these fulfill religious obligations and serve the needs of community. If the appearance of *tsara'at* on the walls of a house is likewise a sign of uncleanness, it is still possible to separate the contents of the house from the building itself, so as to allow for some leniency in sparing the possessions of the person whose house is thus afflicted. This poses no risk to the occupant or to the community, as it is clearly consistent with God's law.

Given that *tsara'at* has subsequently been viewed as a sign of serious moral transgression, the subtlety and restraint required in rendering a diagnosis of uncleanness is particularly noteworthy and suggests some lingering doubt about whether guilt or innocence can reliably be determined. Or perhaps the doubt hinges not so much on the question of guilt or innocence as on the fact that the sin in question—if indeed it is *lashon hara*, or evil talk—is possibly the most common of all sins and the most difficult to resist. Any one of us, at any time, might well be guilty of those same deeds and might become the *metzora*, as happened to both Moses and Miriam.

Although Miriam's case serves as an example and a warning, it is noteworthy that the *tsara'at* is removed after the point has been made, and even the recollection in Deuteronomy 24:8-9: "Remember what the Lord your God did to Miriam"—appears to be an admonishment about following the proper steps to cure the skin affection, rather than a warning about avoiding it in the first place.

Care is taken to ensure that the potential of being declared clean remains a possibility in most situations, and the state of ritual impurity, where possible, is to be considered temporary.

The notion of separation or isolation is treated not only as a physical separation from the community in space but also as a separation in time, with carefully marked checkpoints at weekly intervals. This is consistent with the importance of marking, categorizing, and sanctifying time that pervades Jewish ritual practice. The period of seven days of isolation pertains both to the *metzora* and to the woman who has given birth, the menstruating woman, and the man declared unclean on account of seminal discharge. The text wastes little time assigning blame or making distinctions among the various root causes of impurity, even though some are viewed as punishment for sin, whereas others carry no such stigma. Instead the emphasis is on the ritual to be completed at the end of the period of impurity.

Furthermore there are striking parallels between the purification ritual for the individual and the *Yom Kippur* ritual atoning for the sins of the community. On *Yom Kippur*, one of the two goats is designated as a sin offering for God and its blood is used in purifying the Shrine, the Tent of Meeting and the altar. The other is sent into the wilderness, carrying the sins and the iniquities of the Israelites with it (Leviticus 16:5-22). In the cleansing ritual for the *metzora*, two live birds are chosen. One is slaughtered and its blood is used to purify the *metzora*, after which the other is set free in the open country (Leviticus 14:5-7). One might argue that, just as the entire community, including the righteous, needs to atone and to be forgiven vows on Yom Kippur, so too an otherwise righteous person may have afflictions, both spiritual and physical, for which cleansing is needed.

Leibowitz cites Sforno: "Since this disease is a kind of punishment, the periods of isolation are designed to prompt the victim to repentance . . . . " (p.119) She also cites Maimonides on the occurrence of *tsara'at* in houses as "a sign and a wonder that existed in Israel in order to warn them away from evil talk." (p.136) She continues with a reference to Alshikh:

> "*the plague teaches us that society should take notice of the first sign of misconduct, however small. Just the same as a disease begins with hardly noticeable symptoms and can be stopped if detected in time, so a moral disease in society can be prevented from spreading, if immediate steps are taken. Otherwise, it will spread throughout the community.*" (p.138)

Thus the occurrence of *tsara'at* is viewed not merely as an affliction or a punishment, but as an opportunity that will move the sufferer toward repentance and purification, in turn protecting the community.

On the eighth day after the initial purification ritual, a second ritual uses the blood of a male lamb together with a log of oil as a guilt offering, and the former *metzora* is anointed with the blood and the oil in a manner (Leviticus 14:14-18) that closely resembles the anointing of Aaron and his sons as priests (Leviticus 8:23-30). Thus he rejoins the community with the full status accorded to all male worshipers (JPS Commentary on Leviticus, p. 88), just as Miriam rejoins the community at the end of her appointed period of isolation. This transition from outcast to anointed may be read as striking evidence not only of God's power to punish, but also of the human capacity for change.

Andrew J. Miller is Associate Professor and Chair of the Department of Geography & Environmental Systems, University of Maryland, Baltimore County. He currently serves as chair of the Rosenbloom Religious School Education Committee and as a member of Chizuk Amuno's Board of Trustees.

Acharey Mot
Michael S. Novey

A pervasive theme of *Parashat Aḥare Mot* is the exclusivity of permissible forms of sacrificial worship. The first portion of the *parashah* alludes to the death of Aaron's sons Nadab and Abihu and uses that allusion as an introduction to detailed restrictions on when and how the High Priest may enter the Shrine. The second portion continues with a prohibition on sacrifices away from the central altar and on secular use of the potential animal components of the sacrificial service.

The actual story of Aaron's sons, however, occurs three parashiot earlier: "Now Aaron's sons Nadab and Abihu each took his fire pan, put fire in it, and laid incense on it; and they offered before the LORD alien fire, which He had not enjoined upon them. And fire came forth from the LORD and consumed them; thus they died at the instance of the LORD." (Lev. 10:1–2) In this *parashah*, however, although the incident gives the *parashah* its name, it is only introductory: "The Lord spoke to Moses after the death of the two sons of Aaron who died when they drew too close to the presence of the LORD." (Lev. 16:1–2) Rashi, following the *Sifra*, states that the sons' fate is an object lesson and a warning to comply exactly—and exclusively—with the sacrificial commandments about to be delivered.

These commandments concern the expiation service by the High Priest on the Day of Atonement and the exclusive use of the inner Shrine for that purpose: "Tell your brother Aaron that he is not to come at will into the Shrine behind the curtain, in front of the cover, that is upon the ark, lest he die; . . . . Thus only shall Aaron enter the Shrine . . . ." (Lev. 16:2–3) And the atonement service follows.

The second portion of the *parashah* contains as a central theme a prohibition of decentralized sacrifice. This prohibition is directed not only to the people Israel but also to the non-Israelite

140

hangers-on who were traveling with them. "If anyone of the house of Israel or of the strangers who reside among them offers a burnt offering or a sacrifice, and does not bring it to the entrance of the Tent of Meeting to offer it to the LORD, that person shall be cut off from his people." (Lev. 17:8–9)

Preceding these verses is an analogous rule (although there is controversy over how similar the two rules actually are):

> "(I)f anyone of the house of Israel slaughters an ox or sheep or goat in the camp, or does so outside the camp, and does not bring it to the entrance of the Tent of Meeting to present it as an offering to the LORD, before the LORD's Tabernacle, bloodguilt shall be imputed to that man: he has shed blood; that man shall be cut off from among his people. This is in order that the Israelites may bring the sacrifices which they have been making in the open—that they may bring them before the LORD, to the priest, at the entrance of the Tent of Meeting, and offer them as sacrifices of well-being to the LORD; that the priest may dash the blood against the altar of the LORD at the entrance of the Tent of Meeting, and turn the fat into smoke as a pleasing odor to the LORD; and that they may offer their sacrifices no more to the goat-demons after whom they stray." (Lev. 3–7)

The source of the controversy is that the word for slaughters (SH-H̲-T) could refer either to sacrificial slaughter only or also to killing an animal in a secular context for use as food. If only sacrificial slaughter is meant, why is such a similar requirement restated in verses 8–9, this time extending to strangers as well as to Israelites? On the other hand, if secular slaughter is covered as well, we have to explain an apparently contradictory passage in Deutoronomy 12. This latter passage states:

"When the LORD enlarges your territory, as He has promised you, and you say, "I shall eat some meat," for you have the urge to eat meat, you may eat meat whenever you wish. If the place where the LORD has chosen to establish His name is too far from you, you may slaughter any of the cattle or sheep that the LORD gives you, as I have instructed you; and you may eat to your heart's content in your settlements. Eat it, however, as the gazelle and the deer are eaten: the unclean may eat it together with the clean."
(Deut. 12:20–22)

The two passages can be reconciled by treating the *Aḥare Mot* prohibition of secular slaughter as a requirement applying only to the time before the people entered the land of Canaan. In the wilderness, because the central altar was reasonably close to everyone, any slaughter of a potentially sacrificial animal (an ox or sheep or goat) was to be made in a religious context and treated as a sacrifice. Otherwise, there was too great a risk that an Israelite might sin by being tempted spontaneously to effect the slaughter as a surreptitious idolatrous sacrifice. The rule in verses 8–9, which govern strangers as well as Israelites, would still have been necessary to prevent overt idolatry. Once the central altar was at a distance, however (and once the generation that had known Egypt had died out), Deuteronomy made secular slaughter permissible for Israelites.

Three aspects of the text from Deuteronomy support that interpretation. First, the permission for secular slaughter of potentially sacrificial animals is introduced, and implicitly justified, by a reference to the distance from some Israelites' settlements to the central altar. Second, the analogy to eating gazelle and deer would have been unnecessary and exotic if Leviticus had already allowed secular slaughter not only of wild animals but also of

142

potentially sacrificial animals. Third, the explicit permission for both clean and unclean people to participate in eating cattle or sheep suggests that, previously, any such meal had been treated as the consumption of a sacrifice. This point of view is consistent with Rabbi Ishmael, who understood the verses from Leviticus as barring secular slaughter. (BT Hullin 16b)

Rashi, however, articulates the more accepted view that, even in the wilderness, secular slaughter was permissible so long as the animal was not a consecrated animal. *Sifra* had taken this view (chap. 188), and Rabbi Akiba is reported to have believed that secular slaughter was never forbidden. (BT Hullin 17a)

Both the passage in Leviticus and that in Deutoronomy continue with a prohibition on eating blood. As we shall see below, however, the passage from *Ahare Mot* contains a distinctive justification for the prohibition, a justification that is consistent with the parashah's general emphasis on the exclusivity of permissible sacrifice.

The prohibition is stated first with a familiar justification: "And if anyone of the house of Israel or of the strangers who reside among them partakes of any blood, I will set My face against the person who partakes of the blood, and I will cut him off from among his kin. *For the life* (Heb. *nefesh*) *of the flesh is in the blood* ... ." (Lev. 17:10, emphasis added) This thought runs from the first book of the Torah to the last. In the first, Noah is told, "You must not, however, eat flesh with its life-blood (*naf sho damo*) in it." (Gen. 9:4) In Deuteronomy, Moses continues the passage quoted a few paragraphs above by saying:

> "But make sure that you do not partake of the blood; for the blood is the life (hanefesh), and you must not consume the life (hanefesh) with the flesh. You must not partake of it; you must pour it out on the ground like water: you must not partake of it, in order that it may go well with you and with your descendants to

come, for you will be doing what is right in the sight of the LORD." (Deut. 12:23–25)

In fact, *Ahare Mot* uses language that stresses this familiar justification. Verses 10–12 constitute the third of five major thoughts in this portion of the *parashah* (slaughter only at the central altar; sacrifices only at the central altar; blood not to be eaten; blood of hunted animals to be covered and certainly not eaten; and animals that died or were torn by beasts not to be eaten). In general, the universality of these mandates is expressed in Hebrew by the phrase "ISH-ISH" (roughly, any man, or every man). In the middle of our prohibition on eating blood, however, the same concept is repeated using a very different Hebrew term. "Therefore I say to the Israelite people: *No person* among you shall (literally, *every person* among you shall not) partake of blood, nor shall the stranger who resides among you partake of blood." (Lev. 17:12, emphasis added) At this point, the universality of the prohibition ("every person") is expressed in Hebrew as "KOL NEFESH." That is, Torah refers to the universal human with the same word that it uses to refer to the life-force of the blood of an animal. Eating blood would make people not merely carnivores but almost cannibals.

This usage is not limited to *Ahare Mot*. *Nefesh* is used elsewhere to refer to a person who is eating. See, for example, Lev. 7:25 ("the person who eats (fat)"); *ibid.* 7:27 ("anyone who eats blood, that person shall be cut off from his kin"); Lev. 17:15 ("Any person . . . who eats what has died or has been torn by beasts"). The word is also used as the embodiment of the desire to eat. See Deut. 12:20–21 ("you have the urge," "whenever you wish," "to your heart's content").

What is distinctive about *Ahare Mot*'s justification for not eating blood is the clarity of an additional thought: People must not eat blood because of blood's potential role in the sacred service of expiation. "For the life of the flesh is in the blood, and I have

144

assigned it to you for making expiation for your lives upon the altar; it is the blood, as life, that effects expiation." (Lev. 17:11). Just as a potentially sacrificial animal (according to Rabbi Ishmael) was to be slaughtered as part of a sacred service or not at all, so blood that might have been used to make expiation on the altar is to be given no secular use.

The rule for fat is similar. "You shall eat no fat of ox or sheep or goat. Fat from animals that died or were torn by beasts may be put to any use, but you must not eat it. If anyone eats the fat of *animals from which offerings by fire may be made to the LORD*, the person who eats it shall be cut off from his kin." (Lev. 7:23–25, emphasis added) Not only must there be no sacred service except one conforming exactly to Divine command, but the potential raw materials for such a service must not serve a non-sacred purpose. Consumption of blood is forbidden not merely because it embodies the life of a creature very much like ourselves. Rather (perhaps because of that very similarity), it has the potential for expiating the culpability that might otherwise have cost us our own lives. At some level, the animal's death was a substitute for our own.

This thought brings us full circle to the opening of the *parashah*. Nadab and Abihu present a problem to the rabbis because, although they performed a sacred service in an impermissible way, the text of the Torah seems to leave open the possibility that their motives were innocent. Thus, many *midrashim* try to justify the deaths of this pair by hypothesizing a variety of egregious transgressions (for example, drunkenness, failure to wear the required vestments, failure to wash, and conceit so severe that they had refused to marry). One *midrash*, however, seems to assume that, despite their fatal error, Aaron's son's were righteous men. Rabbi Hiyya the son of Rabbi Abba wondered why their death (which occurred at the beginning of Nissan) is mentioned in the Torah in connection with the Day of Atonement. "It is to teach us that just as the Day of Atonement achieves atonement, so the death of the righteous achieves atonement."

(*Lev. Rabbah, Parashah* 20:XII.2.B) If they were indeed righteous men, the fate of Nadab and Abihu serves not only as a warning to future officiants at the Day of Atonement services mandated by *Aḥara Mot*. It may also be a tragic facilitator of the very expiation that those services seek to bring about.

Michael S. Novey is a graduate of the Rosenbloom Religious School (then called the Chuzuk Amuno Hebrew School). In more recent years, he has taken informal courses for adults at Chizuk Amuno (often with Rabbi Zaiman), at the Baltimore Hebrew University, and at the District of Columbia Jewish Community Center.

Kedoshim
Heller & Ari Zaiman

Parashat Kedoshim has often been called the holiness code, a how-to manual, and an abridged Torah. God's most dramatic mandate begins the parashah:

> *"The Lord spoke to Moses, saying: Speak to the whole Israelite community and say to them: You shall be holy, for I, the Lord your God, am holy." (Leviticus 19:1)*

This requirement is followed by a litany of prescriptions that apply to individuals within the community and to the community at-large. Kedoshim is spoken to the entire congregation, so that each individual may understand how it applies to him or her. It details our responsibilities as individuals and as members of a community. Kedoshim, among other things, requires observance of Shabbat, reverence for our parents, and care of the less fortunate. Further, we are instructed, "You shall not hate your kinsfolk in your heart. Reprove your kinsman, but incur no guilt because of him." (Leviticus 19:17)

The Merriam-Webster Dictionary defines the word, "reprove" as, "to correct gently or with kindly intent." Why is reproof so important? As individuals and members of the community, what are we obligated to do?

A community is based on shared beliefs. The Jewish community, based on Torah, maintains rules and standards its members are required to know and to follow. While the community is the centerpiece, the individual is essential. According to Rabbi Simeon ben Yohai, every individual act affects the community. This is reflected in his parable:

> *"A number of people were seated in a boat, and one of them took out a drill and began drilling a hole beneath*

> *where he sat. The fellow travelers shouted: 'What are you doing there?' The person with the drill shouted back, "What does it matter to you? Aren't I drilling under my own seat?" The others answered: "It is absolutely our business. If the water fills the boat, we will all drown." (Midrash Rabbah)*

As each individual affects the entire community, members of the community have a stake in their neighbors' actions.

Perhaps more than ever, the world we live in perpetuates a conflict between the individual and the community. Straying from relationships and community occurs all too easily as we are driven to achieve personal autonomy and success. This pursuit causes us to lead separate lives.

On the other hand, we speak of relationships and the desire for community; we search for an environment that envelops us and nurtures our need to belong. While "it takes a village (community)" to raise a child and a friend "is all you really need," what is required of us, not only to be a member of a community, but also to be a real friend? An answer is found in *Parashat Kedoshim*'s mandate of reproof.

Reproof recognizes that individuals are not perfect. People make mistakes, fall short of their potential, and behave poorly. Also reflected in the concept of reproof is the way we as individuals and as a community are to respond when confronted with a wrong committed by another. The colleague who cheats in a business deal, the friend who contemplates an affair, the parent who fails to support their child . . . . The mandate to reprove does not ask the question, "Should we respond?" In fact, the injunction to admonish dispels the myth that we can choose not to respond when we witness a wrong or injustice. Silence is a response.

We rationalize our inaction by saying: " . . . I don't want to make waves," or "It's really not my business." We stay quiet and keep to ourselves because we don't want to embarrass our "friend." We remind ourselves of the maxim: "People who live in glass

148

houses should not throw stones." We don't want to judge, because who knows what we would do if we faced the same circumstances?

The short-term impact of our walking away or ignoring the wrong, is one of relief. An awkward situation has been avoided. Take, for example, the "friend" who shares with you the confidence of another. Instead of stating, "I am uncomfortable with you sharing this information because this was meant to be confidential," and risking the possibility of an argument or being accused of self-righteousness, we sit and nod politely. In our silence we think, "If they can do it to someone else, they can do it to me." It is during moments like these that we begin to build walls to distance ourselves from that person.

The long-term impact of our inaction is the decay of trust. We stop communicating and our relationships wither. The witness, the wrong-doer, and the community are diminished as a result of an injustice. The person who has committed the wrong becomes isolated from the community. By ignoring the action, the witness becomes, in part, responsible for the original offense, "Whoever can stop. . .the people of his city from the sinning, but does not. . .is held responsible for the sins of the people of his city." (Babylonian Talmud, Shabbat 54b) The community, in turn, loses an individual created in God's image.

According to *Parashat Kedoshim*, the appropriate response to a wrong is reproof. The Rabbis understood the difficulty and the fear associated with reproving another. It is a delicate situation. Rabbi Tarfon reflected: "I wonder if there is anyone in this generation capable of accepting reproof . . . ." Rabbi Elazar ben Azarya said, "I wonder whether there is anyone in this generation who knows how to reprove" (without humiliating the one being criticized). (Babylonian Talmud, Arakhin 16b)

Reproof requires great care. Be certain of your motives. "Reproach not a neighbor for a blemish that is yours." (R. Nathan, B. Bava Metzia 59b) Further, Maimonides offered these guidelines: administer the rebuke in private, speak to the offender gently and tenderly point out that he is only speaking for the wrongdoer's own good." (Moses Maimonides, *Mishneh Torah*, "Laws Concerning Character Development and Ethical Conduct," 6:7) Respect the person and stress your concern about him or her. Be clear that it is the action being judged, not the person.

After King David took Bathsheba and had Uriah, her husband, killed, the Prophet Nathan went to David and told a well-known parable. "There were two men in the same city, one rich and one poor. The rich man had very large flocks and herds, but the poor man had only one little ewe lamb that he had bought....One day, a traveler came to the rich man, but he was loath to take anything from his own flocks or herds to prepare a meal for the guest who had come to him; so he took the poor man's lamb and prepared it for the man who had come to him." (Samuel II; chapter 12 1-4) King David became irate and began to proclaim judgments. Only then did Nathan say, "That man is you!" Nathan did not start with accusations. He did not share David's acts with the public. Instead, Nathan went in private and spoke to David in a manner he could understand.

We are not alone. We belong to the Jewish community. Nathan's reproof demonstrates how community can be helpful. Nathan allows David to understand his inappropriate actions in order for him to seek teshuva, forgiveness. As individuals, we rely on others to help us grow and mature. It has often been said, that a person can only develop into an individual within a community where there are others to help, to tell us we can do better, and to keep us from loosing faith in ourselves.

Anne Lamott, in *Crooked Little Heart*, tells of a young girl, Rosie, lacking good family support. She was a perfectionist and she played tennis well. However, during a few of her matches she cheated. No one saw except Luther. She thought of herself as a cheater. Is this not common? When we do something wrong, we are often unable to dissociate ourselves from our actions. In a private exchange, Luther says, "I'm just saying that you don't need to see yourself as a cheater. Because that is not who you are. You're someone who cheated. There's a difference, and you should try to get that difference, or that's who you will grow up to be." (p. 277).

We witness an injustice and become paralyzed. Move in any direction and we are in danger of loss. The risk is constant, but only with reproof is there the potential to enhance community and relationships. R. Yose bar Hanina once said, "Reproof leads to love, as it is said, 'Reprove a wise man, and he will love you.'" (Proverbs 9:8)

Heller & Ari Zaiman are members of Chizuk Amuno Congregation where they both take advantage of the many educational opportunities available. The also both benefit from having Chizuk Amuno's Rabbi, Joel Zaiman as their father-in-law and father respectively.

Emor
Dr. David Roffman

Parashat Emor contains the *mitzvot* which command us in the observance of the *shalosh regalim*; *Pesah, Shavuot,* and *Sukkot*, as well as those mitzvot concerning the observance *of Rosh Hashanah* and *Yom Kippur*. Included among these commandments are *mitzvot* concerning the use of numerous ritual items, such as *matzoh, sukkah, lulav* and *etrog*, and *shofar*. Of these ritual items, perhaps none signifies the relationship between God and man so much as *shofar*. Even the sight of the *shofar*, absent hearing its sound, provokes the image of *t'shuvah*—repentance, an act as inherently Jewish as any commanded by God. Surely our clearest memory of *Rosh Hashanah* as children is of our parents holding us up, or leading us to a place where we could not only hear the *shofar* as it was being sounded, but where we could clearly see the *shofar* being blown. And what child, after having heard the *shofar*, does not try to imitate the sound of *"teki'ah"*? Long before we reach the age at which the concepts of self-reflection and repentance can be understood, we are able to conjure up the image and the sound of the *shofar*.

The word *"teru'ah"*—a reference to blowing the *shofar*—appears three times in Torah, twice in connection with *Rosh Hashanah* and once in connection with *Yom Kippur* of the Jubilee year. The *Mishnah* in *Rosh Hashanah* explains the way *shofar* is to be blown: "The manner of sounding is three of three each (*teki'ah, teru'ah, teki'ah*). *Teki'ah*, the first *shofar* note, and the note perhaps most easily recalled by adults as well as children, is the note which we associate with the sounding of the *shofar*, not only on *Rosh Hashanah*, but also at other times in our history. For many contemporary Jews, it is the sound we associate with the call at Sinai, and with the alarm that warned the Israelites in the desert of impending danger. In the *Shofarot* section of the musaf service on *Rosh Hashanah*, we recall "On the third day, as morning dawned at

Sinai, there were peals of thunder and flashes of lightning, a dense cloud on the mountain, and loud blasts of the *shofar*; everyone in the camp trembled. The blast of the *shofar* grew louder and louder." Hearing the *teki'ah* sound of the *shofar* on *Rosh Hashanah* not only harkens us back to the day when God revealed God's self to the people Israel, but for many the sound opens a portal through which God can be revealed to our very presence, in our time and in our lives. The intensity of the sound increases until it reaches its peak with *teki'ah g'dolah;* so does the intensity of our struggle reach farther and farther into our own lives so that we can uncover the truth of how we have lived in our relationship with God, with our fellow man, and with ourselves.

The power of the *shofar* to heighten the intensity of the Israelite's belief in the strength that God brought to them in their conquest of Caanan is best described in Joshua: "Do this (march around the walls of Jericho) six days with seven priests carrying seven rams horns preceding the ark. On the seventh day, march around the city seven times with the priests blowing the horns. And when a long blast (*teki'ah*) is sounded on the horn, as soon as you hear the sound of the horn, all of the people shall give a mighty shout. Thereupon, the city wall will collapse and the people shall advance, every man straight ahead." On *Rosh Hashanah*, the sound of *teki'ah* as described by Maimonides has a profound meaning—"it says awake you sleepers and ponder over your deeds; Remember your Creator and go back to Him in penitence. Be not of those who miss realities in their pursuit of shadows and waste their years in seeking after vain things which can not profit or deliver." The wake up call of *teki'ah* on *Rosh Hashanah* is like the blast sounded at Jericho. It serves to crumble the walls that separate us from our ability to stare into our most inner self and discover there the qualities that keep us from "advancing straight ahead" in the path of *t'shuvah*.

The *Gemarah* relates the three notes to the number of times that the word "*teru'ah*" appears in Torah. The question is then posed: "How is the *teru'ah* note blown?" According to Kehati, opinions varied in the Gemarah about whether *teru'ah* represented the sound of a person sighing when his heart is greatly distressed (i.e. what we call *shevarim*), or whether it should be compared to the sound of women wailing, (what we call *teru'ah*), or perhaps sighing and wailing together, for wailing is usually preceded by sighing. For a time in our history, the *teru'ah* note was sounded differently in various communities, depending upon the interpretation of how the sound of distress was expressed within that community. R. Abahu therefore decreed in Caesaria that the *shofar* should be blown so as to fulfill all of the requirements according to all options: *teki'ah, shevarim teru'ah, teki'ah*, three times; *teki'ah, shevarim, teki'ah*, three times; and *teki'ah, teru'ah, teki'ah*, three times. The total number of notes adds up to thirty, an allusion to which was found in the passage "it is (*yihyeh*) a day of blowing the horn." The numerical value of the word "*yihyeh*" is thirty.

The first of the two references to *shofar,* in connection with *Rosh Hasanah,* occurs in *Parashat Emor*: "In the seventh month, on the first day of the month, you shall observe complete rest, a sacred occasion commemorated with loud blasts—*zichron teru'ah*. You shall not work at your occupation; and you shall bring an offering by fire to the Lord." The second reference occurs in *Parashat Pinchas*: "In the seventh month, on the first day of the month, you shall observe a sacred occasion. You shall do no work at your occupations. You shall observe it as a day when the horn is sounded." Since the Rabbis have taught that there is a reason for what appears to be duplicative wording or phrases in Torah, and that there is a specific purpose for *every* word in Torah, there must be a purpose in this seeming repetition. The terminology used in *Emor,* "*zichron teru'ah,*" may also be translated as "a mention of *shofar* blast" or "a memorial proclaimed with the blast of the horn." Rashi 's commentary on this phrase expands the interpretation to "*zichron p'sukae zichronot*"—a mention of verses of remembrance, i.e. verses which refer to God's remembrance of His mercy toward Creation; "*u'p'sukae shofarot*"—and verses of *shofars*, i.e. verses that refer to the *shofar*; "*lizkor lachem ...*"—to remember on your behalf the binding of Isaac in whose stead a ram was offered. Rashi is referring here to the *Mishnah* that teaches us that this verse in *Emor* commands us not only to blow the *shofar*, but also to recite verses that refer to *shofar* blowing. It teaches us also that "*zichron*" is interpreted both as "mention" and "remembrance," so that on the basis of this verse in *Emor*, the Rabbis obligated us to recite verses of remembrance. Verses of *malchuyot*—"sovereignties," i.e. verses that proclaim God's sovereignty over the universe—are related in the *Rosh Hashanah* liturgy. These verses are alluded to in *Parashat Bhaalotcha* (Numbers 10:10): "And on your joyous occasions—your fixed festivals and new moon days—you shall sound the trumpets over your burnt offerings and your sacrifices of well-being. They shall be a reminder to you before your God: I, the Lord, am your God." The obligation to recite these three sets of verses, *malchuyot, zichronot,* and *shofarot* have thereby become an integral part of the *Rosh Hashanah* musaf service. As the first reference to "*teru'ah*" is interpreted as the obligation to recite verses pertaining to *shofar*, the second reference to "*teru'ah*," from *Parashat Pinchas,* "*yom teru'ah yihyeh la'chem*"—it is a day of blowing the horn unto you—may then be interpreted as a direct commandment for blowing the *shofar*, thus differentiating the two seemingly repetitive verses.

Sincere repentance is not an act that is taken lightly in our tradition, not an act that can be turned on and off with a moment's notice. The entire month of *Elul* is therefore ordained as a month of liturgical and spiritual preparation for *Rosh Hashanah* and *Yom Kippur*. As part of that preparation, the *shofar* is blown immediately following the *shaharit* service every day, with the exception of Shabbat, during the month of *Elul*, until the morning before *Rosh Hashanah*. The *shofar* is not sounded on the day prior *to Rosh Hashanah* in order to differentiate its rabbinically ordained daily sounding during *Elul*, from the commandment in Torah to blow the *shofar* on *Rosh Hashanah*. We come to the synagogue *on Rosh Hashanah* with the clear expectation that the process of repentance will be emphasized with the awe-inspiring sound of *shofar*. In post-

Rabbinic times, we must wait until the musaf service in order for that defining moment to occur. The *Mishnah* states that *on Rosh Hashanah*, "the second one (the reader for *musaf*) orders the blowing." The *Gemarah* explains that originally the *shofar* was blown during the *shaharit* service, until there was once a massacre of Jews as a result of the Romans misunderstanding the earlier sound as a signal for revolt. Since that risk no longer exists, perhaps reinstituting that practice of sounding the *shofar* during *shacharit* might draw more people to the synagogue at an earlier hour on *Rosh Hashanah*.

As the process of introspection and repentance is highlighted with the sound of the *shofar* on *Rosh Hashanah*, and anticipated by its blowing during *Elul*, so then is the ritual of *Yom Kippur* concluded with the sound of "*teki'ah g'dolah.*" It is the sound that lingers with us as a reminder of our hope that God has heard and accepted our offering of repentance, and has inscribed us in the Book of Life for the coming year. As we meet in our homes to partake of the break fast meal, we ask each other how the synagogue experience was for each of us this year. Routinely, we mention the *shofar*—how well it was sounded, how it contributed to our High Holy Day experience, and perhaps how we wished that we would take the time this year to learn to blow the *shofar* ourselves. May the sound of the *shofar* continue to be one of the symbols that brings man closer to God and to each other, and may that sound awaken in each of us the opportunity for renewal and rebirth.

Dr. David Roffman is a long-time member of Chizuk Amuno Congregation. A graduate of the Florence Melton Adult Mini-School, he is past-president of Chizuk Amuno Brotherhood, is a Shaliah Zibbur at High Holy Day Services at the shul, and an active learner(in all elements of) Chizuk Amuno's adult education program.

Behar
Sandee & Dr. Barry Lever

This is the penultimate *parashah* in the book of *Vayyikra*, (Lev. 25:1-26:2). Except for the last two verses, this *parashah* deals almost exclusively with the institution of *shemittah and yovel*, enumerating the regulations of the sabbatical and jubilee years. Rules are set forth for *not* working the Land of Israel, the return of real property, and the remission of debts, as well as the manumission of bondmen and slaves. Lev. 25:10, . . . "And you shall proclaim liberty throughout the land unto all the inhabitants thereof."

However, in this parashah we wish to focus on the concept of wrong-doing as expressed by the word "tonu." The word, "tonu," occurs in only three places in the entire H̱umash, all of them in *Vayyikra*.

In Lev.25: 14, the text states:

> *"When you sell property to your neighbor, or buy any from your neighbor do not wrong* (tonu) *one another." Subsequently in Lev.25: 17, the text states: "Do not wrong* (velo tonu) *one another, but fear your God; I the Lord am your God." The final appearance of the word is in Lev.19: 33-34: "When a stranger resides with you in your land, you shall not wrong him* (lo tonu oto) *...I the Lord am your God." The type of wrong-doing in each of these verses is amplified in Rabbinic texts, outside the H̱umash, where the legal concept of "ona'ah bid'varim," verbal wrong-doing, is established.*

The word *"ona'ah,"* never appears in the Bible. Its first appearance is in Tannaitic texts: the Sifra and Mishnah. The word "ona'ah" has the same root as the word "tonu," the stem. The concept of verbal wrong-doing, "ona'ah bid'varim," however, is a new legal construct.

By carefully following the explication in Baba Metzia Chap.4 Mishnha 10, we will reveal and concretely illustrate the creativity of the Mishnaic sages. We will discover how they captured the underlying spirit of Torah and used it as the source to create entirely new applied law.

In Lev. 25:14, the sages took note that this verse is warning against aggrieving (tonu) one's fellow when buying or selling. Therefore, their first legal construct deals with "ona'ah b'meckach um'memkar," "wrong doing in buying and selling." This concept first appears in Baba Metzia, chapter 4, Mishna 3.

Mishna 10: however states the following: "k'shem sh'ona'ah b'meckach um'memkar, kach ona'ah bead'varim;" "Just as there is wrong doing in buying and selling, so too is there wrong doing with words." How do the sages arrive at this added statement?

They derived it from a discussion in a Baraita from the Sifra, on Lev. 19: 33. Here the sages state that the wrong doing (tonu) inflicted on the proselyte is the (tonu) wrong doing with words, "ona'ah bead'varim." This must be the case, since wrongdoing by buying or selling, "ona'ah b'meckach um'memkar," has already been dealt with in Lev. 19:14.

In Lev. 25:17, the wrong doing (tonu) is unrelated to a definable act, therefore there is no applied law. The sages, however, noted the parallelism between this verse and Lev. 19:33-4. In both of these verses the word, "tonu," is reinforced by a concluding warning phrase:"ani ha'shem elohakem…I the Lord am your God."

Using this same Baraita, the Gemara to Mishna 10 further describes a number of examples of verbal ona'ah. The sages explain that since a speaker's intent is not always clear, the same words may be either helpful or destructive, therefore it is practically impossible to enforce this law.

"In cases such as these, the matter is entrusted to a person's own heart…And concerning any matter that is entrusted to a person's own heart the verse says: 'And you shall fear your God.'

For he who knows a person's innermost thoughts and intentions will enforce his law."

To understand the influence of these two legal concepts emanating from the three verses in *Vayyikra* one has only to realize that the Babylonian Talmud has 138 separate citations either to *"ona'ah b'meckach um memkar,"* or *"ona'ah bid'vaream."*

What is even more fascinating and revealing about *"ona'ah bid'vaream"* being established as a distinct *halakhah* is the radical self-awareness of the sages about what they were doing. This is most clearly seen by following the discussion in BT, *Seder Nizkin,* Tractate BM, 4:10, Encompassed within pages 58B-59A of this *Gemara* is one of the most important theological discussions in the entire Talmud.

The question involves the ritual purity of a type of pottery oven, known as *"tanur shel Achnai,"* the "oven of *Achnai.*" The commentaries explain how such an oven was made and on what basis it could become impure.

The most important element of the story, however, is the intense debate between Rabbi Eliezer ben Hyrcanus, and the other sages of the Sanhedrin. Rabbi Eliezer ruled that such an oven was not subject to ritual impurity, and the other sages disagreed.

Using a *Baraita,* the Talmud details the intensity of the dispute. Rabbi Eliezer seeing that he could not persuade his colleagues with logical arguments to accept his position "said to them: 'If the *Halakhah* is in accordance with me let this carob tree prove it.' The carob tree immediately uprooted itself and moved one hundred cubits—some say four hundred cubits—from it original place."

Continuing the dispute, "the Sages said to him: 'Proof can not be brought from a carob tree.' Rabbi Eliezer then said to the Sages: 'If the *Halakhah* is in accordance with me, let a channel of water prove it.' The channel of water immediately flowed backward against the direction in which it usually flowed. The Sages said to him: 'Proof can not be brought from a channel of water either.'"

"Rabbi Eliezer then said to the Sages: 'If the *Halakhah* is in accordance with me, let the walls of the House of Study prove it.' The walls of the House of Study then leaned and were about to fall. Rabbi Yehoshua, one of Rabbi Eliezer' chief opponents among the Sages, rebuked the falling walls, saying to them: 'If Talmudic scholars argue with one another in their discussions about the *Halakhah,* what affair is it of yours?' The walls did not fall down, out of respect for Rabbi Yehoshua, nor did they straighten, out of respect for Rabbi Eliezer, and indeed those walls remain leaning until this day."

Unwilling to surrender his *Halakhic* position "Rabbi Eliezer then said to the Sages: 'If the *Halakhah* is in accordance with me, let it be proved directly from heaven.' Suddenly a heavenly voice went forth and said to the Sages: 'Why are you disputing with Rabbi Eliezer? The *Halakhah* is in accordance with him in all circumstances!' Rabbi Yehoshua rose to his feet and quoted a portion of a verse (Deut. 30:12) saying: '*Lo ba'shamayim he,* The Torah is not in heaven!'"

To clarify this *Baraita,* the *Gemara* explains through the words of Rabbi Yirmeyah, that since the God already gave the Torah to the Jewish people at Mt Sinai, he could no longer intervene in *Halakhic* disputes. These matters were now resolved by a majority vote of the Rabbis following an open debate.

Subsequently the Gemara relates, that generations, later Rabbi Natan met the Prophet Elijah and asked him: "What did the Holy One Blessed be He, do at that time when Rabbi Yehoshua refused to heed the heavenly voice?" Elijah replied: "God smiled and said: '*Nitzckhuni banai, Nitzchuni banai,* My sons have triumphed, my sons have triumphed!'"

Rabbi Eliezer, unwilling to accept their opinion, was excommunicated by a majority vote of his colleagues. The *Baraita* goes on to relate the dire consequences inflicted on the world and specific rabbis, because of Rabbi Eliezers's humiliation through "*ona'ah bid'varim.*"

What are we to make of this discussion? It is easy to see that the rabbis through the statement: "*lo ba'shamayim he*" are using this story to assert their authority over those who would reject anything that was not written in the *Torah*.

What is more intriguing, however, are the questions: Why is this *halakhic* dispute over the purity of the oven of *Akhani* so bitter? Why not permit Rabbi Eliezer's opinion to remain a minority opinion as in all other Talmudic disputes? Why is this a unique case? Why do the sages who established the law of *"ona'ah bid' varim,"* flagrantly humiliate Rabbi Eliezer by excommunication? And finally, why would the rabbis even place that part of the story of Rabbi Eliezer in the Talmud at all? The common explanation that Rabbi Eliezer was too stubborn and an example had to be made of him, seems less than satisfactory.

In a weekly Talmud seminar in Stulman Adult Learning Center of Chizuk Amuno with our instructor, Dr. Moshe D. Shualy, we proposed a new explanation of this well-known and dramatic passage. This Talmudic debate about the oven of Akhnai must be understood in its historical setting: Judea, under Roman control following the destruction of the Temple, and preceding the Bar Kochba Revolt in 130 CE. The country seethes with anti-Roman sentiment and guerrilla warfare is a constant threat to their occupation. In spite of the occupation, the Roman authorities permit some semblance of Jewish self-government in the form of the Sanhedrin. The Romans, wishing to put as much pressure on the guerilla forces as possible, want the Sanhedrin to rule that the oven of Akhani is not ritually pure. The reason for their demand is that this type of oven is easily carried and constructed. The pottery rings from which it was made could be quickly assembled and disassembled in the field, thus making it ideal for use by mobile guerilla forces. Rabbi Eliezer had a close relationship with these forces and was known to be an opponent of the Roman occupation.

The Sanhedrin was faced with a Hobson's Choice. Either decide to rule that oven of *Aknai* was now no longer ritually pure, or face its dissolution by the Roman Authorities.

It is clear from the *Gemara* what the Sanhedrin elected to do to maintain a central organized Jewish community. It was forced to reverse the long standing *Halakha* on the ritual purity of the oven of *Akhnai*. More than that, it was forced to publicly repudiate Rabbi Eliezer when he would not abandon his position. Without him reversing his opinion the future of the Sanhedrin was imperiled.

We propose that this entire *Gemara* about the excommunication of Rabbi Eliezer was inserted to mask the Sanhedrin's bitter choice. The existential imperative of making bitter and difficult choices are costly yet necessary. Politically the Sages could not openly acknowledge their dilemma. However, by inserting this *Gemarah*, future generations might recognize the terrible price that the Talmudic Sages had to pay to persevere in their mission.

Sandee & Dr. Barry Lever are grateful to their teachers for helping them to arrive at their present level of attainment. The Levers are longtime members of Chizuk Amuno Congregation and are both students of Rabbi Zaiman. For 27 years, Sandee served as Director of the Goldsmith Early Childhood Education Center of Chizuk Amuno Congregation.

162

Behukosai
Hadassah & Dr. Levi Gordis

This *parashah* lays out God's requirements and rewards for following His commandments and punishments for not following His directions. The details are presented in two discrete sections: The *parashah* begins with a conditional sentence, "If by My laws you walk, and My commands you keep, and observe them."

What is missing in this verse is the 'then'—that is, the consequence of the action. These consequences are given instead in the next 10 verses. The separation of the conditions and the consequences into separate verses—both for the rewards and for the punishments—serves to heighten the dramatic quality of the presentation.

Following this section, in verses 14 and 15, we have the introduction to the punishments or curses:

> "But if you do not hearken to me, by not observing all these commandments. If my laws you spurn and my regulations you repel by not observing all my commandments, by your violating my covenant."

Again, the 'then. . . .' is missing in both of these introductory conditional verses. The consequences are listed after this introduction, which this time is two verses long, compared to the single-verse introduction of the rewards section, and the evil consequences take up the next 31 verses. Thus God details the 'good' in 10 verses, but the 'evil' in 31 verses. Not only is the description of punishment longer than of reward, but it is also more graphic— e.g. "you will eat the flesh of your sons and daughters."

Rabbinic commentators rejected the idea that the punishment section is greater than the rewards section and stressed that the rewards are stated in broad, general terms, while the punishments are presented in considerable detail. The rationale presented is that, if Israel observes the commandments, all the

163

blessings and rewards will come together. But if they do not observe, punishments will come little by little, in order, perhaps, to give them an opportunity to return from their evil ways before the full array of punishments is put into effect.

Nevertheless, more verses are used for the punishments than for the rewards. Why is the section on punishments so much longer than that on rewards? Perhaps this parallels our own lives— as human beings we take the good for granted when we have it and we generally don't think about our good fortune until it is gone. When we are ill or in trouble, financially, socially or politically, we are aware of the details of every problem that has come our way and we look back nostalgically to the 'good old days.' (It has been said that human beings tend to forget that, when those days were not very old, they were also not very good.) Indeed, we often only recognize good by the absence of evil rather than by positive attributes. On the other hand, we recognize and feel every detail of evil events which remain with us over time and stay in our memories, if not in our consciousness even after they are gone.

One interesting contrast in the listings of rewards and punishments is God's use of the terms, panai (my face) and paniti (I turned my face). In the rewards section (verse 9) we read, "I will turn my face toward you, making you fruitful and making you many, and I will establish my covenant with you." The same root is used in listing the punishments (verse 17), "And I will set my face against you, you will be hit by plague in the face of your enemies; those who hate you will have dominion over you, you will flee with no one pursuing you!" Thus God's turning to you does not necessarily imply the same positive compassionate result in all situations; rather the outcome varies with the circumstances.

It is interesting to contrast this section with *Dvarim*, chapters 27-28, in *Parashat Ki Tavo*. Israel was divided into two groups—one stood on Har Gerizim to recite the blessings and rewards and the other group stood on Har Eval to recite the punishments. Chapter 28 also first lists the rewards and then the punishments but unlike our *parashah*, Verse 28:1 begins with a condition but ends with the overall consequence in the same verse.

> *"Now it shall be: if you hearken, yes, hearken, to the voice of YHWH your God, taking care to observe all his commandments that I command you today, then YHWH your God will make you most high above all the nations of the earth."*

The rewards are listed in the next 13 verses.

Verse 15 introduces the punishments, "But it shall be: If you do not hearken to the voice of YHWH your God, by taking care and by observing all his commandments and his laws that I command you today, then there will come upon you all these curses, and overtake you."

An interesting difference between the recitations of rewards and punishments in *Behukotai* and *Ki Tavo* is in the introductory conditions. In Ki Tavo, the rewards and punishments are predicated on Israel's observing or not observing the commandments. In Behukotai, however, the Rabbis pointed out that, while the rewards come upon Israel for their having observed God's commandments, the punishments are not meted out solely for non-observance. The punishments come to pass only if non-observance is accompanied by a deliberate rejection of God's commandments, "if my laws you spurn and my regulations you repel." Isolated non-observance can be relatively easily reversed by beginning observance. However, non-observance resulting from intentional rejection of the commandments and a deliberate spurning of tradition is much more difficult to overcome.

Hadassah and Dr. Levi Gordis are longtime learners and members of Chizuk Amuno Congregation.

·NUMBERS· במדבר

TO DO THE WILL OF YOUR FATHER WHO IS IN HEAVEN.~

BE BOLD AS A LEOPARD & LIGHT AS AN EAGLE, SWIFT AS A DEER & MIGHTY AS A LION

ANGELA MUNITZ. 1999

Bemidbar
Rabbi Mark Loeb

The Five Books of Moses are, above all else, the Jewish people's record of the history of its relationship with God. But they are also more than that. They are also a depiction of the Jewish people's place in the context of the history of the human family. That is why the Torah begins, as Rashi notes at the very outset of his remarkable commentary, not with the Exodus (a Judeo-centric event) but with the Creation (a universal concern). This teaches us that, while the Torah is given to God's covenanted people, its message is nevertheless intended ultimately for the entire human race and is meant to serve as a spiritual blueprint for all of God's children.

The sweep of its rhythm is compelling not only because it feels so truly inspired but also because it seems so rational and sensible as it evolves. The early books focus on the history of the human person, on the metaphysical structure of the world, on the proclivities of human society, and on God's underlying hope and purpose for humankind—the creation of a world in which we—and He — work together to sanctify life and establish a moral order through ethical living. These tasks are difficult. First there is the chaos of the human personality and the family that need to be confronted—fratricide, jealousy, relational conflict. Then the struggles of the first Jewish families which lead to 70 souls in Egypt who grow in numbers but become trapped in slavery for centuries. The agonies of slavery rob them of their dignity and of an awareness of the supreme calling to be a moral vanguard for humanity through lives consecrated to God.

There follows the redemptive experience of the Exodus under the leadership of Moses that seems to lead inevitably to the theophany at Sinai where God's final plan is revealed. Israel, the people is told, must lead a life based on a code of religious behaviors in order to become a *Goy Kadosh* (Holy People) and an *Ohr*

LaGoyyim Light unto the Nations). The challenge is clear: to take a band of slaves raised in a pagan society and transform them into a collectivity capable of attaining the spiritual dignity required by monotheistic faith.

To achieve these goals, Moses proceeds in a highly sensible way. For one thing, he leads his people on a lengthy, time-consuming journey in order to give them time to develop a new group psyche. Aware that, in order to do this, he must satisfy their sense of religious authenticity by providing links to their pagan past, he bids them build a Tabernacle with familiar elements of ritual that they could recall from Egypt. Thus, the sacrifice of animals on the altar was, as Maimonides would later note, not an intrinsically sacred act, but a way to begin to wean the Israelites away from paganism. The creation of an hereditary priesthood (yet one denied the right to own land), further created a sense of religious familiarity with their past even as it moved them to a more progressive system where the religious elite did not enrich themselves at the expense of the faithful.

Most critically, he elaborates the laws not only of sacrifice but the statutes that govern all aspects of life. By the end of Exodus and Leviticus it has become clear that the Torah intends for the laws to become both Constitution and Code as Moses tries to build a faith community which, hopefully, all humankind will seek to join and/or emulate. It is at this point, where ideals have been depicted and the way to live has been articulated, that we come upon Bemidbar (Numbers) the fourth of the Five Books.

Suddenly, we realize, the agenda has changed. It is one thing to know what we as a people want to be. It is quite another matter to be able to create a society in which this vision can be realized. Thus Moses now turns to the practical challenges of community-building—organizing the people by tribal units, taking a census, establishing a defensive perimeter, and preparing the Tabernacle for daily worship. These tasks are critical even though seemingly mundane.

First, by organizing the people through tribal allegiances, he affirms that a nation needs to sense its rootedness in the extended nuclear family. The clan is an appropriate middleman between family and country. The notion of family as sacred center is reinforced.

But the real message of the Torah portion (Bemidbar) is in the Torah's insistence on detailing the census with such intense specificity of both names and numbers, even to the point of calculating the number of adult males (603,550). The number is incredible. If this number were accurate, then there would have had to be literally millions of Israelites in the Exodus, something which our rational sense tells us is impossible. (So argues Professor Zvi Herzog, the eminent Israeli archaeologist, who has been a major advocate of demythologizing the biblical text in recent years.) So what do we make of this text? Some argue that the Bible is simply *retro*jecting the numbers of later generations into a cherished past. Or perhaps the Torah is *pro*jecting the Deuteronomist's vision of all the generations being at Sinai together to receive the Torah and therefore counting the future as well as the present generations. In any event, there is one point no one will dispute: namely that when trying to build a community, the leadership must begin by seeing who is really there. Leaders need to know with whom they are working, who are those with commitment and on whom can they rely as they endeavor to respond to God's call. How can their people be inspired to live by the faith they represent? Thus the number, whatever its accuracy, more likely represents not human *quantity* but human *quality*.

The next phase is when Moses arranges the tribes in a defensive perimeter. Here his brilliance as a leader truly reveals itself. Rather than ordering the people to face *outward* from the center to the perimeter, a normal maneuver for defense, he instead tells them to face *inwardly to the center* towards the Tabernacle. By focusing on the locus where God dwells, the people will be driven by spiritual hope and faith, far greater forces with which to defend themselves than mere military maneuvering. By engaging themselves to the core of faith, they become proactive for God and truly safe.

These principles form a prescription for Jewish life today. Yet, for too many of us, the modern Jewish community is built upon crises and fears that, however real, are not likely to be overcome by hyper-reactivity. A crisis mentality does not build a community, only a frightened bunch of well-intentioned folk unprepared to preserve the Jewish heritage.

To find leaders who can help to sustain such a community we need people who have figured out, as Moses did, who is really there and what they can be led to achieve, who can affirm the *positive* paths to survival—knowledge, study, religious practice. As in every generation, there are few who are capable of such leadership, but Rabbi Joel Zaiman, friend and colleague, is clearly one such leader. For two decades he has demonstrated to us all the ways to forge a vision of Jewish life rooted in authentic Jewish ideals. He is a remarkable human being whose religious vision embraces the Jewish people and the human family, and whose integrity and sincerity are a blessing to our people. We may well thank God for his presence in our lives. May he continue to serve among us for many years to come.

Rabbi Mark G. Loeb is Rabbi of Beth El Congregation in Baltimore.

Naso
Rabbi James Rosen

Those familiar with modern computer word processing have undoubtedly met the little helper that can save enormous embarrassment. It's called spell check and makes certain that when you are indeed typing that impressive word you read some place but can't quite remember how to write, you will emerge as articulate as you intend.

Be forewarned. Spell Check has a very difficult time with Hebrew words transliterated into English letters. I've seen "Shabbat" come back as "subterranean."

But even with English words, you sometimes get significant results—results that unintentionally teach. Mary Ann Brussat, co-editor of *Spiritual Literacy*, writes: "The day the spell checker tried to substitute 'hopelessness' for 'homelessness' I was challenged to do something to break that automatic association. Being married to a minister I had to laugh when the program stopped on 'pastor' and suggested that better terms might be 'pasturing' (as in tending a flock?) or 'pestering' (all that emphasis on moral laws?). I decided that my program was too inclined to maintain the status quo when it suggested that 'alikeness' was a better word than 'aliveness.'

Sarah Maitland, author of *A Big Enough God*, writes: "The spell check program in my word processor which I have to say is both pagan and right-wing does not care for the word 'sacred.' Every time I ran this text through the program it wanted to change the word 'sacred' to the word 'scared.'"

Think about that one. An inability to see the word "sacred" without seeing something scary. You need to wonder: Does the computer grasp what we intuitively know? That which we don't understand evokes fear.

Fear has a unique power. For many, it leads to superstition, a kind of magical mischief—making that marks our fears. Rabbi Chanan Brichto used to say tongue in cheek, "The difference between religion and superstition is that superstition is the other person's religion."

I suppose for many of us it is. But whether it's avoiding cracks on the sidewalk, not walking underneath ladders, avoiding cats who walk in front of us, knocking on wood (which, by the way, comes from Christian sources of knocking on the cross) or tying red ribbons on babies' cribs to avoid the evil eye (that's an authentic Jewish one), superstition all has something else in common—it's an escape from reality. It forms an appeal to something magical, some power inherent in the universe or in things that will do our bidding. Mind you, that power is not God. And the link between the deed and the result is utterly automatic.

In fairness, there is a strong folk tradition within Judaism, and we have more than our share of superstitious elements that have crept into our lives.

But we who fashion ourselves as intellectuals tend to frown upon all such manifestations. It's one thing to have a Mezzuzah on the door to remind us of our desire to have a Godly home. It is quite another matter to think of it as a magical amulet that will automatically protect our house from all ill. Superstition is the other guy's religion, the ultimate escape. It's what motivates cults: separate from life, worship a guru-like leader, find some way of storming the gates of heaven through bizarre rituals designed to force the divine hand in bringing the millennium. We want nothing to do with it. And if our word processors come out with "scared" every time we think of "sacred" maybe that's because "sacred" all too often leads to superstitious, frightening nonsense.

From the Torah reading of Naso: A man wants to separate himself and becomes super-pious. He will be a Nazirite, separated unto God. Avoiding wine and strong drink, not cutting the hair, he will live a life of consecration, removed from all contact with the dead, holy unto God.

From Chapter 6, verses 13 and 14: "And when the period of Naziriteship is over …, he shall present one ewe lamb in its first year without blemish for a sin offering." A sin offering? Why? Is this not a desired piety? Nachmanides, with his mystical leanings, says something we might expect. "The act of forsaking the Nazirite vow is the sin." Of course, if one wishes to attain a sense of the sacred in life, you have to strip away the material. A Nazirite surrenders it all. To then abandon the potential for human divine encounter is a serious matter. To be sure, the about-to-be-former Nazarite must bring a sin offering.

Maimonides says something we rational moderns prefer: The sin is in trying to become extra pious in the first place. The Commandments as they are, are enough. "Our sages commanded one to deny the self only things denied by the Torah. One should not inflict on the self-vows of abstinence on things permitted. As it is said… 'Do not be overly righteous'…." For Maimonides the sin is in trying to become a Nazirite in the first place.

Solomon Astruc, in *Midrishai HaTorah,* adds another dimension: "The fact that his passions got the better of him till he was driven to abstain from wine to subdue his material desires and bodily wants and deny himself the legitimate enjoyment of wine that makes glad both God and man." According to him, the sin is not in becoming a Nazirite or in ceasing to be one. The sin is that which preceded the Nazirite vow. If one reaches the point where the only way one can avoid becoming intoxicated by wine is to become a total teetotaler, then indeed that compulsion is a very sad thing indeed. The Nazirite vow was often necessary, but extreme, medicine for spiritual ills for the failure of moderation.

We who live in a culture of some twenty million alcoholics, countless substance abusers and, especially poignant for the Jewish community, those addicted to gambling, can't help but be struck by the insight and relevance of Astruc's perception. And to these tragic addictions we have added a whole list of escapist habits. Shopping, romance, and to return to our friendly computer, the Internet. For all of our vaunted attempts to downplay the superstitious and to uphold the rational in modern life, to reject those elements of religion that encourage escapism and silly flights of fancy, for all of our realization that this is a world where the sacred really means scary, the irony is it is we who are the greatest escape artists of all. The television is on in the average American home four to seven hours a day. The highest paid people in this country are, for the most part, not researchers who find cures for terrible illnesses, not the teachers who touch lives forever, not the people who defend our borders, nor those who make our laws, but those who entertain us. Be a model, be an actor, be a sports hero, do one of those things that help get American minds off of their own pedestrian and dull lives for just a few minutes, and you will be rich and famous.

We consume more pills than any other country on earth. We are driven to succeed by a culture that applauds compulsive drives for success and workaholism. What a splendid way to avoid real and genuine human intimacy.

A Peanuts cartoon has Linus asking Snoopy, "Being a World War I flying ace must be very dangerous—have you considered what you would do if you were captured?" Snoopy thinks and says, "It happened once, I said I would never talk but then they offered me this big marshmallow sundae." The temptation to cope with the pressures of our lives, with food and pill, drink and the highs of risk—these are all so great.

Lord knows there is nothing wrong with fun and release, with forgetting it all for just a little while. But our culture thrives on raising escapism to the highest possible art. We have bartered it for meaning.

But one of the supreme ironies is that it is religion that roots us in this world. You may want to pray all day, you may want to ascend into the heavenly spheres, but you also have to give Tzedakah because there is a Mitzvah system that says, "We care about each other and care for each other as well." Says the Talmud, "For a person to be God-like, that person must be a partner in the act of creation." We are reborn each day. As Rabbi Harold Kushner puts it: "Feeding the hungry, supporting the poor, comforting the sick and lonely. These are not things that God does, these are the things that we do, and when we do them, God is present in our lives."

It's no wonder that so many find their way out of addictive behaviors by attaching themselves to religious sources. Jewish 12-Step groups now abound. And their message always is, "For those who have become lost in this world, there is a way out." And it is not only believing, it is doing and knowing that we are not alone. There is God and fellowship and the loving link between them. These groups teach that the sacred is often not scary at all but fully within our reach. Holiness is in our hands.

None of us needs to be a Nazirite. We need not become zealous and do more than what Torah requires of us. But it is religion that reminds us that we have been put on this earth to serve and not simply have fun, to run towards helpful duty and not away from challenges, we are here to embrace the sacred and comfort the scared.

Tradition is the guide. Not to help us soar heavenward but to transform the world.

That is the ultimate task, and the ultimate L'Chaim—anyway you spell it.

James Rosen, the Rabbi of Beth El Temple in West Hartford, Connecticut, is also a member of the Conservative Movement's Commission on Jewish Law and Standards and the President of the Connecticut Valley Region of the Rabbinical Assembly. He was privileged to serve as Assistant/Associate Rabbi with Rabbi Joel Zaiman at Chizuk Amuno Congregation from 1983-1992.

Behaalosecha
Rabbi Gila Coleman Ruskin

Did Aaron, Miriam, and Moses ever sit down with their families at Seder? Did they get together to celebrate birthdays or to reminisce about Mom and Dad on their *yahrzeit*? The *Tanakh* does not record any of their family gatherings; indeed the only time we get a glimpse into their personal relationship as adults is during *Parashat b'ha-alotka*. Clearly, all of them were public figures with their own constituencies, which makes for a complicated sibling relationship and the *Tanakh* generally preserves their privacy and dignity.

The episode during Chapter 12 of the Book of Numbers gives us a rare glimpse into the sibling relationship of the children of Yocheved and Amram. It also raises many questions about family relationships among public figures, and specifically this "First Family," about sin and punishment, and about the uniqueness of the bond between God and Moses. Also in this chapter we are introduced for the first time to the concept of an original prayer of kavannah for healing, a paradigm which has inspired renewed interest in the contemporary Jewish healing movement.

> " When they were at Hazerot, Miriam spoke against Moses because of the Cushite woman he had married: 'he married a Cushite woman!'
>
> They said: 'Has the Lord spoken only through Moses? Has He not spoken through us as well?' And the Lord heard it.
>
> ...The Lord came down in a pillar of cloud, stopped at the entrance of the Tent, and called out 'Aaron and Miriam! Hear these My words. When a prophet of the Lord arises among you, I make Myself known in a vision...Not so with My servant Moses...with him I

speak mouth to mouth …and he beholds the likeness of the Lord. How then did you not shrink from speaking against My servant?'

…there was Miriam stricken with snow white scales. When Aaron turned towards Miriam, …he said to Moses, 'O my lord, account not unto us the sin which we committed in our folly. Let her not be as one dead.'

So Moses cried out to the Lord, saying: 'El na rfa na la. O God, pray heal her!'

But the Lord said to Moses: "If her father spat in her face, would she not bear her shame for seven days? Let her be shut out of camp for seven days and then let her be readmitted." (Numbers 12, JPS translation)

Before focusing specifically on the prayer uttered by Moses, let's analyze the story itself. The questions that naturally arise are: 1. What exactly was the sin of Aaron and Miriam for which they are taken to task by God? 2. Why was Miriam punished with leprosy and Aaron not? 3. Why did Aaron turn to Moses to utter the prayer rather than turn to God himself? After all, he was the High Priest.

From the text itself, we learn that Aaron and Miriam were speaking against Moses regarding his wife. They also challenge the justice of God's recent communication to the people exclusively through Moses. Aaron and Miriam consider themselves to be prophets as well, who have in the past been the recipients of God's word. The text does not address the issue of why only Miriam was stricken, or why Aaron approached and beseeched Moses to pray for Miriam's healing.

The commentaries expand on the issue of Miriam and Aaron's comments about Moses' wife. From the Midrash collection of *Sifre* comes this interpretation:

> *"The criticism of Moses had to do with his ceasing to have sexual relations with his wife, Zipporah. Now how did Miriam know that Moses had ceased to have sexual relations with his wife? She realized that Zipporah was not making herself up with women's ornaments. She said to her: "How come you're not making up like other women?" She said to her: "Your brother does not pay any attention to such things." Miriam realized and told her brother (Aaron) and both of them spoke against Moses.*

> *"Now it is an argument a fortiori (kal v'homer) if Miriam, who intended to speak against her brother not to his detriment, but to his credit, and not to lessen procreation, but to increase it, and who spoke only in private, yet she was punished, if someone intends to speak ill of his fellow and not in praise, to diminish and not to increase procreation, and speaks not in private but among others, how much the more-so will such a one be punished." (Sifre on Numbers 99, part 13 translated by Jacob Neusner)*

The Midrashic collection *Deuteronomy Rabbah*, apparently making the opposite assumption that Miriam's intentions were not all honorable, makes the specific connection between slander and leprosy:

> *"R. Hanina said: Plagues of leprosy come only on account of speaking calumny. For, as the sages said, you can see for yourself that such plagues come on account of calumny. Even the righteous Miriam, who*

*spoke calumny of her brother, Moses, plagues clung to
her, as a sign (and a warning) to all given to speaking
calumny. Hence, "remember what the Lord thy God
did unto Miriam" (Deut. 24.9)." (Deuteronomy
Rabbah 6:8)*

The above commentaries, plus the well known *notarikon* of *metzora* (leprosy) as *motzi shem ra* (slander), establishes that the sin for which Miriam is punished with *metzora* is one of slander or a similar sin of *lashon ha-ra*. Even in the above passage from *Sifre*, where Miriam's intentions were actually recognized as constructive, she was nonetheless still punished for speaking against her brother about a private matter. This commentary establishes the premise that the prohibition against *lashon ha-ra* even applies to private conversation which is not meant to be derogatory. ("Even though they tell the truth, they ruin the world." Maimonides, *Hilchot Dayot* 7:2)

Then why was Aaron not punished with leprosy? W. Gunther Plaut offers the suggestion that Aaron was also punished, not "corporally, but mentally . . . Aaron doubtlessly undergoes great anguish because of the divine rebuke, but also he suffers keenly from guilt when he sees his sister disfigured hideously while he who had committed the same offense is apparently let off free." (p. 1101, *The Torah: A Modern Commentary*) What could be more agonizing than watching one whom we love suffer?

Plaut also cites an even worse punishment that is visited upon Aaron: humiliation. "Aaron has pretended to be the equal of his younger brother and now has to humble himself utterly." (ibid.) He addresses Moses as "my lord," begging his forgiveness and asking him to intercede with God for Miriam's healing.

Why does Aaron approach Moses instead of praying himself? In the Shulchan Aruch, it directs us to not only offer our own prayers for the sick but also to request a prayer from a sage:

"Rabbi Phineas, the son of Hama, preached: "Whoever has a sick person in his house, should go to a sage and ask him to plead for mercy in his behalf, as it is written (Proverbs 16:14): "The wrath of a king is as messengers of death, but a wise man will pacify it." (Ganzfried, Kitzur Shulchan Aruch Volume 4 Chapter 192)

So we now come to the prayer itself, uttered by Moses, for Miriam's healing, at the request of Aaron. *"EL NA R'FA NA LA . . .* Please, God, pray heal her."

My involvement in the Baltimore Jewish Healing Network has exposed me to the hypnotic power of this brief prayer. The Baltimore Jewish Healing Network is a local group, one of dozens nationwide, that have become involved in the teaching of Jewish healing texts and providing support for those suffering from illness and caretakers. This short prayer has become a well-known and loved chant. The words are poetic and elegant in their simplicity, rhythm, and rhyme, and have been set to music by Debbie Friedman and Hanna Tiferet Siegel. I have personally witnessed the participants in our classes and support groups, many of whom are not familiar with the liturgy, become enthralled and moved by this prayer.

It is only the second prayer of *kavannah* (spontaneous) intention we find in the Bible, the first being Eliezer's request for God's graciousness in granting a sign to demonstrate who will be the right wife for Isaac. These prayers of *kavannah* (Eliezer's, Moses' and later Hannah in I Samuel) are unusual in that there is no accompanying sacrifice on an altar, which would generally be part of a petition or thanksgiving.

The commentaries about the brevity of this prayer range from Jacob Milgrom, who believes that Moses must have been unmotivated to create a longer prayer because of his anger at his siblings (JPS Tanakh), to Rabbi Eliezer in the *Babylonian Talmud* (Berakhot 34a) who calls such a spontaneous prayer "genuine supplication." Rabbi Joshua, also in a passage from the Talmud, maintains that "when one is in a dangerous situation, one should recite a short prayer." (Berakhot 28b)

In the Midrash collection of *Sifre*, this prayer is held up as a paradigm of the proper format for prayer. "One must first say a few words of supplication (*EL NA*) and only then lay forth his requests. (R'FA NA LA)" (op.cit. Sifre Numbers 105)

In *Sifre's* response to the issue of why the prayer is so brief, we encounter a rabbinic construct which is cited over twenty five times by Rashi in commentary on the Pentateuch " so that the people will not say . . ."

> *"On what account did Moses not draw out his prayer? It was so that the Israelites should not say, 'it is because she is his sister that he is standing and laying forth abundant prayers.' (a complaint that he would not take the time to recite such a prayer for the average Israelite). Another reason: it is so that the Israelites should not say: 'his sister is in trouble and he is standing and saying a lot of prayers."*

In these two comments which provide opposing reasons for the brevity of Moses' prayer, the commentator puts forth the explanation that certain things happen the way they do in the Torah as a precaution against *lashon ha-ra*. The nations of the world, and the Israelites as well, seem poised to judge God's actions (and sometimes Moses') by verbal indictment. This portrayal depicts them as harsh critics, who will jump at any opportunity to condemn.

Below are some examples of the *shelo yomru* (so the people will not say) construct cited by Rashi.

> *"Why was only one human created at the beginning? So that the pagans would not say there are two powers in the heavens." (Genesis 2)*

"Why were the firstborn of the captives in Egypt also slain during the tenth plague brought by God? So that they would not claim that their gods brought the plague upon the Egyptians." (Exodus 11)

"Why does the text read "and the Israelites saw the Egyptians lying dead on the shore of the Red Sea"? So that the Israelites should not say that just as we have come out of the sea on this side, so the Egyptians came out of the sea on the other side." (Exodus 14)

"Why does every passage which mentions Moses' death also cite the reason he was not permitted to enter the Land of Israel? Moses requested this so that the people would not assume that it was the same reason the rest of the generation of the wilderness were not permitted to enter the Land (because they did not believe the positive report of the spies Joshua and Caleb)." (Numbers 20 and 27)

"Why does the text emphasize that the produce for the fifth year is especially abundant? Because of the human and his yetzer ha-ra which will accuse God "for four years I sacrificed this fruit for nothing!?" (Leviticus 19)

"Why do Moses and Joshua together speak to the people in the discourse in Deuteronomy 32? So that the people would not say to Joshua after Moses' death "during your teacher's lifetime, you were afraid to speak."

Apparently the commentators have a poor opinion of human nature. According to them, these textual safeguards are a scrupulous attempt to head off the strong tendency towards *lashon ha-ra*, especially as it pertains to God and other authority figures. The assumption seems to be that the people, whether they be pagan or Jewish, are quick to judge and indict, and that the Torah must guard against this tendency.

The Torah itself has Moses using this argument in his plea with God to reconsider destroying the Israelite nation after the construction of the Golden Calf. "Why should (You encourage) the Egyptians to say: for evil did he bring them out, to slay them in the mountains and to consume them from the face of the earth?" (Exodus 32:12) Moses reminds God that as an authority figure, one's reputation can easily be ruined by gossip and innuendo.

After these illustrations from rabbinic literature about the tendency towards *lashon ha-ra*, perhaps the punishment of leprosy does not seem so harsh after all. Aaron and Miriam were challenging Moses' authority and criticizing his domestic life. Even if their conversation were held in private, how soundproof could those tents in the wilderness have been? The spreading of rumors about Moses could have undermined the entire operation of moving the whole Israelite nation of over 600,000 through the Sinai Desert.

And what of the prayer of Moses? "And Moses cried to the Lord saying, *EL NA R'FA NA LA*" Please God, pray heal her." Moses knew only too well the fishbowl of leadership and the sacrifices of family and personal life. He pleaded with God, "You know, God, just how lonely and stressful it is at the top. None of us is perfect, so have compassion upon her. You and I have been in that spot ourselves. I am speaking now from my heart. Answer me from Yours."

Rabbi Gila Colman Ruskin serves as the spiritual leader of Congregation Chevrei Tzedek in Baltimore. She also teaches eighth grade Bible in the Krieger Schechter Middle School and is an instructor in the Florence Melton Adult Mini-School at Chizuk Amuno. She considers Rabbi Joel Zaiman to be a mentor who has helped guide her on her rabbinic path, and a valued colleague and friend.

Shelach Lecha
Linda G. Blumenthal

"The Lord spoke to Moses, saying, 'Send men to scout' . . ." (Numbers 13:1). From the opening phrase, *Shelach lecha* is a study in responses to the challenges of faith. "Our Sages said: 'Man is led on by the path he wishes to pursue.' This is what the Torah meant to imply when it stated: *Shelach lecha anashim*—Send thou men." (Nehama Leibowitz, *Studies in Bamidbar*, p.135) In this *parashah*, the issue of faith is a recurring theme throughout the disturbing narrative of the twelve scouts. Spiritual weakness culminates in sin and rebellion, encompassing an entire generation.

The tradition recorded in Deuteronomy 1:22 clearly ascribes the initiative to send out scouts to the people. 'The plan originated with the people; it commended itself to Moses; and was sanctioned by God." (Dr. J. H. Hertz, *The Pentateuch and the Haftorahs*, p.740) The literal translation of *Shelach lecha* is 'send for yourself'. In effect, God disassociates Himself from the scheme, which Moses endorses. The scouts are chosen by Moses, further indicating God's distance from the plan.

Commentators understand the Hebrew *anashim* to refer to important and brave men. The men selected to reconnoiter the land "were not ordinary military scouts, but distinguished leaders of each tribe who were chosen to witness God's truth by verifying the virtues of His land. According to this tradition, then, the venture was more a test of faith . . ." (*The JPS Torah Commentary*, Numbers 13:2) Since God has already scouted the land, the mere suggestion of the expedition constitutes a breach of faith, a manifestation of rebellion. Apparently, the Israelites prefer to trust in spies rather than in Divine Providence.

Moses dispatches distinguished leaders, representatives of each tribe, to investigate the military, economic, human, and natural resources of the Promised Land. Upon their return, the scouts are unanimous in their praise of the magnificent land promised by God. Bearing fruits, they describe a land flowing with milk and honey and abundant natural resources. "However," the spies qualify their report, and the tone shifts ominously from fact to fear, from the positive to the negative, as ten of the spies warn of peril. They describe powerful and massive inhabitants who dwell in heavily fortified cities. Their words negate hope, convincing the people that the land is unattainable. To convey their complete lack of self-confidence, the spies cry out to the Israelites, "And we looked like grasshoppers to ourselves, and so we must have looked to them." (Numbers 13:33)

The scouts assess their plight as impossible. They lack sufficient faith in themselves to believe that even God can enable them to conquer the land. As leaders, the scouts could have urged the people to strive for worthiness. Instead, they sabotage their responsibility, permit cowardice to overtake reason, and misuse their power to incite the people who rely on them for guidance. In effect, they betray the trust of their people, their leaders, and God.

R Menahem Mendl of Kotzk commented, "Did the spies lie? The truth is not necessarily as things appear, but stems from the depths of the heart, from the sources of one's faith. Truth and faith go hand in hand . . . The spies . . . preferred their limited and deceptive vision to God's promise, which is the absolute truth - and that was their great sin." (Aharon Yaakov Greenberg, *Torah Gems*, p. 64)

Nehama Leibowitz (*Studies in Bamidbar*, pp. 135-146) suggests that the sin of the ten scouts is that they repudiate trust in God. Leibowitz cites Rashi's commentary on Numbers 13:31, which understands *mimenu* to refer to God, rather than to the Israelites, as is usually suggested. It is not just that the inhabitants of the land are too strong for the Israelites to conquer; they are too powerful for the Israelites to prevail even with God's help. Thus, the sin of the ten scouts is their lack of faith in God, not their lack of self-respect.

The distorted picture described by the ten scouts causes the people to falter. Spurning the many miracles they had witnessed, the generation of the Exodus readily believes the worst about themselves. Driven by their slave mentality, hampered by their own insecurities, and demoralized by the slander of the spies, the fragile Israelites easily succumb to doubt and panic and descend into despair.

The Israelites' despair escalates from inadequate confidence in themselves to loss of faith in the leadership of Moses and Aaron, who maintained their unwavering conviction that the power of God would prevail. This loss of faith is exacerbated by the ten scouts who deliberately deliver their negative report directly to the people. "They went straight to Moses and Aaron and the whole Israelite community . . ." (Numbers 13:26) Their decision to go public, without affording Moses and Aaron the opportunity to comment and advise, effectively positions the people against their leaders, thus undermining Moses' authority. "All the Israelites railed against Moses and Aaron." (Numbers 14:2)

"Then Moses and Aaron fell on their faces," (Numbers 14:5) utterly dismayed at the insurrection of the people. Censured by the people, their power diminished, Moses and Aaron renounce their leadership. Moses ultimately loses faith in the people he leads, recognizing that their dedication does not equal his. The repeated complaints and pessimism call into question whether this people can ever form themselves into the special nation envisioned by God.

Only Caleb and Joshua, inspired by their faith in God, believe that the Israelites will conquer Canaan as promised. They exhort the people to believe that the land is good, that God is with them, and that they will emerge triumphant. By repudiating Caleb and Joshua as well as Moses and Aaron, the people also repudiate God. "But the truth of the matter is that it wasn't the land they were rejecting, but God Himself; they were retreating from the heights of spiritual glory." (Isaac Arama, *Akedat Yizhak*) The extent of the Israelites' apostasy is expressed in their willingness to reject freedom and Torah and willingly return to Egypt—to slavery and idolatry.

186

"And the Lord said to Moses, 'How long will this people spurn Me, and how long will they have no faith in Me despite all the signs that I have performed in their midst?" (Numbers 14:11) In response to the Israelites' rebellion, God proclaims His intent to destroy all Israel except Moses. He would have destroyed them all, were it not for Moses' intervention. Moses beseeches God to forgive the people's lack of faith. God mitigates the punishment. Rather than annihilation, He decrees that the Israelites will wander for forty years, one year for each day of the spies' expedition. The generation liberated from Egypt is condemned to die in the desert. The ten scouts suffer unnatural deaths. Only the children, led by Joshua and Caleb, are to inherit the Promised Land. They have the potential to develop immutable trust in God, so lacking in their parents, and the privilege to preserve and fulfill the covenant.

Overcome with remorse, the people subdue their fears and prepare to occupy Canaan, in a futile attempt to appease God. They defy the Divine injunction to turn away, and pay no heed to Moses, who warns them not to proceed without Divine guidance. Failing to recognize that conquest is possible only with God's help, the obstinate Israelites are doomed to suffer a shattering defeat. Harvey J. Fields (A Torah Commentary for our Times, p. 42) writes, "We can only conquer 'Promised Lands' when we have regard for our talents and believe in our creative powers."

The people indulge their own self-doubt, deny God's power, and allow their destiny to be thwarted by the spies. "For everything which they had experienced in Egypt and in the wilderness had no other purpose than . . . to plant deep and unchangeable in their hearts and minds that fear of God and that trust in God which thereafter made them fear nothing else in the whole world, and trust nothing else in the whole world other than God." (Samson Raphael Hirsch, The Pentateuch, Numbers 14:23) In Shelach lecha the people capitulate to the machinations of the spies, misplace their trust, and suffer the consequences.

In God in Search of Man, Rabbi Abraham Joshua Heschel writes ." . . the greatness of man: to be able to have faith. For faith is an act of freedom, of independence of our own limited faculties . . . ." (p. 118) Our challenge is to confront the obstacles to faith, to ground our choices in truth, and to fulfill the destiny of our people with strength and honor.

Linda G. Blumenthal is Director of Development for Chizuk Amuno Congregation. She is a graduate of the Florence Melton Adult Mini-School and is privileged to study Torah with Rabbi Zaiman.

Korach
Marcia Manekin

"You are only as free as the master you serve allows you to be" (Rabbi Joel Zaiman, November 26, 1996, quoting Frederick Buechner, Christian theologian, Chizuk Amuno Adult Bat Mitzvah class discussion). "We all serve a master." Rabbi Zaiman explained that he chose God as his master because serving God allowed him maximum freedom. Would that Korah had studied with Rabbi Zaiman! Perhaps then, he and "his band" might have been spared their fearful fates. But Korah chose to serve his ego, thinking it would give him freedom, power, and status; instead, his ego served him up as an example of evil, self-centeredness, and wrong-doing—allowing him only the legacy of an impossibly tarnished name.

Who exactly was Korah? The Torah tells us he was the son of Izhar, son of Kehath, who was the son of Levi. As a Levite, Korah thus had special status to "perform the duties of the Lord's Tabernacle, and to minister to the community . . . ." (*The Torah, A Modern Commentary*, edited by W. Gunther Plaut, UAHC, New York, 1981, *Numbers 16:9*, p.1127) But it was not "enough" for him as Moses noted in the same verse, " . . . yet you seek the priesthood too! Truly, it is against the Lord that you and all your company have banded together." (*Numbers 16:10-11*) Moses understood that Korah's real rebellion was against God, who had chosen Moses as leader of the people and Aaron as its high priest.

In *Parashat Korah*, the Torah describes a single story of revolt organized by Korah who also recruited Dathan, Abiram, On, all descendants of Reuben, and 250 "chieftains" of the Israelite community. Modern biblical scholars, however, see the story of Korah's rebellion as a fusion of at least two rebellions. *The JPS Torah Commentary* (Numbers, Commentary by Jacob Milgrom, 1990, pp. 414-415) cites four rebellions which were then combined and recorded after the incident of the spies. These rebellions are the Levites against Aaron; Dathan and Abiram against Moses; the tribal chieftains against Aaron; and the entire community against Moses and Aaron. The Levite Korah is cited as the arch-villain because he is the main instigator and is connected with all four groups.

According to the *Plaut Commentary*, the story of Korah's rebellion was the most serious challenge faced by Moses and Aaron during the forty years of wandering through the desert. The various stories of rebellion may have been consolidated because they shared two common themes: (1) dissatisfaction over the loss of first-born status and (2) self-interest as motivation for revolt. As a first-born, Korah was angry when his first cousin, Aaron, and his sons were designated to replace the first born as the only ones who would perform the sacrificial service. He was also resentful because Aaron was made *Kohen Gadol* (High Priest) and another cousin, Elizaphan, was made head of the Kehatite family. Since the other Israelites had their own related gripes, these common threads could be woven into one story for a powerful lesson on the perils and consequences of rebellion against God and His Torah.

A discussion in *Pirke Avot* (Chapter 5:17) illuminates the difference between just and unjust disputes and confirms why Korah's dispute is unjust. The discussion states that there are two kinds of disputes: one that is pursued for a "heavenly cause is destined to be perpetuated; and that which is not pursued in a heavenly cause is not destined to be perpetuated." The arguments between Hillel and Shammai are cited by the rabbis as "heavenly" because they always sought to understand God's will in the matters of ritual on which they disagreed. The controversy of Korah and his congregation is given as an example of selfish and unworthy controversy. Korah's dispute is not "heavenly" because it has has nothing to do with the authentic effort to determine God's will; it has everything to do with Korah asserting his own will against that of God.

Nehama Leibowitz (*New Studies in Bamidbar*, Hemed Book, Inc., pp. 181-185) concurs with Malbim's analysis that

Korah and his followers "were simply a band of malcontents, each harbouring his own personal grievances against authority, animated by individual pride and ambition, united to overthrow Moses and Aaron and hoping thereby to attain their individual desires. What would really happen, however, would be that they would quarrel amongst themselves, as each one strove to attain his selfish ambitions."

Korah truly earned the title role in this saga of egotism. His brand of egotism was nothing short of idolatry. This interpretation is derived from *Numbers 16:3* where we read that Korah and his followers combined against Moses and Aaron and said to them, ." . . For all the community are holy, all of them . . ." Korah believes that God has granted holiness to the people; because they were "chosen," Korah argued, they have no responsibility to earn this designation. They are already holy. Harvey Fields (*A Torah Commentary for our Times, Volume 3*, UAHC Press, 1993, p.50) presents Martin Buber's view that for Moses, holiness was the goal. Generation after generation must choose "between the way of God and the wrong paths of their own hearts; between life and death." Korah failed to see that it is only by continually striving for holiness that we can stand in relationship to God.

Indeed, Yeshayahu Leibowitz (*Notes and Remarks on the Weekly Parashah*, Hemed Books, 1990, pp. 142-143) notes the profound difference between the demand to be holy found at the end of the Shema in the commandment to wear tzitzit, and Korah's holiness in which "the person absolves himself of responsibility, of the mission imposed upon him and of the obligation to exert himself; he is smugly sure that he is already holy." The difference between these two views of holiness is the difference between faith in God and idolatry. The master Korah served neither desired nor required any absolute authority outside of himself ; in his ego, Korah worshipped a jealous master who left no room for a relationship with God.

In the verse, " All the congregation *are* holy," "(rather than '*is* holy'), Nehama Leibowitz (*Studies in Bamidbar*, p.183) interprets the plural to mean 'every one of them'—each one taken individually. The assertion of individual, selfish ambitions outweighs their group feeling as a "kingdom of priests and holy nation." Korah spurned the privilege of serving the community as a Levite, because it was not "enough" for him. He separated himself from the community rather than staking a claim in it and serving it as a member of a "holy nation." At the same time, he used his entitlement as a platform to advance his own cause, under the guise of speaking for "all the congregation."

As Korah twisted the meaning of holiness, so did he scorn the intent of other laws of the Torah in his quest for power and fame. Rabbinic tradition claims that Korah argued with Moses about ritual fringes, asking Moses: "Since the Torah claims that tzitzit must be made with a blue thread, does it mean that a person wearing a shirt made of blue threads need not wear tzitzit?" In another example, Korah asks, " If a house is filled with Torah scrolls that contain all the words inside a mezuzah, does the house still require a mezuzah?" Attacking the sense and logic of the Torah, Korah endeavored to undercut Moses' authority through public ridicule and embarrassment; in so doing, he "battled not merely Moses but the God of Moses." *(Plaut Commentary*, p.1132) Even Korah's manner of arguing with Moses might be seen as a blasphemous mockery of the format for talmudic argument.

Midrash claims that Korah also distorted the meaning of Torah in an attempt to convince the Israelites that its laws were too difficult and demanding. He told them the story of a poor widow who was harassed by Moses and Aaron with legal claims. With an elaborate and devious spin, Korah debased the Torah's overriding concern and protection for the widow and the orphan. Thus, Korah corrupted his gift for effective and persuasive speech; he became a demagogue, creating divisiveness in the Israelite community and distrust of Moses and Aaron. He accused Moses of fabricating God's laws and of nepotism in promoting Aaron and his sons to the priesthood.

Rejecting God's choice of Moses and Aaron as leaders of

the Jewish people was even more sinful than rebellion—it was tantamount to a denial of God. Korah refused to acknowledge the special qualities of these leaders; their uniqueness and singularity reflected nothing less than the image of God. But Korah was unable to recognize God; the images he saw reflected only his own desire for power.

In the end, Korah's sins were so grievous that they nearly caused the destruction of an entire people. An astounding number of Israelites died in Korah's rebellion. Dathan and Abiram and all their households were swallowed alive by the earth and the 250 chieftains were consumed by divine fire. In addition, 14,700 more Israelites died in the plague. The rest of the community was saved by Moses' and Aaron's intercession. Although God wanted to annihilate the whole community, Moses prayed that they not be punished for the sin of one man. As for that man, Korah, there is a great deal of Talmudic speculation as to whether he met his fate in the earthquake or by fire. But all agree that his rebellion grew out of evil, self-centered motives and his punishment was deserved.

Korah's self-centeredness was like a total eclipse of the soul, blocking the light of God's presence and darkening the road to redemption. His ego enslaved and consumed him. From the enormity of Korah's arrogance and the human destruction left in his wake, we learn how important it is to struggle to restrain our own egos. Korah was unwilling to accept any limitations on his individual liberty; since he was already "holy," he felt entitled to do whatever he pleased. As Fields points out, Korah confused individual freedom and the limits to that freedom which living in society imposes. Freedom carries with it responsibility and living in a community requires some sacrifice of personal liberty.

Belonging to the Jewish community, a community of belief in God and His Torah, requires even more sacrifice. But in return for choosing God as our master, we are offered a life infused with purpose and meaning. Through our genuine participation and work in community, we have an opportunity to elevate ourselves, to acquire not the fleeting, superficial status sought by Korah, but the more enduring power of holiness. God's gift of Torah, while it is filled with difficult demands, offers us maximum freedom for the pursuit of both our individual and communal creativity, growth, transformation, redemption, and peace.

Marsha Manekin was a student in Chizuk Amuno's Adult Bat Mitzvah Class of 1998. (This is her first D'var Torah.) She is grateful for the gentle guidance and moral support of Judy Meltzer, Director of the Stulman Center for Adult Learning; for creative suggestions from her husband, Richard, and editorial assistance from her son, Michael, and especially, for the life-affirming wisdom and inspiration of Rabbi Joel Zaiman.

Chukkat
Mimi Blitzer & David Mallott

Once upon a time, a man grew up in luxury surrounded by toiling slaves. Leaving this life of leisure to wander in the wilderness, he returned some time later to lead a people out from under the control of a mighty king and through many battles. He died shortly after the death of his brother while a new nation launched itself on the world stage beginning with a conquest of new lands and a novel set of laws. The man in the story is George Washington, and within a year of his death an etching was produced by an American artist depicting him as Moses leading his fellow citizens and delivering the United States Constitution to an odd assortment of Thirteen Colonies.

George Washington, the Father of Our Country, the first President, the Commander of the Army, the Presiding Officer at the Constitutional Congress, a Leader. He was a thoroughly American character of modest formal education, seemingly born to the role of leader. People followed him, fought for him, voted for him, and honored him. After he died, his new citizens wore mourning clothes for months. He continues to personify the American Revolution and has achieved sainthood in the American Religion.

Yet the etching depicting Washington as Moses seems somewhat amiss. Perhaps it is because Abraham Lincoln, not Washington, has been granted the leading role in the liberation theology known as the United States. Maybe Washington better fits the role of David as the slayer of Goliath and king of Israel. He did, after all, defeat the British and was offered a crown to serve as king of the United States. Or, perhaps the real problem with the etching is that Moses is not a leader in our minds the way Washington is.

Moses our greatest Prophet, Moses the Lawgiver, Moses our Teacher—these are the roles that we have taken into our hearts for

Moses, especially Moses our Teacher. Our access to the wisdom of God is through Moses, for he delivered the Torah, our guide to life. However, the title Moses our Leader doesn't quite fit. Perhaps it is because his motley crew of Egyptian quasi-slaves treated him so badly with their constant complaints and demands. Perhaps his other attributes overpower any appreciation of his leadership. Or, perhaps brilliant teachers are more important than great leaders.

In *Chukkat* we see the leadership of Moses and Aaron tested by the people Israel, as they once again become thirsty. The vignette of Moses striking the rock instead of speaking to it provides an encapsulated study of Moses in the wilderness and his subsequent life in the Jewish collective consciousness.

Jacob Milgrom, in his commentary and excurses of the JPS Translation of *Numbers*, deals extensively with the incident of Moses and the rock. He reviews different explanations of the "sin" of Moses and Aaron while citing commentators that focus on the actions of Moses (striking the rock), the character of Moses (his temper, his cowardice, or callousness), or the words of Moses (doubting God, calling Israel rebels, or using the word "we" to usurp credit from God for the water). So many commentators and so many hypotheses make one wonder if a sin was even committed. Milgrom continues by noting that modern commentators claim that the sin has been deliberately obscured or deleted from the text. He then lines up behind the usurpation of credit hypothesis, contending that Moses used "the fatal pronoun" *we* in addressing the people Israel while water was in fact provided by God.

To further examine the "sin" of Moses and Aaron, let us consider Numbers 20:6-13, Exodus 17:5-7, and Psalms 78:15-31. Numbers and Exodus relate two, shall we say, strikingly similar accounts of Moses and the issuance of water from a rock. So similar are these versions that some commentators think that they may be different accounts of the same event. Whether they are the same incident hardly matters, for they are recorded as different events and must be considered as two distinct threads of teaching. Multiple differences in the accounts have been studied and scrutinized. However, at least one major difference and one major similarity seem to stand out. In the Numbers account, Moses and Aaron repair to the Tent of Meeting in the face of an angry crowd. In the Exodus version, Moses calls to God openly, demonstrating his leadership to the elders. It is Moses' panicky helplessness in seeking God's reassurance and his flustered reaction to the crowd that lead to his "punishment," not so much a punishment as a private message (perhaps even a gentle whisper) that Moses and Aaron would not lead the Israelites into the land. There is, in fact, no sin but a painful lack of leadership. In both the Numbers and Exodus accounts, it is the Israelites that are ultimately assigned the blame of quarreling with God. Psalm 78 reinforces this view by telling the story in verse with no mention of Moses, much as the *Haggadah* tells the story of redemption without Moses.

What about the view of Milgrom (and by extension *Bekhor Shor*) that the problem was "the fatal pronoun?" The word "we" does not refer to Moses and Aaron instead of God. If that were true, the punishment should have been harsher and more public than is reported. If Moses openly credited himself with performing this miracle, would we expect a private message without dire consequences? Rather, the "we" refers to Moses and Aaron instead of Miriam. It is Miriam who, according to the Midrash, is the keeper of the well, provider of water in the wilderness and whose recent death filled the people with new worries about their own survival. The "we" refers to Moses and Aaron instead of Miriam, for the Midrash states that Moses represents Torah, Aaron represents *Avodah*, and Miriam represents *Gemilut Hasadim*. Miriam the prophetess and Aaron the spokesman fill the gaps in Moses' leadership as the newly freed slaves move through the desert. Moses the Lawgiver has a number of lapses of leadership while he toils to understand the ways of God and transmit them to the people. That is because he is first and foremost a teacher.

Moses was and is our teacher. Throughout *Chukkat*, Moses continues his teaching and his leadership. However, it is the Red

197

Heifer rather than the victory over Og that catches our eye. We identify Moses with Torah, not the Book of the Wars of the Lord.

By the time of the events of Numbers 20, Moses is almost finished as the leader. *Chukkat* reports the deaths of Miriam and Aaron, the chief aides to Moses. New leaders must be found for a people literally thirsting for leadership, new leaders that build monuments to the previous generation of leaders to honor and venerate them.

What monuments have we built to Moses? If we want to find David, we can go to Jerusalem. If we want to find George Washington we can go to his plantation, look at a quarter, or visit Federal City, now called Washington, D.C. In Baltimore we can go to the huge "main-mast" described in the novel *Moby Dick* memorializing his leadership towering over us, a habit of tower building that Herman Melville traces back to the Egyptians and Babel builders. Leaders are given and richly deserve such monuments. Yet, what monuments have we built to Moses?

None. Teachers don't inspire monuments. If they are lucky, their students remember them. If they are really lucky, their students' students know of them. Their best ideas live on in lectures and books, often some other teacher's lectures and books. We may name a school after a teacher that soon becomes a name that the students themselves hardly recognize. However, our teachers do live on and on. Each student is a living monument, and each student's student is further testimony to that teacher.

Teachers can lead, and leaders can teach. Our archetypal leader, George Washington, in his farewell address to the nation, gave a series of brilliant insights to guide the new country including, "Of all the dispositions and habits which lead to political prosperity, religion and morality are indispensable supports." He recognized that the charisma of leadership and the strength of an individual are not enough. *In Siddur Sim Shalom* we don't ask for our leaders to be given courage, we ask that they be taught the insights of Torah.

Fortunately for us, teachers mostly just teach.

"Our Masters taught:
A sage takes precedence over a king of Israel;
If a sage dies, we have none like him—
If a king dies, all Israel are eligible for kingship."

Joshua, the son of Perachyah, said, "Provide yourself a teacher."

Mimi Blitzer and David Mallott are long-time members of Chizuk Amuno Congregation. Students in the Florence Melton Adult Mini-School, they are both active in the Chizuk Amuno's lay leadership and enjoy learning Torah from Rabbi Zaiman.

Balak
Judy Meltzer

Parashat Balak, or as the Talmud calls it, the Book of Balaam, is the story of a seer who cannot see, a dumb animal that utters words of wisdom, and blessings that become curses. Amid the magic and the contradictions, a theme emerges: seeing may be believing, but vision is not always reality.

The cast of characters includes a king, a prophet, and a donkey. Only the donkey has eyes that see. Seeing, in fact, is what this parashah is all about. Robert Alter points out, in *The Art of Biblical Narrative*, "the very first word of the Balaam story is to see, which appropriately becomes the main Leitwort in this tale about the nature of prophecy or vision." (p.105) In one form or another, the verb appears 36 times.

Balak, a Moabite king, sees what Israel has done to the Amorites, how strong and many they are, and how ominously immanent their presence. Israel is viewed as a powerful and intimidating force, causing fear and trepidation among the Moabites. But in their ignorance, Balak and the Moabite people are blind to the source of Israel's strength. They can neither see nor understand God's active providence.

Instead, to alleviate their fears and insure their country's security, the Moabites resort to their belief in the power of magic. Balak dispatches Elders from Moab "with the means of divination in their hands." (Num. XXII:7) They seek to persuade Balaam, an eminent soothsayer with a reputation for delivering efficacious curses, to return with them to Moab to curse the Israelites.

This is a tempting job offer for Balaam. He asks the Elders to stay overnight so he can "sleep on it." Despite the fact that he is a sorcerer, Balaam relies on the Hebrew God for advice. So far, so good. God comes to Balaam and inquires about the credentials of the visiting Moabite dignitaries. A logical question, but not coming from God. God would already know who they were, so why did He ask? For the same reason that we ask leading questions of our children when we prefer not to deny their request directly. We are encouraging them to think carefully. Our hope is that they will make the right decision on their own.

But Balaam doesn't get the message. He is blinded by his self-interest, as he will be at other times in the story. So God makes His position very clear: "Do not go with them; thou shalt not curse the people, for they are blessed." (Num. 22:12) Balak, however, is unwilling to take "no" for an answer. He sends more messengers of even greater stature with the promise of even greater rewards. Despite God's initial refusal, Balaam again turns to Him for permission to go to Moab. Balaam is looking for loopholes so that he can accept the assignment and collect the Moabites' money. God, the parent, is irritated at His child's unwillingness to accept His original response. He tells His persistent child, Balaam, that he may go, but only if he follows God's rules.

According to Samson Raphael Hirsch, in spite of the definitive warning he had received from God, Balaam was convinced that he would still succeed in pronouncing the curse and collecting his reward. So, the next morning, Balaam arose early, saddled his donkey, and left with the princes of Moab. Three times on the journey, an angel of God, brandishing a sword, places himself in Balaam's path. Three times the donkey turns and twists to protect his master from the angel's wrath. Balaam is unable to see the angel. Each time, Balaam beats the innocent animal unmercifully. "What have I done to you that you should beat me three times?" asks the donkey. So solipsistic is Balaam's worldview that he is not even surprised to hear the animal speak. Instead, Balaam turns on the faithful animal and says, "Because you have acted willfully against me, I wish there were a sword in my hand, for now I would have killed you." (Num. XXII:29)

Finally, God "unveiled the eyes of Balaam, and he saw the angel of God standing in the way." (Num. XXIII:31) The angel tells Balaam that the donkey has saved his life. Balaam confesses;

he has sinned. At last he is beginning to "get it." God's spirit, as well as His words, has begun to permeate Balaam's being.

This episode has been variously interpreted as a dream or vision (Maimonides), or as "a masterpiece of ancient Israelite narrative art." (Noth, Martin) "Many expositors, both in ancient and modern times, take the account of the miracle in these verses literally." (Hertz, Joseph H., *The Pentateuch and Haftarahs*, p. 671) The philosopher Franz Rosenzweig wrote that Balaam's talking ass may be a mere fairy tale all the days of the year, but not on Shabbat "wherein his portion is read in the synagogue, when it speaks to me out of the open Torah." Whatever our interpretation, we can conclude that it is possible for an animal to see things to which an obdurate human being is blind.

In the third part of the story, Balak welcomes Balaam to Moab, at the same time reproaching him for not responding at once to his first invitation. It is evident that while Balaam is just beginning to see the light, Balak is still blind. Despite the fact that Balaam insists that he has no power to utter words other than those that are placed in his mouth by God, Balak stubbornly refuses to give up. He is determined that Balaam will curse the Israelites.

Accordingly, Balak leads Balaam to the heights of Baal. Balaam instructs him to build seven altars and prepare seven oxen and seven rams for a proper sacrifice. The concept of monotheism is not unknown to the two men, but they still believe that they can use magic to influence God. Three times Balak leads Balaam to a different vantagepoint. Each time they carry out elaborate ritualistic preparations, and each time, Balaam blesses, rather than curses, the Israelites.

Nehama Leibowitz points out that in his first blessing, Balaam explains what a mortal king has demanded of him, and what, in contrast, the King of Kings desires of him. But it is not only God who prevents Balaam from cursing God's people. Balaam himself sees the origins of the people and acknowledges their uniqueness. Rashi says he sees them "firmly founded and as strong as the rocks and hills through their forefathers." Balaam is clearly impressed by the historic continuity of this imposing people, and by the strength and continuity of their traditions.

In a second attempt to exact a curse from Balaam, Balak takes him to the Field of Seers. This time, the selected site is higher; perhaps a loftier lookout point will provide Balaam with a different outlook, more in line with that of Balak. Balaam responds by enhancing the blessing and predicting disaster for the Moabites. At this point, it is Balak's turn to "get it." He is willing to decelerate and reduce his demands. He says, "Neither curse them at all, nor bless them at all." (Num. XXIII:5) These words provide the source for an expression that is quoted frequently in Hebrew and in Yiddish: "I don't want your kiss, and I don't want your bite."

But Balak is still not quite ready to give up. He takes Balaam to the top of Peor, where they can see the entire desert. At this point, Balaam is not only mouthing the words of God. "Balaam saw that in God's eyes it was good to bless Israel. He went not, as at other times, to meet omens, but set his face towards the wilderness." (Num. XXIV:1) At last Balaam's eyes and soul are truly open. Imbued with the Divine spirit, he delivers a powerful and eloquent message. For the first time, he addresses the people Israel directly, in a poetic passage that has become part of our liturgy: *"Mah tovu, ohaleha Yaakov, mishkenoteha, Yisrael."* (Num. XXIV:5) "How lovely are your sanctuaries, people of Jacob, your study houses, descendants of Israel."

Balak, the Parashah about seeing, begins with a seer who cannot see and concludes with his visionary praise of God and the Jewish people. As his "eyes are unveiled," Balaam sees that magic and sorcery cannot compete with the power of the Almighty. A people who put their faith in God are assured that curses can become blessings.

Judy Meltzer is Director of the Stulman Center for Adult Learning and Coordinator of the Florence Melton Adult Mini School at Chizuk Amuno Congregation. She studies Torah with Rabbi Zaiman in his women's study group.

Pinchas
Gil Abramson

Parashat Pinchas poses the disturbing question of the role of the zealot in a society ordered by laws. When is it appropriate, if ever, for a person to take the law into his own hands? How can an act in contravention of the written law be permissible?

Parashat Pinchas reprises and valorizes a stunning tale at the end of *Parashat Balak*. In a murderous attack, the high priest Pinchas, grandson of Aaron, kills a publicly copulating couple: Zimri, chieftain of the Tribe of Simon, and Cosbi, the daughter of the Midianite chieftain, spearing them directly through their genitalia. Pinchas acted on his own volition to eradicate what he saw as a threat to his people. His act of zealotry pacified God, ended a plague, and earned Pinchas divine commendation, in the form of protection against retribution from the family of Zimri and God's promise of "an everlasting priesthood" for his descendants.

There are a number of crimes, according to the Mishnah (Sanhedrin 81b), which are beyond judicial remediation, but which are amenable to non-judicial action. For example, a murderer who cannot be convicted because there are no witnesses may be incarcerated and force-fed until he dies. The same holds true for "(o)ne who cohabits with an Aramean (a non-Jewish) woman . . . . (Z)ealots may kill him." (*Sanhedrin* 81b).

How is one to make any sense out of this paradoxical situation? The sanctity and preservation of human life unquestionably is an important value in Jewish law. One may not murder (Ex. 20:13; Deut. 5:17). One may not stand idly by the blood of a fellow Jew. (Lev. 19:16). Thus, the zealot, acting extremely and emotionally, operates extralegally, threatening the ordered integrity of law, creating a tension between the rule of law and the rule of God.

There have been other examples of murder, which have escaped legal consequences. Moses slew the Egyptian taskmaster.

Abraham would have killed Isaac but for the intervention of God's angel. Mattathias, like Pinchas a High Priest, speared a fellow Jew who was about to defile his religion, invoking the zealot's rallying cry, "All who are for God, follow me!"

The *Gemara* poses a solution. While Jewish jurisprudence recognizes that "Nothing stands in the face of preserving life," exceptions are made in the cases of "idolatry," Mattathias' act, "murder," Moses' act, or "illicit sex," Pinchas' act. (*Tosaphot Shabbat* 15:17; *Sanhedrin* 74:9).

But the zealot cannot act completely unchecked. Judicial immunity is not automatic. The *Gemara* states (Sanhedrin 82b) that the zealot, in effect, must act at his own peril and strictly on individual initiative. Thus, if the zealot seeks counsel prior to committing his act, he receives no support or protection of law. The Mishnah's ruling is construed to apply "only to one whose zealousness is self-inspired," conduct which emanates from the heat of the moment.

Then, focusing specifically on Pinchas' act, the *Gemara* observes that, if Zimri had ceased copulating even moments before Pinchas attacked and killed him, Pinchas would have been liable for capital punishment as a murderer. Further, if Zimri, even while still engaged in the act of copulating, had defended himself successfully against Pinchas, killing his assailant, he would not face capital charges, "because (Pinchas) is considered a pursuer." Explaining this apparent anomaly, Rashi explains that Zimri would be allowed to kill Pinchas in self-defense, because Pinchas, while permitted to kill Zimri, was nonetheless not authorized to kill Zimri. Rashi continues that no other person was allowed to stop Pinchas by killing him, inasmuch as his actions were permitted. Thus, if one sees a zealot in action, it is not easy to stop him and prevent his act.

Applying these principles to Pinchas' conduct, Rashi and Tosafot explain that Pinchas' act was unpunishable. He acted on the spur of the moment upon witnessing Zimri in an act of infidelity, slaying Zimri immediately, without deferentially consulting his mentor, Moses, beforehand. Pinchas felt it was urgent to take immediate punitive action, so as to prevent the people from concluding erroneously that Zimri's deed was permitted.

Perhaps recognizing the incongruity of sanctioning extralegal conduct taken in the name of God, the Torah offers a symbolic admonition that such conduct may not be completely acceptable. In verse twelve of the Parashah, the word *"shalom"* is left separated, the *"vav"* omitted. This gap, this *"vav katua,"* indicates, according to Rashi, the ambivalence with which Pinchas' act should be viewed and understood.

Gil Abramson is a member of Chizuk Amuno Congregation and is honored to be able to call Rabbi Zaiman his rabbi.

Mattos
Rabbi Aaron Gaber

As we enter the twenty-first century C.E., we are struggling to understand and define the roles that Diaspora Jews and Israeli Jews play in the Jewish community as a whole. Just 60 years ago, individuals from Baltimore and around the world helped smuggle arms and people into a land called Palestine. Many of us felt then that the Jewish community of Palestine needed all the help we could give in order to become the State of Israel, as it did in 1948. Even after the founding of the State of Israel, we felt that Israel needed our support in a variety of ways; that without it, Israel would die. Now, however, the Jewish communities of the world are struggling to define their roles in relation to the community of Israel that is no longer a poor third-world nation; it is a nation of high-tech and high-speed commerce. Israel is no longer treated as a pariah state. It is now a nation seeking to find peace with its neighbors and with itself.

In light of current world events, *Parashat Mattot* speaks to both Diaspora and Israeli Jewry, teaching us that the relationship between both communities is sacred and important. It also teaches us that both are necessary to create a strong worldwide Jewish community.

Chapter 32 opens with the following request from the Tribes of Gad and Reuben,

> *"The Reubenites and the Gadites owned cattle in very great numbers. Noting that the lands of Jazer and Gilead were a region suitable for cattle, the Gadites and the Reubenites came to Moses, Eleazar the priest, and the chieftains of the community, and said . . . 'the land that the Lord has conquered for the community of Israel is cattle country, and your servants have cattle. It would be a favor to us...if this land were given to*

your servants as a hold; do not move us across the Jordan.'" (Numbers 32:1-5)

After 40 years of wandering through the Wilderness, the Tribes of Reuben and Gad made an economic decision to keep themselves, their families, and their cattle in the land on the east side of the Jordan. They decided not to enter the Land of Israel promised to them since the time of Abraham.

Angry at their request, Moses asked them, *"Are your brothers to go to war while you stay here? Why will you turn the minds of the Israelites from crossing into the land that the Lord has given them?"* (Numbers 32:6-7) Moses continued to berate them by drawing a parallel between them and the spies who had entered the land, asking if they were frightened of the obstacles they had to face the giants and monsters reported by the spies. Moses even invoked the possibility that God would bring wrath and calamity against all of Israel because they (the Reubenites and Gadites) had "turned" away from God.

Then in a moment of intimacy, the tribal leaders stepped up to Moses and said,

> *"We will build here sheepfolds for our flocks and towns for our children. And we will hasten as shock-troops in the van of the Israelites until we have established them in their home, while our children stay in fortified towns . . . We will not return to our homes until every one of the Israelites is in possession of his portion. But we will not have a share with them in the territory beyond the Jordan, for we have received our share on the east side of the Jordan.(Numbers 32:16-19)."*

Moses agreed with their compromise formula and repeated to them clearly that they must support the tribes that were entering the land of Israel. Unless they did so, they could not return to their homes and families.

The modern commentator Pinchas Peli writes that the request/demand by the Reubenites and Gadites represent a serious "separatist" threat to the Jewish people.

> *"Moses' concern was . . . with the ethical implications of the seceding of the two tribes from a war that should be fought by all of Israel. The conquest of Eretz Yisrael was not incumbent only on those people who planned to live on the land. It was, in the eyes of Moses, the culmination of the drama of redemption that should be acted out in full by all the tribes that came out of Egypt.*(Fields, Harvey, *A Torah Commentary for Our Times,* UAHC Press, New York, NY 1993, page 87)

This threat was so serious that Moses believed that it could bring a calamity to the Israelites and prevent them from inheriting what had been promised to them. He saw an even more serious threat: if these two tribes decide to possess the land outside of Israel and not join the rest in battle, then the other tribes may also find reason not to enter the land of Israel, deciding not to fight under one united banner. Thus divided, the Israelites would be defeated and destroyed.

Nachmanides believes that Moses overreacted and misunderstood these tribes. He believes that they were seeking what was best for themselves and for the whole nation. They were not looking to set up a confrontation; they saw a way for themselves to benefit from settling in a land that was fertile and good for their cattle. They were also willing to serve as the lead force for the Israelite army. The tribes of Reuben, Gad, and Menasseh wanted to and did fulfill their responsibilities to the community.

Notice, if you will, the difference of opinions: Nachmanides, a Diaspora Jew, saw the necessity of supporting Israel as of paramount import to these tribes; Pinchas Peli, an Israeli Jew, saw their refusal to settle in the Land as disrespectful.

Once the Reubenites, Gadites, and the half-tribe of Manasseh have fulfilled their obligation of service to the Israelite nation, the Book of Joshua reports their release from service. They returned to their families and their homes on the east side of Jordan River. Before they returned home, they gave much of the wealth they had collected from the war to the other tribes to be used in the Land of Israel.

The story of these tribes does not end with their release from service. The end of the Book of Joshua records a narrowly averted civil war because the tribes of Gad, Reuben, and Manasseh set up their own place of worship, which the other tribes viewed as an affront to God and to the rest of the tribes. The tribes who had settled in Israel wanted to destroy those who lived outside of the Land, and if it were not for the efforts of Joshua, they might have done so. Joshua sent a delegation of tribal leaders, led by Phineas the son of Eleazar, to talk with the Reubenites, Gadites, and Menashites about why they had set up their place of worship. Indignant at the accusations leveled against them, the Reubenites, Gadites, and the half-tribe of Manasseh replied,

> *"God, the Lord God! God, the Lord God! He knows, and Israel too shall know! If we acted in rebellion or in treachery against the Lord, do not vindicate us this day!. . .We did this thing only out of our concern that, in time to come, your children might say to our children, 'What have you to do with the Lord, the God of Israel? The Lord has made the Jordan a boundary between you and us, O Reubenites and Gadites; you have no share in the Lord!' Thus your children might prevent our children from worshiping the Lord. So we decided to provide (a witness) for ourselves by building an altar—not for burnt offerings or (other) sacrifices, but as a witness between you and us, and between the generations to come—that we may perform the service of the Lord before Him . . . Far be it from us to rebel*

against the Lord, or to turn away this day from the Lord and build an altar . . . other than an altar of the Lord our God which stands before His Tabernacle. (Joshua 22:22-29)"

"What have you to do with the Lord, the God of Israel?"

The tribes of Gad, Reuben and Menasseh worried, and perhaps with good reason, that the Israelites in the Land of Israel might decide that they could no longer be part of the inheritance from their common ancestors Abraham, Isaac, and Jacob. They built an altar to God so their children and their children's children *"will be able to perform the service of the Lord."* They built the altar as a *"witness between you* (Tribes in Israel) *and us,"* in order to physically remind themselves and everyone else that they, too, were an essential part of the Covenant between God and Israel. They would always have a share in the inheritance of the Jewish people. This action of legitimization helped both parties to know and understand that both together formed the community of Israel.

The Israelite reaction to these two-and-a-half tribes that chose to live outside of Israel is played out today between Israeli Jews and Diaspora Jews. Israelis ask, "How can you turn away from Israel, the Jewish homeland, and settle in this place (Outside of Israel) and worship in those Houses of Worship which are not like ours here (in Israel)?"

Our answer should be that we are not denigrating the significance of Eretz Yisrael; rather, we are building upon it so that our children and our children's children will be able to witness the importance of God in our lives and in the lives of the whole Jewish community. Joshua and the Israelites, after years in the Wilderness, did not enter the Land of Israel only to lose all that they had learned from Revelation at Mount Sinai. Most certainly the tribes of Reuben, Gad, and Manasseh would not have led the Israelites into the land if they were not committed to the fulfilling of God's promise to their ancestors of inheriting the Land of Israel as their own and to the well-being of their own families. Those of us who are committed to the building up of Israel and to the continued building of a community in the Diaspora are dedicated to God, Torah, and to Judaism. As the Reubenites, Gadites, and the half-tribe Manasseh flourished in their lands outside of Israel, may we flourish and prosper in our lands. May Israeli Jews and Diaspora Jews work together to build a stronger State of Israel and a stronger Jewish community, based upon a shared witnessing of Revelation at Sinai and of God's presence in all of the Jewish Community, as we enter the 21st Century.

Rabbi Aaron M. Gaber is Spiritual Leader of Adat Chaim, Reisterstown, Maryland.

Massey
Rabbi Richard Camras

The family gathered around to share with me the story of the life of their father who, at the age of 92, had just died. Searching through his personal belongings, they discovered a stack of diaries that he had kept during his lifetime. More than simply recording the events of his life, they were reflections on the trials and tribulations of his life and the lessons he learned from his experiences. He was a man who had traveled much in his life, beginning in New York and, ultimately, after many years and a multitude of hardships, settled in Los Angeles. With each upheaval, he related his journeys back to his New York beginnings. That became the lens through which all his experiences were reflected. It seemed that the memory of his beginnings helped him to overcome each of the hurdles he faced in his life.

The family was overwhelmed and grateful for these diaries, as they offered a glimpse of the difficulties their father (grandfather) had faced and how he had conquered each of them. Finding strength in reading his diaries, they remarked that they would use this legacy in their own lives for inspiration, direction and courage.

Parashat Massey opens, "These were the journeys of the Israelites who started out from the land of Egypt, troop by troop, in the charge of Moses and Aaron. Moses recorded the starting points of their various journeys as directed by the Lord. Their journeys, by starting points, were as follows…" (Bamidbar 33:1).

Some would say that of all the *parashiot* this one is clearly the most difficult to understand in terms of purpose. Why do we need to read about the 42 stopping places of the Israelites on their long trek through the desert, with little information offered other than the names of the encampments? Why would God direct Moses to record these journeys in such detail?

In his commentary, Rabbi Yehudah Leib Alter of Ger, the

Sefat Emet, reads "journeys" as "comings forth" and "starting points" as "goings forward." He further comments, "notice that the order is reversed from the beginning to the end of the verse. Scripture is telling us that all this going forward (i.e. starting point) depends upon coming forth (i.e. journeys) from Egypt. Only after all those journeys is the Exodus from Egypt complete; with each going forward they got farther from Egypt, until they reached the Land of Israel." (Arthur Green's translation)

Therefore, the reason God instructs Moses to record each of the 42 places of encampment is that each stop was another moment of self-discovery for the Israelites. Each point was necessary in order to reach the final destination of their journey. And what was their final destination? The Promised Land and the recognition of the Oneness of God.

According to our sages, Egypt was more than simply the place our ancestors were enslaved for 400 years. Egypt represented a place devoid of God and spiritual awareness. A place or people that has no recognition of God can have little, if any, recognition of the importance of human dignity or the value of human life. For the Israelites to become partners with God in God's plan they had to remove the shackles of slavery from their hearts and their minds. Their journey to the Promised Land was a journey to discovering and believing in the One God.

Such a journey cannot be accomplished instantaneously, and the 42 encampments were each stages along this path of enlightenment, of moving from godlessness to awareness of the Oneness of God. Each encampment along the way, each "going forward" represented another breakthrough in the emotional journey from slavery to freedom. These were not endpoints but rather moments on the journey of continual discovery. Tosefet Berachah suggests that *motzaheihem*, their "goings forward," derives not from *yitzeyah*, exit, but rather from *matza*, find, recalling all of the events as in "all the travail that had found them" (Shemot 18:8). To move beyond a point we must be cognizant of that place in which we are currently.

And for all of us who would later read of the Israelites' journeys, these diaries would help us on our own journeys of discovering God. The legacy these diaries leave us is the recognition that the journey to enlightenment is a difficult one, wrought with moments of despair and moments of faithlessness. And at the same time, these diaries offer us hope as we travel from our Egypts to the Promised Land.

We further come to understand that as God instructed Moses to record the experiences of our ancestors' journey, so are we wise to do the same for those who follow us. What of our journeys do we want to transmit to the next generation? What are our "comings forth" and "goings forward?" How might they help those who follow us to construct their own journeys? Moreover, how do we (or do we at all) articulate them: through our writings? through our stories? through our actions and behaviors?

The family mourning their father was blessed that he left them diaries of his "coming forth" and his "goings forward," as a beacon of light that would guide them in their own paths. May each of us reap the benefits of the richness of our ancestral history and may we do the same for our own families for generations to come.

Richard Camras is currently Rabbi at Shomrei Torah synagogue in Los Angeles, California. Prior to his current position he was Associate Rabbi under Rabbi Joel Zaiman for 7 years.

Chizuk Amuno Congregation

Devarim
Dr. Chaim Botwinick

The Book of Deuteronomy (*Devarim*) is comprised of the teachings that Moses gave to the Children of Israel just prior to his death. "These are the words that Moses spoke to all of Israel beyond the Jordan in the wilderness...." (Deuteronomy 1:1-3)

Although *Devarim* contains numerous *mitzvot* and commandments, it is by and large regarded as a *Parashah* of admonishment and discipline.

In his recapitulation of prior events, Moses recalls vividly the manner in which he protested to God as indicated in the *passuk*: "I am not able to bear the burden of this people alone." (1:12) As a result of this perceived inability to lead, God counsels Moses to identify and select wise men, judges and military administrators from the assembly to assist him in fulfilling his leadership duties and responsibilities.

According to Rashi, it is almost inconceivable that Moses, who performed all the miracles of the Exodus and the events that followed, was unable to judge Israel. Rather, he meant to say that God had elevated Israel to such a level of greatness that a judge whose error caused an unjustified loss is worthy of death. That is a burden that even Moses could not bear by himself.

Nevertheless, the question still remains. Why had it suddenly been necessary to give Moses assistants? Had his own leadership and greatness diminished?

Ramban and Ibn Ezra provide a fascinating insight into what Moses was experiencing—was it a perceived lack of leadership? In reality, Moses was providing the Children of Israel with a level of leadership and greatness, which, according to many commentaries, transcended his leadership capacity when leading the Children of Israel out of Egypt.

According to Ramban, many of the commandments and mitzvot Moses had imparted to the Children of Israel when they left Egypt are now being repeated. But why the repetition? The response to this question, which also clarifies Moses' leadership role, is two-fold: (1) several *mitzvot* are repeated in order to clarify further the manner in which to perform them; and (2) others are repeated to add a warning that had not been articulated to the generation that left Egypt.

So, the burden and difficulty experienced by Moses was not a result of waning leadership, but rather of the difficult task of teaching the laws and their deeper meanings and implications.

Rambam informs us that although all of the commandments and *mitzvot* had already been taught to Moses during the first year of the Exodus, he had not yet imparted them to the Children of Israel. Several of the *mitzvot* were not relevant until the Children of Israel were about to enter the land; other mitzvot and commandments were only relevant to those who would eventually live in the land of Israel. Therefore, these commandments are first introduced in this *parashah*.

A true leader is one who not only provides strong and powerful direction and vision, but one who leads with humility, compassion, insight and respect for those he leads. Moses' greatness was indeed his ability to lead the Children of Israel out of Egypt with the strong hand of God, but it was also his profound respect and understanding of human nature, an appreciation for the talents of those who surrounded him and his deep unswerving commitment to loving-kindness.

Dr. Chaim Y. Botwinick is Executive Vice President of the Center for Jewish Education in Baltimore, Maryland. In that capacity, he has the opportunity to work with Rabbi Zaiman on a variety of educational endeavors in the Baltimore area.

Vaetchanan
Joanne Fritz Kraus

With the permission of my teacher…

Parashat Vaetchanan, read on *Shabbat Nachamu*, the first of the *Shabbatot* of Consolation which follows the observance *of Tisha B'Av*, has embedded within its first word the notion of *"chen,"* of *"grace."* Hirsch translates *Vaetchanan* "And I besought." A reflexive of the verb, Plaut suggests that it might also be read, "and I got myself to plead," referencing Moshe's petition that he be allowed to cross over into the Promised Land. Rashi comments that Moshe requests it, not because he merits God's intervention, but as an act of grace. *Vaetchanan* is one of many words that we Jews have for prayer, one that implies God's grace. "Said the Rabbi of Tsams, in like manner: 'Before I begin to pray, I pray that I may be able to pray.'" That is certainly the intent when we begin the Amidah with the words, *"Se-fa-tai tiftach oofee yagid tehilatecha."* "Open my mouth, O Lord, and my lips will proclaim Your Praise!" The ancients had sacrifices, the *korbanot*, which enabled them to make peace with our God, to re-establish their damaged relationship. In the wake of the Temple's destruction, we were left with the substitutes of prayer and deeds of lovingkindness. Torah, the prophets, and our own *Avodah* coalesce to help us to understand that *"chen"* is central to our relationship with God, even as it was central to Moshe Rabbeinu.

Some moderns, though, have begun to clamor that the prayers have become inflexibly fixed, "petrified." The ancient Talmudic debates between *"keva"* and *"kavanah,"* between fixed and spontaneous prayer, have re-emerged cloaked in contemporary colors. The black and yellow cover cues us to the ubiquitous reference series published by the International Data Group. Titles such as *Windows 3.1 for Dummies, Windows 95 for Dummies,* and *Windows 98 for Dummies* assist the "technically challenged" who want to be "technically competent." No longer are they the secret hidden resource of the "nouveau-techies." With the emergence of titles such as *Gardening for Dummies* and even *Wine Tasting for Dummies*, they have broken from the purely technical mode and become something of a cultural icon. We appear to be poised to go into the next century with these aids, perhaps a reflection of or a response to the "dumbing" of America. So, why not, *Davening for Dummies*? After all, the Siddur can be construed as a kind of technical manual, and a black and yellow "Cliff noted" edition, at that, one which directs what is *"keva,"* what is fixed, in prayer. Only *"kavanah"* need be added to make our prayer complete. *Davening for Dummies*? What does it mean to be dumb?

When I first faced the "dummy" titles, I was hesitant to be seen even handling the volumes. To do so was to admit inadequacy, and I do not like seeing myself as inadequate. Most of us prefer to see ourselves as fully competent in all aspects of our life, including ritual, and we shy from our failures. However, we have all been caught at one time or another "without a prayer." I have vivid memories of the quickened heartbeat and abject terror when once I stood in front of a Congregation of 600 to recite the Musaph. My intention strayed. I lost the *nusah* and with it prayer's powerful mnemonic. I finished reciting the *kedusha* without a note. In Jewish parlance, being "dumb" is not the absence of intellect or knowledge and the sense of competence that they encourage. What it means to be "dumb," that is speechless, caught without a prayer, is to witness the destruction of the Temple all over again, to lose our ability to connect with the divine in prayer. In a way that parallels the experience of our ancestors who saw the Temple stones up-ended, fractured, and charred, if we are unable to offer the prescribed language to our Creator, which is "keva," we lose our ability to establish or repair our relationship with God.

Being dumb in prayer potentially teaches more than being able to fly fluently through the liturgy. *"Tefillah"* is derived from the verb *"l'hitpallel,"* to judge oneself, in relationship with the values and the *Mitzvot* of the Tradition. *"Ethchanan"* on the other hand, has its root in *"chen"* gifted by God. Rashi asks why *"Vaetchanan"* is used and not *"vayitpallel"* and then explains, "Even though the righteous could base their request on their good deeds, they beg of the Omnipresent only an act of grace." Moses asked God for the grace that he be allowed to "go over and see." God answered: God enabled Moses to see, but from afar.

Gematria, a form of numerology, one of the 32 sanctioned methods of interpreting Torah, works remarkably well in understanding the equivalencies in terminology. This cosmic calculus is intriguing. The numeric values of *"ethchanan," "t'fillah,"* and *"shira"* each sum to 515. Add to any of them 26, the value of *"yud, hay vav, hay,"* the unpronounced name for God. The result is 541, the numeric value of "Yisrael." The *Chatam Sofer* concluded, "If Israel clings to God in prayer, it will gain true life." The semantic connection Rashi proffers and the equivalencies of the mystic complement one another, but these two systems only scratch the surface of the understanding conserved in the tradition.

The reinvigorated search for Jewish "spirituality" that has captured the headlines of many of our periodicals has spawned wonderful learner's minyans and opportunities for studying the texts, but frequently we explore individual meditation at the expense of communal prayer. We "moderns" express our frustrations with "petrified prayer" and with speed that trivializes each word. We do daven too fast, just as we eat too fast, drive too fast, flying through our busy lives at breakneck speeds. For some, finding and keeping pace and place in the Siddur become more important than finding meaning there. On the other hand, the babies of the boom generation and their children have grown up with the secular emphasis on the individual, on ME. We have felt the need to respond to our contemporary spiritual needs with contemporary techniques borrowed from Madison Avenue, from Disney, and from Spielberg. Those techniques offer tricks to improve performance and heighten the individual's worship experience. In this milieu, we breed a New-Age spirituality that is distinctly different from the Jewish tradition, with its emphasis on community.

Without an appreciation of the tension between the secular emphasis on the individual and Judaism's emphasis on community, worship may be reduced to a self-centeredness that borders on narcissism instead of a centering of self in the midst of the values of the community and the *Mitzvot* that God gave to us so that we might attain those values and add holiness to our lives. As difficult as "center" is to assess, it can only be understood in a communal sense as we move from "me" to "we."

The *Birkat haShalom*, the last of all of the benedictions of the *Amidah*, is a liturgical response to our need for and promise of consolation and "wholeness." For me it has provided "center." "*Sim shalom tova u'veracha, chen, vachesed, verachamim.*" "Grant peace, but read also, wholeness, from the root shin, lamed, mem, well being, blessing, grace, the same "*chen*" which anchors the word "*va'etchanan,*" loving-kindness, and mercy upon us and upon all Israel, Thy people." Its Temple parallel was the priests' blessing of the people at the completion of the sacrifice. The message of consolation that I draw is that the opportunity for wholeness and grace exists in our world. Wholeness, "*shelemut,*" need not be a concretized physical reassembling of what was. For the most part, it can't be. Those dead whom we mourn don't physically walk with us.

The shattered shards' of the wineglass broken at the wedding ceremony and preserved and suspended in Plexiglas for the young couple do not hold drink; nor is reestablishing the Temple Service critical to our relationship with one another or with God. Prayer that gets us to center, *mitzvot* that get us to share our values in a behavioral way, are critical. Wholeness and unity are much more in the perceptual realm than in the physical one...and I believe that they are accessible in our world as a result of God's grace.

How do we know that we are where we need to be when we daven? How do we know that we are "to center" and not simply centered in ourselves? I'm not sure, but it has to be more than a "hot sync" of our palm pilot (or is that our prayer pilots?) that has us starting and finishing the *Amidah* together. It's not enough to be on the same page, to sing the same nusa<u>h</u>, and to finish on the same note. So how do we know that we are "to center"? I'm not sure but let me describe what happens to me when I think that I'm successful in my davening. I don't always get there, but it's a matter of establishing the horizon line outside of myself.

This analogy may be a stretch, but what happens to me on those occasions that I feel that my davening is successful is that the words *"Sim Shalom b'olam tovah u'veracha, chen, vachesed, verachamim"* emerge in 3 dimension; like seeing them through a stereopticon, a Viewmaster, or imbedded in one of those "Magic Eye" pictures that were popular a few years back. Something called "deep vision" teases the brain into interpreting depth from the two-dimensional representation. Once the image is seen, you felt as though you could reach in and cup it. Seeing value concepts in prayer that way, I can sidle up to the concepts, crawl underneath and behind them or view them from on top. With that dimension, with that perspective, I get myself to center. It's a reflexive form, like, *"va'etchanan,"* "I got myself to plead." Prayer, it seems, if it is to transform our lives, involves moving ourselves in relationship to God so that we can emulate qualities like *"chesed,"* deeds of loving-kindness. Abraham Joshua Heschel wrote, "The issue of prayer is not prayer; the issue of prayer is God." He wrote as well, in the spirit of the *hasadim,* "To pray is to know how to stand still and to dwell upon a word."

Not all of our *t'fillah* is prescribed and fixed. Not all of it is *keva.* We are also obligated to bring to it our *kavanah,* our intention. Bring to it an educated and informed vitality and it will be vital. Reading the "cliff noted" edition may not be sufficient for you. After *Birkat haShalom,* there is ample room for a quiet plea or personal note of thanksgiving. I'll share one of mine with you. "Adonai...May we continue to be blessed with language, the choice words which are our offering. May we know the *Mitzvot,* the tools that prepare our offering, and may we be endowed with the deep vision to fire our sacrifice. Blessed are you whose grace gives us center."

Joanne Fritz Kraus encountered Chizuk Amuno Congregation while searching for a community in which her daughters could be educated. She found there, Rabbi Joel Zaiman, who has become her teacher and her Rabbi. She currently serves the congregation as secretary on the Executive Committee and Chair of the Ritual Committee.

Ekev
Larry Shuman

> *"V'haya Ekev . . . And if you obey these rules and observe them carefully, the Lord your God will maintain faithfully for you the covenant that He made an oath with your fathers."* (Ekev, 7:12)

So begins Parashat *Ekev*, Moshe's covenant reminder and benefits speech—and one of his final addresses to the Israelites before they are allowed to enter the Promised Land.

Moshe begins this outline of the benefits package offered by God to the Israelites—which includes your usual biblical fare: the guarantee of fruitfulness (of both the womb and of the land), good health and victory over enemies—with the word *Ekev*.

A curious choice of words, *Ekev* has received quite a bit of attention over the years from scholars and sages. From "if only" to "if you do," to the more literal "as a consequence of," "foot," or "on the heels of," *Ekev* has been defined in a variety of ways over the centuries.

The Baal Shem Tov understood *Ekev* (etymologically) as "heel" in the sense of the end of something . . . on the heel end of . In the context of the commandments, the Baal Shem Tov believed that the use of the word *Ekev* implied that it was incumbent upon each of us to perform each *mitzvah* as if it were our last. Similar to the more recent adage, "living life as if it were your last day on earth," performing *mitzvot* in this mindset would heighten one's willingness to perform the mitzvah as well as heighten the *mitzvah's* effect on the individual and the community at large.

This mindset can also be seen as a priority for approaching each mitzvah with the joy and willingness that it is due. According to *Leviticus Rabbah* 11:7, the word *"v'haya"* connotes joy wherever it occurs in biblical text. Consequently, it is by means of joy that you will come to such a point that "you will obey these rules and observe them carefully...." Together the two words *"v'haya Ekev"*

225

suggest that only through a motivation of joy in serving God—and the urgency of performing the *mitzvah* as if it were our last—will we be able to obey the commandments carefully and successfully.

Just as the heel is the end of the foot, it is also the beginning of a step. With each swing of your leg, it is the heel that first plants itself in the ground, which sends you on your way towards the next step. Within Moshe's words of "covenant cause and effect" can be found what the publishing industry might title "Moshe's Guide to Walking the Jewish Path: A Step by Step Guide to Living a Jewish Life." The *mitzvot* can be viewed in these terms as the roots from which Jewish life will blossom. By carefully planting our heel—performing the *mitzvot*, taking one step at a time, approaching each *mitzvah* joyously and completely—we cause the Jewish path to make itself apparent.

As Moshe continues his address, he reminds the Israelites that God gave them manna to eat "in order to teach you that man does not live by bread alone, but man may live on anything that the Lord decrees." (*Ekev*, 8:3) Taken literally, it means that our sustenance and fulfillment is in the hands of God alone. A more thoughtful reading may reveal a continuation of "Moshe's Guide to Walking the Jewish Path."

Even though manna was received every day, it was not enough to satisfy the Israelites' hunger. In that lingering hunger, Moshe may well have chapter two of his "Guide." Although manna was enough to curb the Israelites' physical hunger, it nevertheless left them unfulfilled—spiritually. What remained after the physical satiation was a yearning for God's presence, leading to the lesson that taking care of our bodies is one thing, nourishing our souls is quite another. Taking in the goodness that God has to offer by doing His commandments and acknowledging His influence: these are the ways to maintain a well-fed physical and spiritual existence. The joy that follows the completion of *mitzvot* helps not only to feed the spiritual hunger in all of us, it keeps the desire for God's closeness at the forefront of our consciousness.

226

It is no wonder that Judaism offers us such joyous blessings for food. Celebrating the food that we eat as both a physical necessity and as a spiritual obligation is at the heart *of Birkat Hamazon*. Talmudic commentators, in fact, point to Moshe's address in *Ekev* as the catalyst for the *Birkat Hamazon*. The rabbis created Birkat Hamazon as a way of fulfilling their debt to acknowledge God's (physical and spiritual) gifts to us.

Birkat Hamazon is not the only blessing to trace its origins to *Ekev*. We also learn of three additional *mitzvot* that make their way into our *siddur*. Each of these *mitzvot*—to wrap tefillin, to teach our children, and to affix *mezuzot*—help us to bridge elements of the physical and the spiritual in Judaism.

> *"Bind them as a sign upon your hand...and let them be a reminder above your eyes.' (Ekev* 11:18)

The *mitzvah* of wrapping *tefillin* actually brings elements of the spiritual in contact with the body. Symbolizing the relationship of the Jewish people to God and His commandments, wrapping *tefillin* on the head and arm also represents the dedication of mind and body (spiritual and physical) to God's service.

> *"And teach them (My words) to your children." (Ekev* 11:19)

The commandment to teach children about the connection between the physical world and the spiritual world is incumbent upon every Jewish parent. By performing this *mitzvah*, parents are enabling children to experience their own discoveries of Judaism, to take their first steps on the Jewish path.

> *"And inscribe them on the doorposts of your house . . . ."* (Ekev 11:20)

More than an affirmation of one's identity, the *mezuzah* symbolizes the home as sacred—a commandment facilitating the bridging of the physical and spiritual. The commandment to affix a mezuzah brings God into the physical structure of the home, making the physical structure a spiritual dwelling place as well.

As you piece together the chapters of Moshe's "Guide," the theme of recollection emerges. Although much of our modern day existence is based on the here and now of the physical world, the key to living a Jewish life is found in the lessons and experience of the past. So important is this concept of recollection that Moshe goes on to remind the Israelites that it was God who freed them from Egypt, who led them through the terrible wilderness and parched land. And even though they triumphed over these trials, and are now poised to enter the Promised Land, it was God who tested their resolve and it will be God whom they will thank for their prosperity.

Moshe warns them that even though they may produce great wealth and live prosperous lives in the Promised Land (according to their covenant (benefits package) with God), the Children of Israel must always remember to whom their gratitude is due. For Moshe, recollection is also a running anxiety throughout his address. His overwhelming concern is that the Israelites, upon achieving wealth and prosperity in the Holy Land, will disregard God's influence and indulge their own feelings of great pride. His constant reminders to them are what Rabbi Moses ben Nachman (RaMBaN), a 13Th century Spanish scholar, calls Moshe's antidotes to arrogance. Moshe was aware of how fickle the Israelites could be (especially after the events of Mount Sinai), and he also realized that a little prosperity after forty years of harsh wilderness could go to their heads. It is natural, following that logic, for human beings to take pride in and ownership for their accomplishments. Moshe is trying to get the point across that it is all right to appreciate your own hard work, but it is essential to remember who enabled you to work hard.

For Moshe, and in fact for most of us, the inference of history (or experience) serves as a humbling tactic and, perhaps more importantly, as a means of putting one's current situation in perspective. Used in this way, history need not always be on such a grand scale as in the history of a nation's trek through the wilderness. But within each of our own personal histories (both great and small), God's presence must be recognized as being front and center. That is basically what Moshe is asking of the Israelites: to give credit where credit is due. To be thankful for what you have and how you attained it.

The covenant between God and the Children of Israel is embedded in every aspect of our physical and spiritual being. It is the guiding force in our blessings, liturgy, traditions and observances. This is why Moshe repeats his comments "to remember the covenant" over and over again throughout the Ekev address. The covenant is our link to the past, our companion in the present and the key to our future.

Larry Shuman is Director of Communications for Chizuk Amuno Congregation and teaches in Rosenbloom Religious School's High School program. He points to working with Rabbi Zaiman as one of the major "perks" of employment at Chizuk Amuno.

Re'eh
Kathy & Sanford Shapiro

Re'eh, Moses' reiteration of laws and religious precepts, oddly is distinguished by its structural rambling, inattention to critical detail, and lapses in focus; it seems hardly a comprehensive code for an entire society. On further inspection, "Re'eh" presents a psychologically more persuasive appeal, highlighting key principles and values, dramatizing, emphasizing and repeating. Clearly meant for mass consumption, "Re'eh" trades thoroughness of content for strength of appeal. There is throughout as much emphasis on the *why* as on the *what*. Through the lens of the rhetoric, one develops insight into the picture of the audience addressed as one needing to be constantly refocused.

In the preamble, Moses summarizes what's at stake in the laws he is about to lay out. Exhorting, "See, that I place before you a blessing and a curse." (11:26) Significant in this very first line is the singular "re'eh" and then the plural throughout. Why the turn? By addressing the individual, Moses is reminding the people that they each must discriminate carefully in their individual choices. One can not hide behind the collective deeds. There is no compromise, no averaging out the good among the people. Quite the contrary, the entire nation is held responsible for the sins of the individual. (See in Judges, where the individual's actions are referred to as "Israel has sinned.") "Re'eh" speaks to both in their symbiotic relationship. Before you are situations that require great judgment, and restraint. It is the individual who must act, holding the responsibility for the whole.

In contrast, the Midrash Tanchuma states that prior to the giving of the Torah to Israel, individual lives were subject to the behavior of the whole. Members' lives were spared even if their own actions weren't worthy. But here, in "Re'eh," this singular "See" distinguishes a new time. The fate of the whole depends on each individual's actions. Then why the shift to the plural at all? As individuals, we are to remember that we also operate as a people, collectively bound to each other in the unique covenantal relationship with God.

"See, that I place before you a blessing and a curse." While setting the tone for the stern consequences of the people's actions, the opening lines simultaneously promote the desired outcome by speaking with an underlying respect. Note that blessing in the singular and the curse in the plural. The singular, "tovah," the good, the unified beneficence that emanates from God, and the plural, "ra'ot," evils, come from the unexpected actions of disobedience. In the plural is an implicit diminutive, a lesser status and expectation that these will occur. Also Rashi implies in his note that, ." . . the blessing *that* you obey" means ." . . the blessing, on condition that you obey."God is giving man the benefit of the doubt. He assumes that man will obey.

The first section of the laws (Deut. 12:1-19) starts with the single place of worship. Even though the structure is truncated (it starts with the single sanctuary, then jumps to uprooting Canaanite traces, sacrifices, offerings, the bringing of your households, and then returns to the centralization of the sanctuary idea), there is a general associative link between the disjointed parts: single place of worship to destroying worshiping idols. The stronger tie throughout is rhetorical, sensitive to the audience's psyche. Note the style of command in the negative.

> "*You shall not act at all as we now act here . . .* "
> *(12:8)*

> "*Take care not to sacrifice your burnt offering in any place you like . . .*" *(12:13)*

> "*You may not partake in your settlements of the tithes . . .*" *(12:17)*

The negative construction reveals an awareness of what the people currently do, what their tendencies are, how they tend to rationalize aberrant behavior. "I know you." It's hard to overestimate the power of the voice constantly reminding the people, "I know you."

After almost every section listing the prohibitions (e.g. the centralization of sacrifice, distinguishing between sacrificial slaughter and slaughter for food, the prohibition to inflict wounds upon oneself in mourning, etc.), there is the repetition of the motivation: "For you will be doing what is good and right in the sight of the Lord your God," (12:28); or, "For you are a people consecrated to the Lord your God: the Lord your God chose you from among all other peoples on earth to be his treasured people." (14:2)

The constancy of the refrain echoes parental conversations in which parents are advising, demanding and expecting a long list of rules of the children, and then stop periodically to remind them of the context, "It's because I love you." Implied throughout "Re'eh" is the recognition that the requests are stringent and often without reinforcement or confirmation. The constant reminder of the special relationship implicitly recognizes the very human tendency to stray, to lose track, and thus to need to be kept on track.

Later, in the section on false prophets, Moses employs a dramatic technique of persuasion to reach his audience.

> *"If there arise in the midst of thee a prophet*
> *or a dreamer of dreams—*
> *and he give thee a sign or a wonder,*
> *and the sign or the wonder come to pass,*
> *whereof he spoke unto thee—saying:*
> *Let us go after other gods,*
> *which thou hast not known,*
> *and let us serve them;*
> *thou shalt not hearken unto the words of that prophet,*
> *or unto that dreamer of dreams;*
> *for the Lord your God putteth you to proof,*

*to know whether ye do love the Lord your God with all
your heart and with all your soul." (13, 2-4)*

Why does Moses call this instigator to other gods a
"prophet?" He uses the provocation purposefully, to dramatize how
powerfully mesmerizing is the experience of a person with
extraordinary gifts. Rather than telling the people that he knows
how susceptible to astonishment they are, Moses offers the
hypothetical event by presenting the experience *as it comes*. And
then, he walks you through the progression dramatically. First you
see a prophet, then he gives signs, and then those very things come
to pass ("Aha! confirmation," you think) and then, (crash!) the
bottom line. The mission is revealed, but only after you are
hooked. Rather than telling us that's how the ruse works, he *shows*
us in the drama. It is all the more persuasive because he enters the
subjective experience.

"And the sign or the wonder come to pass." How can the
false prophet make signs and wonders come to pass? R. Akiva
even tries to rationalize this away by arguing that this false prophet
is a true one turned false. Calling a person a prophet with real
power doesn't authenticate his godliness. It simply acknowledges
that people experience people with gifts as if they are divine. And
evil forces do hold potent qualities that confuse and distract. Their
presence offers an opportunity for growth and discovery. The false
prophet must have real power, power to allure, for there to be
testing of any kind. The success of the trick is precisely the point.
Trickery is successful, yet only in its own terms. As Maimonides
suggests, signs and wonders, *per se*, mean nothing in terms of
authenticity. When signs come to pass, they are validated when
they are shown to be of the work of God, and they are immediately
invalidated when the mission is revealed to be trickery.

Instigation to worship other gods comes not only in the
form of astonishing prophets bringing signs and wonders, but in
the privacy of the safe harbor of our own homes: "If your brother,

your own mother's son, etc." (13:7) Look, not only out but within. "See."

The forthrightness is powerful, the message is clear: you are forbidden to stand by passively ("do not shield him" (13:9), you must actively participate in his death. The injunction takes center stage: you own nothing. Nothing of yours is sacred when it comes to saving the soul of Israel. You must make an example by public capital punishment, so that "all Israel will hear and be afraid, and such evil things will not be done, in your midst." (13:12) The *parashah* does not stop to instruct about the details of the judicial procedure (the kind of inquiry, the number of witnesses required, etc.). The contrast is stunning. The charlatan prophet dazzling with his powers, to the intimacy of your own home. No place is invulnerable. "See."

The pull to other gods can come in small steps and virtually invisible aberrations. When a prophet suggests that even one mitzvah is false, you must not even listen. The suggestion is that you should not even engage your ears, lest you might be willing to enter a discussion. *Sefer Ha-Chinuch* explains that one's intellect is simply not up to the task. In discussion, by even listening, or entertaining the presence of the other, one might be tempted to imagine for a split second the possibility of other gods, and then the window is cracked. The stakes are simply too high.

The vividness of the portraits, the repetition, the knowing voice, the potency of the rhetoric throughout "Re'eh" paints a living testament to the ideals within the laws, far more powerful than a letter-perfect list of do's and don'ts.

Kathy and Sandy Shapiro have been members of Chizuk Amuno for many years and both play an active role in the lay leadership of the synagogue community.

Shofetim
Shoshana Shoubin Cardin

Parashat Shoftim (Judges) establishes the framework for a civil, land-based society; it delineates the division of the governing powers and their exercise of authority, as well as the responsibilities of and limitations on authority. Many of the rules and admonitions are relevant to today's democratic and civil societies.

The power to govern and exercise authority is divided into categories: the power of the king-political and economic;the power of Kohanim and Levites to teach Torah and attend to the Temple rituals; and the authority of the Judges.

Earlier, in Shemot, Exodus 18:14-26, we learned that Moses was advised by Jethro, his father-in-law, to establish a system of lower and higher courts to deal with any controversies arising during the Israelites' wanderings in the desert. In Shoftim, the Torah states clearly that lower courts should be established in each city that the Lord gives to the tribes, an implication that the judges should be from their own tribes, known and close to the people. In addition, there should be a higher court, comparable to a Sanhedrin, for those cases in which a decision cannot be concluded in the lower courts. Torah implies that there should be officers of the court who would enforce the decisions of the judges and would circulate among the populace to ensure that violators would be brought to justice.

It is in this *Parashah* that we learn that oft quoted: "*Tzedek, tzedek, tirdof*—Justice, justice thou shall pursue." Today we translate *Tzedek* as "justice" but *Tzedek* is also sometimes translated as "righteousness." Rabbi Brenam of P'shis'cha interpreted the repetition of the word "*Tzedek*" to say that righteousness alone is not sufficient. Righteousness must be pursued through righteous and honest means. That "righteousness" is necessary behavior if the Israelites are to live on and possess the land that God gives them.

Parashat Shoftim delineates the responsibilities of judges and the importance of *justice* as a basis for a civil society. "Judges. . . shall judge the people with righteous judgement." Therefore, those selected to be judges were to be both qualified and righteous, for the community would be held responsible for their judges' decisions and actions. We also learn that judges not only must judge righteously, but must "pursue" all the evidence and "make a thorough investigation" (12:4) in order to render a just decision.

This theme of justice as the basis for society has been repeated and emphasized throughout our history. The prophet Zachariah stated: "You shall administer truth, justice and peace within your gates." Rabbi Shimon ben Gamliel—much later—stated: "The world is established on three principles: truth, justice and peace." Righteousness or justice requires that no judge can accept a bribe, "for the bribe will blind the eye of the wise and make just words crooked." No judge can give preferential treatment or show favoritism to any party.

The need for witnesses and their responsibilities are also clearly articulated. Against any person, man or woman, accused of "evil in the eyes of God" (the most serious offense of all) there must be at least two credible and trustworthy witnesses; and if the accused is found guilty, the two witnesses are the first to mete out the punishment, i.e. stoning to death. Only then can the people add their own punishment. No one can be sentenced to death upon the testimony of a single witness. Further, the sentence was to be carried out in the city in which the accused committed the evil offense, for the populace to see and remember, thereby serving as a deterrent. Should a witness prove to be a false witness, the sentence which would have been meted out to the accused is rendered upon the witness.

"Evil in the eyes of God" was defined as one of the following: idol worship, which is the "ultimate violation of God's covenant"; desecration of the altar (later the Temple); and using invalid animals for offerings or using stolen funds to purchase offerings.

Shoftim clearly states that the decision rendered by the judges must be followed without "any deviations, right or left" for it has been rendered by a Kohen, Levite or Judge in a place chosen by God,

236

therefore representative of God. Any violation of this admonition would result in death, as an example for the entire people not to rebel against judicial authority.

The *sedrah* clearly defines the Torah as "The Law," equivalent to our Constitution of the United States. The Torah governs the lives of the people and societal behavior, including kings and priests as well as civilians.

The Torah explicitly states that once the Israelites have arrived and settled in the land the Lord has given them, they are to request a king as sovereign, one who will be chosen by the Lord from among them. No foreigner, non-Israelite, could qualify as king. (No foreign-born individual can be president of the United States.) Further, the king has limits on his powers: the king should not own numerous horses; he could take only eighteen wives and not amass excessive wealth. The king, himself, was subject to the Torah, the Constitution. In fact, the king was to write or own two copies of the authoritative Torah, one of which he was to study and read daily. The other he was to carry with him at all times to remind him that he, too, had to obey its dictates. The king was not above the law, nor were the people, his subjects; rather they were his *achim*, brethren. This also limited any inclination towards dictatorship. It is interesting to note that the wisest of kings, King Solomon, violated all three of the limitations of power, for which his kingdom was divided upon his death, not handed down to his sons, with ten tribes forming an independent kingdom of Israel.

As the king represented political power, economic power and leadership, the domain of power and authority vested in the Kohanim (the priests) and the Levites was religious and social. These groups were responsible for teaching the Torah, for managing the Temple, conducting the sacrifices, explaining Temple worship and ritual purity, as well as providing musical accompaniment and festivals for the holidays.

Their power also had limitations. They were prohibited from owning or inheriting land, so when the land was divided among the tribes, they were not counted. Their inheritance was service to God.

Because they were to devote themselves solely to teaching, religious duties and ritual, it would have been impossible to provide for themselves and their families. Therefore, they were given places to live, and a portion of the crops harvested by the Israelites as well as specific parts of the sacrificial offerings for food.

Prophets also played a very special and significant role in biblical times, even though they did not hold positions of power. Numerous peoples practiced witchcraft, magic, etc. and often engaged in human sacrifice to satisfy multiple gods. The Torah specifically prohibits such practices, and tells the people that, when in doubt about the future, they should consult the true prophets whom the Lord will select from among the Israelites. Shoftim explains how one distinguishes a false prophet from a true prophet and dooms the false prophet to death, according to the word of the Lord. It was vital that the witchcraft and magic so widely practiced by the neighboring peoples not be brought into the life of the Israelites.

To be certain that justice and humanness be respected and observed, Shoftim also reiterates the issue of the refuge cities for blood revenge killers first addressed in Bamidbar (Numbers).

Laws for the conduct of warfare are dictated in Shoftim, too, with specific attention to those who would not be required to fight. Once again we learn that faith in the Lord is mightier than military weapons. When engaging in battle, ."..let not your hearts be faint; do not be afraid, do not panic, and do not be broken before them. For the Lord, your God, is the One who goes with you, to fight for you with your enemies, to save you."

All of these rules, laws and admonitions were relevant and necessary for the transition from a wandering homeless people to a land-based society. With these laws, rules and admonitions, the Israelites were prepared to begin life as a nation—no longer a wandering, conquering people.

An International Jewish Leader and Philanthropist, Shoshana Shoubin Cardin is a longtime member of Chizuk Amuno Congregation.

Ki Tetze
Dr. Barry M. Gittlen

Through the miscellaneous laws of the *parashah Ki Tetze* runs the Biblical imperative of social order, social justice. Here the reader enters deeply into Israel's sense of self as well as of its past. Grasping the rich fabric of Israel's social and political history demands much from the savvy reader: it requires a certain level of knowledge and grounding in Israel's social and legal realia. *Ki Tetze* begs the reader to reread the Torah, to ascend the rich landscape of Israel's experience.

Entering the *parashah*, we confront individual and familial issues effecting the social order. We find the balancing of ritual issues with communal problems, revisiting the frameworks of Exodus and Leviticus with new eyes. In its last wilderness moments, Israel prepares for establishment in the land, the land that had been Canaan. Israel prepares for a land-bound communal existence. Once in its land, Israel needs a socio-legal infrastructure that binds together all elements of society and thereby enables the community to function harmoniously. This community must work. Only once it works internally as a community can Israel redirect its attention to the outside world, can Israel deal with Canaanites, with various foreign states, and ultimately with the Amalekites.

For Israel on the move through the wilderness, survival was paramount. Once settled in its land, inter-personal and communal issues would become increasingly important, and thus the need to codify practice; to ensure the survival of the community. The codification, including our *parashah*, illuminates a rich and vibrant Israelite society. Thus, *Ki Tetze* [as parsed by Jeffrey Tigay, *Deuteronomy, JPS 1996*, pp.194-237] contains some 35 categories of communal interest: those that involve women or children, those that involve animals, those that involve business dealings, those that involve human dignity. The list culminates in Dt. 25:13-16 with an injunction against false weights, which interestingly concludes with the statement that false weights are an abomination to the Lord (Dt. 25:16). There follows a final command that Israel remember what Amalek did to her during the exodus from Egypt and blot out all trace of Amalek (Dt. 25:17-19).

Specific recollection of the Amalekite attack against Israel during the Exodus (Ex. 17:8-16) seems out of place in this final collection of legal material. Yet it fits the context: the legal corpora have reached conclusion; with Israel in the land, the text turns briefly to world perspectives. Israel needs just measures in dealing with the rest of the world. Unjust measures are an abomination. So too, throughout the generations of Israel, have the Amalekites become an abomination. God will obliterate memory of them (Ex. 17:14). Yet the memory and the reality of the Amalekites confronts Israel throughout her history. When settled in the promised-land, when the religious, social and political institutions which govern conduct within the community have been established and are functioning, Israel cannot simply rest on God's beneficent deeds. Rather, Israel must remain on guard, must remember Amalek, the very Amalek the memory of whom God was to erase.

In Exodus, God will erase the memory of Amalek. But in Deuteronomy (25:19), Israel is instructed to erase the memory of Amalek. Thus, in keeping with God's dictate as revised in Deuteronomy, God instructs King Saul to completely obliterate the reality of Amalek, to slaughter the population (I Sam. 15:2-3). Indeed, roughly two centuries after the presumed date of Israel's settlement, King Saul was to exterminate the Amalekites, including Agag their king. Unfortunately, he failed to carry out this task fully and had the kingship wrested from his possession (I Sam. 15). Saul, the son of Kish, failed to slaughter the Amalekite king, but Samuel chopped off Agag's head.

Israel's involvement with Amalek was to continue into and effectively underlie the narrative of Esther. That flowery narrative of queenship, beauty pageants and high intrigue also staged the final battle between Israel and the Amalekites. At the time when

Israel once again seemed settled and in control, albeit in the diaspora, at a time of apparent security, once again Israel needed vigilance. So it developed that Mordecai, direct descendant of Kish (father of King Saul) enabled the impalement of Haman the Agagite (direct descendant of Agag, King of Amalek).

Of further interest here is the method by which Haman was dispatched. The Hebrew text of Esther indicates that he was "hung on a tree," with the implication from Assyrian reliefs that this means impaled on a stake. Here I must take issue with Tigay's commentary on Dt. 21:22: Tigay opines that Israel did not impale, and that the text of Deuteronomy must be taken otherwise. However, it remains abundantly clear that Israel knew of the custom of impaling, whether directly from Assyria or through general knowledge, and that Israel actually employed the practice (Joshua 8:29 and 10:27, possibly also Gen 40:19). Impaling remains the best (and only illustrated, see the famous Lachish Relief) possibility for the Hebrew phrase translated as "hang on a tree."

Raised high on a thick stake or tree trunk, the impaled were often placed near the city gate or in some other prominent position where their predicament could be seen by a large number of passers by. In this way, as well as in artistic representation, Assyria employed impaling as a vital part of its royal propaganda. This tactic of prominent impaling clearly signals every witness: don't mess with the impaler. In the Book of Esther, God brings about the impaling. Also in Esther, God finally brings about what had been promised in Exodus and commanded in both Deuteronomy and I Samuel.

Not only has Israel established itself in the territorial world, but Israel's God has once again demonstrated His extra-territoriality. God does indeed work in history, God does have power and can employ that power everywhere, God does keep His promises to Israel.

Dr. Barry M. Gittlen is Professor of Biblical and Archaeological Studies at Baltimore Hebrew University, internationally recognized archeologist, and teaches Biblical Literature at Chizuk Amuno Congregation. He joined Chizuk Amuno shortly after Joel Zaiman became its rabbi. This commentary is dedicated to Rabbi Joel Zaiman and to his encouragement and nurturing of Jewish learning.

Ki Tavo
Dr. Anne Young

"My father was a wandering Aramean . . . ." This phrase is so familiar that many Jews can probably finish the entire passage from memory. What may be surprising is that hundreds of years ago Israelite farmers were even more familiar with these words, albeit for an entirely different reason. In ancient Israel, the passage was recited as part of the harvest festival; today, of course, it is a centerpiece of the Haggadah. In the interim, the Rabbis of the Talmud discussed the *mitzvah* associated with the recitation of the phrase and the leading Torah commentators of the Middle Ages debated its exact meaning. The transition from harvest festival to Seder table provides a wonderful example of how Judaism has evolved, shaped by people who lived and events that occurred hundreds of years ago. And, certainly, it all begins with the Torah.

The phrase "my father was a wandering Aramean" occurs in the Torah as part of the ceremony for bringing first fruits (*bikkurim*) to the Temple. Although the commandment to bring *bikkurim* was given earlier (Exod. 23:19, Exod. 34:26, Num. 18:12-13, Deut. 18:4), the ceremony itself is described for the first time in *Ki Tavo*. Moses tells the Israelites that when they bring their first fruits to the Temple, they are to say the following:
"My father was a wandering Aramean, and . . . he went down to Mitzrayim . . . . The Egyptians dealt harshly with us and oppressed us . . . . We cried out to *Adonai*, the God of our ancestors and . . . Adonai took us out of *Mitzrayim* with a mighty hand . . . . Then He brought us to this place, and he gave us this land, a land flowing with milk and honey. And now, behold I have brought the first fruits of the land that You, *Adonai*, have given me."

After reciting this capsule version of the Exodus and acknowledging the good land, *Eretz Israel*, the farmer was to present his *bikkurim* to the priest. Reciting this formula is known as "*mikra bikkurim*," or "saying of the *bikkurim*."

It is not particularly surprising that the Torah would command Israelite farmers to have a ceremony in which they were to dedicate a portion of their produce to God. Many ancients had such rites. What is striking is the formula itself. It is not simply an expression of thanks to the Creator for providing the good soil, for causing the rain to fall and the sun to shine at the appropriate times, and for giving the farmer the strength to cultivate the land. Instead, the farmer is to recount his story, or more accurately, the story of his people. As he brings *bikkurim*, he is to remember that he was redeemed from *Mitzrayim*. Not he, himself, literally, of course. But at this pivotal moment in his year, when celebration is in order, the farmer must recognize and remember who he is and where he came from. He does this by telling the central story of Judaism: "Adonai, the God of our ancestors ... took us out of *Mitzrayim* with a mighty hand ... He brought us to this place."

As they did about so many *mitzvot* commanded in Torah, the Rabbis of the Talmud had many questions about bikkurim and *mikra bikkurim*. Exactly what produce must be brought to the Temple? Was it to be all produce or just the seven species mentioned in Deut. 8:8? Who was to participate? What if the farmer did not actually own the land, but rather was simply a tenant farmer? During what period of time were the first fruits to be brought? How was the ceremony to be conducted?

Mishnah Bikkurim is devoted to a discussion of such questions. From the range and depth of the discussion, it is obvious that the Sages took the process of fulfilling this *mitzvah* very seriously. Since God commanded it, it must be carried out in the proper way. It was their task to sort out the details.

The *Mishnah* mentions that originally those who knew the formula recited it by themselves; those who did not, repeated it after a priest. However, over time, this latter group began to refrain from participating, perhaps because they felt self-conscious. As a result, the Sages declared that henceforth everyone would repeat the words after a priest. In this way no one would be embarrassed. For the Rabbis, avoiding embarrassment, especially to one engaged in the fulfillment of a *mitzvah*, was so important that they changed the procedure rather than risk shaming any of the people.

The Mishnah also describes the ceremony itself: "The men . . . gathered together . . . spent the night in the open place of the town and . . . early in the morning, the officer said: 'Arise and let us go up to Zion unto the Lord our God' (Jer. 31: 6). Before them went the ox, its horns overlaid with gold ... and the flute was played before them . . . . When they approached Jerusalem, they sent messengers before them and adorned their first fruits. The officers . . . of the Temple went forth to meet them. . . . And all the craftsmen in Jerusalem would rise up before them and greet them, saying: 'Brethren, men of such-and-such a place, you are welcome!' When they reached the Temple Court, the Levites sang the song: 'I will exalt Thee, O Lord, for Thou hast raised me up, and hast not suffered mine enemies to rejoice over me' (Ps. 30). While the basket was yet on his shoulder, a man would recite *bikkurim*."

The details are wonderful; we can actually picture the farmers bringing their produce. The description also provides an indication of the importance attached to *bikkurim*. At the time of the Mishnah, it was an accepted practice that people stood in the presence of scholars.

Because scholars were so common in Jerusalem, artisans were excused from this custom; otherwise they would been unable to work. However, when the *bikkurim* procession arrived, even the craftsmen would rise and greet them. Additionally, it is fascinating to remember that when Rabbi Judah Ha Nasi redacted the Mishnah, the Temple had been destroyed approximately 130 years before. Neither he nor his teachers had seen this event. Still, the vividness of the story as it was handed down from generation to generation, remains, and it gives the sense of a joyous fulfilling of the commandment.

In the Middle Ages, Torah commentators debated the meaning of the phrase "My father was a wandering Aramean," *Arami oved avi*. The words *Arami* and *avi* are clear, meaning "Aramean" and "My father," respectively. The debate centers on the meaning and tense of the verb *oved*. Rashi interprets it as a transitive verb meaning, "to destroy." Thus he renders the beginning of the verse "an Aramean sought to destroy my father." That is, according to Rashi, the verse means, "the Aramean Laban sought to destroy my father Jacob." This interpretation fits with the Biblical story; Laban was an Aramean and he certainly did pursue Jacob. Those who criticize Rashi do so based not only on matters of Hebrew grammar, but also on the context of the phrase. They ask the question, why would a capsule account of the central story of Judaism include Laban? Moreover, Jacob did not go down to Egypt because of Laban.

Many of those who disagree with Rashi interpret *oved* as an intransitive verb meaning, "to wander." As a result, they translate *Arami oved avi* as "my father was a wandering Aramean." This raises the question, to whom does "my father" refer? Here there is a debate was well. According to Ibn Ezra, *avi* refers to Jacob; according to Maimonides, Abraham. Either interpretation is problematic. Although Jacob resided in Aram for a period of time, he was not really an Aramean. Abraham, on the other hand, was from Aram. From this point of view, focusing on *Arami*, Maimonides' interpretation seems superior.

However, as the Torah makes clear, Abraham did not wander; throughout his journey from Ur to Canaan, God directed him. On the other hand, Jacob certainly did wander. So, from the point of view of *oved*, Ibn Ezra's interpretation seems better. Proponents of Ibn Ezra and of Maimonides bring additional support for their positions based on arguments about Hebrew grammar and other considerations.

Such debates sometimes give rise to the question, "Who cares?" Why should anyone spend time worrying about the opening words of *mikra bikkurim*? After all, the ceremony cannot take place today because there is no Temple. Moreover, it only applies to produce grown by farmers in *Eretz Israel*. In short, there is no Temple, we live in America and we are not farmers. It appears that it does not matter how *Arami oved avi* is interpreted.

246

One response is that the debate is not simply over three words. Rather it is a debate over words of Torah. And that makes all the difference. For our Sages, words are important; those of Torah, the most important of all. Moreover, on a practical level, Maimonides used his interpretation to render an important decision which affects many Jews today.

According to the Mishnah, while converts are required to bring first fruits, they may not recite *mikra bikkurim*. In discussing this statement, the Jerusalem Talmud states that this is the opinion of Rabbi Meir, and that Rabbi Judah disagrees with him. According to Rabbi Judah, converts do recite the formula.

Although the Jerusalem Talmud records the disagreement between the two rabbis, it does not resolve the issue. Centuries later, Maimonides supported Rabbi Judah's position using his interpretation of avi. He said that since *mikra bikkurim* begins with "My father" which refers to Abraham, and since Abraham is the father of all converts, the proselyte farmer should recite *mikra bikkurim*.

For Nehama Leibowitz, this is the only instance when Maimonides issued a ruling in disagreement with the Mishnah. Maimonides used his decision as a basis for another ruling. He received a letter from Obadiah, a proselyte, who asked if he could include in his prayers phrases such as "God of our ancestors" and "who brought us out of Egypt." Maimonides responded that just as converts say "my father" when bringing first fruits, so, too, they recite "God of our ancestors" in their prayers.

This opinion was accepted by the entire Jewish community and is the established practice today of Jews-by-choice. Jews today who hear "my father was a wandering Aramean . . ." usually think of the Haggadah. When the Rabbis selected this passage as one of the bases for telling the Pesah story at the Seder table, they were making an important connection between the past and the future. Just as the farmer in ancient Israel considered this his own story, so, too, do we at the beginning of the twenty-first century view it as our story. It is a story, a history, a heritage, which we pass on to our children and grandchildren.

Dr. Anne Young is the Associate Vice President for Academic Affairs and a Professor of Mathematical Sciences at Loyola College in Maryland. She and her husband David are active members of Chizuk Amuno; it is where they learn and daven with Rabbi Zaiman.

Nitzavim
Barbara Cohen

"You are standing this day all of you before the Lord, your God." So begins the *parashah* (weekly portion), *Nitzavim* (Deut. xxix. 9-28, xxx. 1-20). Moses has assembled the People of Israel, and he lists who is standing there, who is included in the gathering:

> *"your tribal heads, your elders and officers, every man of Israel; your children, your women, and the stranger in the midst of your camp from the woodcutter to the drawer of water."*

Every individual has been so gathered to enter into the covenant with God, a covenant that is being established on this day at this gathering. God is fulfilling the promise to establish these people as His people and the oath He made to Abraham, Isaac and Jacob to be their God. The text continues, specifying with whom this covenant is being made:

> *"Not only with you alone do I make this covenant and its sanctions, but with him that is standing here with us today before the Lord, our God, **and** with him that is not with us here today."*

This covenant is a pact between every individual of Israel, as well as the strangers who have attached themselves to the People of Israel, and God. The text is very clear; all of the People of Israel, old and young, male and female, leader and average citizen, are present at this momentous occasion. The passage, however, continues: "and with him that is not with us here today." Since everyone is present, this cannot refer to the chance individual who may not be present; rather, the reference is to future generations of the People of Israel. The *Midrash Tanhuma* states that "the souls of the whole nation were present at the time of the covenant, and the covenant included all those destined to be born in the future generations." All commentaries concur that "with him who is not with us here today" refers to future generations forever and ever. The covenant is derived not only from the promise made to Abraham, but from the exodus from Egypt, as well. Just as all subsequent generations are indebted to God for the deliverance from slavery personally experienced by their ancestors, so, too, is each generation bound by the original acceptance of the covenant. This covenant is totally inclusive, timeless and everlasting.

The parashah is straightforward, for the most part, and basically succinct. The terms of the covenant are stated clearly in Chapter xxx: 16:

> " ...I command you this day to love the Lord, your God, to walk in His ways, to keep His commandments, His laws, and His rules that you may live and increase and that the Lord, your God may bless you in the land which you are about to enter and to possess."

The specifics of the covenant are not complicated, nor is the language in any way confusing or duplicitous. Love God. Follow His laws, rules and commandments. And what will happen if you follow these directions? You will live, increase and be blessed in your new homeland. The text continues in a tone that is almost pleading in xxx: 19:

> "I have put before you life and death, blessing and curse. U'vacharta bachayim—Choose life so that you and your offspring will live . . . ."

Choose life, that is, a life that is guided by the mitzvot, a life of doing good deeds and cleaving to Him. (Abravanel) These words are very simple and concrete. God explains to the people that this commandment is not too awesome. Rashi defines the word awesome as meaning not hidden from the people, implying that the commandment is something that can be accomplished. Torah explains the accessibility of fulfilling this commandment in very physical terms. It is not too far away. This commandment is not over the sea or in the heavens that some might say "who can go up for us to the heavens and get it for us . . . the thing is very close to you, in your mouth and in your heart, to do it." This last phrase could be the slogan for this parashah: the commandment (to love God and to follow His laws) is set before you. It is explicit, and it is accessible. Just do it, and you will be rewarded.

It is important to note that as explicit and direct as the text is, the covenant is not all about rewards; it also includes sanctions. Torah always emphasizes that there are consequences to every behavior. Choose life and you and your offspring will live and be blessed in that land which you are about to enter. But should you choose not to observe this covenant, should you think in your heart that you can escape the sanctions and not be noticed, *oy vavoy l'cha* —woe unto you! What calamity awaits you! There is no chance of pardon.

> *"The anger of the Lord will be kindled against that individual, and every curse written in this book shall come down on him, and God will wipe out his name from under the heavens."*

The text continues in this vein, with the wrath of God rising like a wave rolling across the sea, gathering momentum as passage after passage describes the destruction that will ensue. Finally, it smashes onto the shore, overwhelming everyone and everything in its path until even the Promised Land, itself, is destroyed, and the people are uprooted and cast into another land. One may read this as a prediction in which God is telling the people that, yes, you will sin and you will be punished. I, God, have been teaching you that you have a choice and that you can make the correct choice. Unfortunately, you always veer the wrong way. And so, yes, you will know the wrath of God.

However, this covenant is a contract that is eternal. It does not become null and void if the People of Israel are derelict in their observance of God's law. And God does not withdraw from this contract when the People do not "choose life." The text continues:

> ." . . when all these things befall you, and you take them (the blessing and the curse) to heart amidst all the nationsto which the Lord has driven you, and you return to the Lord with all your heart and all your soul . . . then the Lord will return you from captivity and have compassion on you."

Compassion! Torah has put forth the plan of action, a plan that can be accomplished. Nevertheless, there is an understanding that human nature is such that the proper course is not always chosen. But never mind; even in the event of an incorrect choice, all is not lost. There is a way back, and when you find that path, God will have compassion on you.

Repeatedly, the terms of the covenant have been very concrete. Torah states that if you follow the commandment, you will be blessed. Choose the wrong path and all manner of atrocities will befall you. And the text states very clearly: no pardon. Nevertheless, in chapter xxx, this aspect of compassion and the concept of t'shuva, repentance, are developed even though that specific word is not used. However, the root shin/vet, shav (return) is used seven times in different forms:

> "...you return them (God's words) to your heart;"
> "...you return to God;"
> "...God will return you (from captivity);"
> "...He will return and will gather you from all the nations;"
> "...you will return and listen to the voice of God;"
> "...God will return to rejoice over you for good;"

"...you will return to God with all your heart and all your soul."

It is possible to translate less literally and to better express the meaning, but the Hebrew root, *shin/vet*, is always the same, and it forms the root word in *t'shuva*, repentance. In *Parashat Nitzavim*, there is every expectation that the people will not make the correct choice and will be punished severely. However, God does not abandon His people. The contract is binding, and the path of return is clearly delineated: Return your heart and soul to God's commandment, and God will take you back. At that time,

"the Lord your God will grant you fruitfulness in all the undertakings of your hand, of your body, of your land and in the offspring of your cattle. . ."

In fact, perhaps in complete understanding of errant ways and the need for enticement to return to the correct path, "He will make you more numerous than your fathers."

It is interesting to note that this *parashah* is usually read in the weekly cycle of Torah reading at the end of *Elul*. During this month the *shofar* is sounded daily to call our attention to the need for *t'shuva* prior to *Rosh Hashanah*. This sound alerts us to the necessity of consciously and conscientiously assessing our behavior. This is a time of the year when we are reminded to right whatever wrongs we can and to find the way to return to the correct path, the ways of Torah.

This is a very powerful *parashah*. The covenant between God and His people, the people of Israel, is explained in precise terms, with its attendant rewards and punishments clearly stated. The idea of free will, choice, is a central theme. If there is any thought of preordained behavior, it is not God that has determined the choice, but rather there is an understanding that poor judgement is part of human behavior. And because the covenant is eternal, there is an "escape clause." The idea of repentance, *t'shuvah*, is clearly specified as an option. Even though this terminology is not used in Torah, the language in chapter xxx is very definitive, and all the behaviors of repentance are laid out for the people to follow. In spite of the vivid description of God's anger in this *parashah,* what stands out is God's capacity for compassion and forgiveness and the repetitive plea to choose life, a life of *mitzvot.*

Barbara Cohen is Judaic Studies Head of Krieger Schechter Day School of Chizuk Amuno Congregation's Lower School where she works with Rabbi Zaiman.

Vayyelech
Susan Vick

At the beginning of Parashat Vayelech, Moses makes a heartrending announcement to Israel: he tells the people he is about to die. He says. "I am a hundred and twenty years old this day; I can not longer go out and come in; and the Lord has said to me: You shall not go over this Jordan." *(V'omer alehem behn me'ah v'esrem shana anochi ha'yom lo u'hal od l'tzat v'labo v'Adonai amar alai lo ta'avor et h'yardan hazeh*. 31: 2) This speech is a prologue to the appointment of Joshua as Moses' successor, and to a monologue that God speaks to Moses and Joshua about the way the people will turn away from God after entering the promised land. This day, identified by Rashi as Moses' date of birth, as well as of his death, was particularly trying: not only must Moses pass the baton of leadership, and not only is he informed that the relationship he has forged between the people and God is about to be strained, but he must also prepare for the end of his days (Fields, *A Torah Commentary For Our Times*, 174, speaks of the fears Moses must have had in giving up leadership; "Giving up authority, power, position, status, and office is difficult, even if you have trained your successor. Moses must have experienced jealousy, bewilderment, resentment, and fear about the unknown future." I would like to add that by choosing his words carefully, Moses delivered the news about his impending death in a gentle fashion.)

A key phrase that elucidates the precise nature of Moses' circumstances is that in which he says, "I can no longer go out and come in." We are told by the text that this is an activity that he has experienced before, but one in which he can no longer participate. These words are repeated elsewhere in Tana<u>h</u>, and an examination of the context in which they are found reveals their meaning.

Although the Torah says that Moses was not ill or infirm at the time of his death, many commentaries on the concept of "going out and coming in" speak of its meaning in terms of his physical capabilities. (Deuteronomy, 34:7 - "And Moses was 120 years old when he died; his eye was not dim, nor his natural force abated.") Hertz and Hirsch both say that the phrase refers to Moses' inability to attend to the details of public life, most notably, leading the people out of the city into battle, and then coming back in safety. This interpretation is supported by a number of texts:

"Let the Lord, the God of the spirit of all flesh, set a man over the congregation, who may go out before them, and who may lead them out, and who may bring them in, that the congregation of the Lord be not a sheep which have no shepherd." (Numbers 27: 15-17)

"And Saul removed him from (being) with him, and made for himself a captain over a thousand, and he went out and came in before the people." (I Samuel 18:13)

"And all Israel and Judah loved David, for he went out and came in before them."
(I Samuel 18:16)

"And Achish called to David and said to him, "As the Lord lives, (I swear) that you are upright, and your going out and coming in with me in the camp, is good in my eyes, for I have not found in you any evil from the day of your coming to me until this day..." (I Samuel 29:6)

"And now, O Lord my God, You have made your servant king instead of David my father, and I (am but) a little child; I do not know (how) to go out or come in." (I Kings 3:7)

256

The explanation of 'to go out and to come in' as being military in nature is logical, but there are other possible meanings as well. Rashi says that Moses was capable of physical activity, but that he was commanded by God not to go out into battle so that Joshua could take over that responsibility. Rashi continues, "Another interpretation of 'to go out and come in' refers to the words of the Torah; it teaches that the traditions and the fountains of wisdom were closed to him." Moses sensed that his intellectual capacity had weakened, and so he could no longer engage in meaningful 'Talmudic' discourse. Rashi explains that a spiritual life was no longer available to Moses, and that the phrase 'to go out and to come in' is simply Moses' way of saying that without a spiritual basis for his existence, he could no longer live. (Other types of physical activity are occasionally associated with this phrase. For example, reference is made to leaving and entering the city gates in general: "And Jericho had shut its gates and was barred because of the children of Israel-none went out and none came in." (Joshua 6:1))

Rashi's interpretation of 'going out and coming in' as having spiritual significance, can be applied to the same words, found in Psalm 121:

> *"I raise my eyes upon the mountains; whence will come my help?*
> *My help is from God, Maker of heaven and earth.*
> *He will not allow your foot to falter; your Guardian will not slumber.*
> *Behold, He neither slumbers nor sleeps -the Guardian of Israel.*
> *God is your guardian, God is your shade at your right hand.*
> *By day the sun will not harm you, nor the moon by night.*
> *God will protect you from every evil; He will guard your soul.*

God will guard your going out and your coming in,
from this time and forever."

The psalm provides consolation and is a reminder of God's constant protection, but these words also clarify the meaning of Moses' message to Israel. In describing the series of actions, the psalmist presents opposites that symbolize all activity that takes place within the space of life. (I wish to thank Rabbi Robert Tobin of Chizuk Amuno Congregation for pointing out the opposite actions that are described in the psalm, and for helping me to understand their significance.) Opposite images are evoked of valley and mountaintop, of sleep and wakefulness, of protecting and saving, and of night and day. By concluding in the final lines that God guards our souls, and that He guards our departure (tz'athah) and our arrival (boehah), the psalmist tells us that God guards all the physical and spiritual moments of our existence. (These actions would include leaving from Torah study to make a living and then returning at a later time (Targum), and leaving exile to enter the land (Radak).) It is living, with all of its diversity, from which Moses will be separated. He stands before the people of Israel and tells them that he can no longer participate in life, in the words of the psalm, "from this time and forever."

Moses speaks of his personal situation at a highly charged emotional moment for the entire nation. Their wanderings are about to come to an end, and they soon will place their feet upon the land for which they have yearned. Moses, however, will not be crossing into this land of promise. He will not be present for the next stage of "coming and going" of the people - he is about to be replaced. In contrast to the image we have of the entire nation—men and women, young and old, scholar and shepherd—noisily crossing the river to encounter their destiny, Moses will ascend Mount Nebo alone with God.

We sense from the text that the ability to 'go out and come in' is desirable, even necessary, to life. Regrettably, Moses had reached the day at which this action, no matter how it is interpreted, would not be possible. When we come to a place in our own lives when we can no longer 'go out and come in' in the accustomed manner, whether it is related to a physical activity or an emotional or spiritual situation, we must evaluate the circumstances. This evaluation is followed by change and by growth: it is, in fact, a time of crossing over into new territory. When Moses says that he can no longer "go out and come in," followed by the statement that he will not "cross this Jordan" with his people, he is telling them that he will not experience their own transformation. On that same day, at the moment of his death, Moses will experience a 'crossing over' of a different kind. (An additional commentary by Rashi is instructive on this point. Deuteronomy 28:6 says, "Blessed you shall be when you come in, and blessed you shall be when you go out."—which Rashi explains as meaning "may your departure from this world be as sinless as was your coming into the world.")

The reading of *Parashat Vayelech* often coincides with *Shabbat Shuvah*, which is between *Rosh Hashanah and Yom Kippur*. It is a time of the year when we examine our own "going and coming," so that we can repair relationships with God, with other people, and ultimately with ourselves. We attempt to return to a more righteous state. Over and over we remind ourselves of the need for 't'fillah, t'shuvah, tzedakah,'—prayer, repentance (return), and charity. Even the Haftorah associated with this parashah begins with the concept of shuvah: "Return, O Israel, unto the Lord your God..." Thus, and finally, we appreciate the fullness of Moses' impending circumstances, because *t'shuvah*, return, implicit in the sequence of events that involves going out and coming in, is one further activity in which Moses will no longer participate.

Susan Vick is the Curator of the Goldsmith Museum at Chizuk Amuno Congregation. She looks forward to a long a meaningful relationship with Rabbi Zaiman, to his ongoing support, and to an evolving exchange of ideas.

Haazinu
Rabbi Robert L. Tobin

> *"Give ear, O Heavens, and I will speak;*
> *And may the Earth hear the utterances of my mouth."*
> (Deuteronomy 32:1)

Moshe Rabbeinu opens his mouth at the end of his life and bursts forth with song. He is no longer the stutterer of his youth, afraid of the path upon which God set him at the burning bush. Here he stands before the people with his full days of service behind him, and the proof of God's faithfulness waiting just across the Jordan River for the people Israel to inherit. He knows where they are going, because he knows where he himself has been with them.

God's promise to Israel is as permanent as the heavens and the earth.

Said the Holy One, blessed be He, to Moses, "Say to Israel, 'Now look to the heavens, which I have created to serve you. Have they ever changed in quality or character? Has the orb of the sun announced, "I shall not rise in the east and give light to the entire world?... let the earth hear the words I utter!" Look at the earth, which I have created to serve you. Has it ever changed in quality or character? Have you ever sowed it, and it has not sprouted? Or have you ever sown wheat and had the earth produce barley?" (*Sifrei* to *Deuteronomy*, Pisqa 306)

Between heaven and earth lie the great sea and waters, and the world of our lives washes in waves against the shores of mortality that God has drawn for us. "And prescribe for it my decree, and set bars and doors and said, Thus far you shall come but no further, and here shall your proud waves stand still." (*Job* 38:10) "And though the waves toss themselves, yet they cannot prevail." (*Jeremiah* 5:22) Through trouble and turmoil we dance in the sea of Talmud, our lives a drop in the deep, and our souls springing up through the earth that we are formed from.

What is to be remembered of the fact that we passed this

way? What is the legacy of a man in history? "When I behold Your heavens, the work of Your fingers, the moon and stars that You set in place, what is man that You have been mindful of him, mortal man that You have taken note of him, that You have made him little less than divine, and adorned him with glory and majesty?" (*Psalms* 8:4-6)

It is to know that the passage of a man leaves footprints, and even though the footprints fill with the driving wind, the world has been changed by the man's walking. "The Rock!—perfect is His work, for all His paths are justice; a God of faith without iniquity, righteous and fair is He." (*Deuteronomy* 32:4)

Among God's works are Creation, the Torah and His people, and none exists fully without the others. "For He believed in the world and created it." (*Sifrei* to *Deuteronomy*, Pisqa 307) "For I have given a good doctrine to you, my Torah, do not abandon it." (*Proverbs* 4:2) "For you are a people consecrated to the Lord your God," (*Deuteronomy* 7:6) and " . . . the Lord set his heart on you." (*Deuteronomy* 7:7)

To live in the world, immerse oneself in living Torah, and love God's people is to embrace God's gifts. This is the only way for a Jew *qua* Jew to tap into eternity and be a full part of God's plan for human history. And Torah is the key that unlocks the potential for the Jewish soul.

"May my teaching drop like the rain, may my utterance flow like the dew; like storm winds upon vegetation and like raindrops upon blades of grass." (*Deuteronomy* 32:2) "Just as showers fall on grass and make it grow and develop, so words of Torah make you grow and develop." (*Sifrei* to *Deuteronomy*, Pisqa 306)

But this life of Torah is not selfish or narcissistic. It is a gift of wisdom and learning dedicated to others, that they may also live and derive sustenance from it.

R. Dosetai b. Judah says, "If you gather together teachings of the Torah the way people collect water in a waterhole, in the end you will acquire merit and see your learning endure, as it is said,

261

'Drink waters from your own well.' (*Proverbs* 5:5) But if you collect teachings of Torah the way people collect rain water, namely in publicly-available springs, ditches, and wells, in the end you will flow forth and give water to others, as it is said, 'And running waters out of your own well.' " (*Proverbs* 5:15)

"He set him atop the highlands, to feast on the yield of the earth; he fed him honey from the crag, and oil from the flinty rock." (*Deuteronomy* 32:13)

Yet growth is not always easy, nor is life always as sweet as honey. Torah takes hard work, and *mitzvot* are a yoke. "Sages say, "Moses said to Israel, 'Don't you know how much anguish I endured for the sake of the Torah, and how much labor I invested in it, and how much effort I poured into it? . . . Now just as I have learned it through much anguish, so you must learn it through anguish." (*Sifrei* to *Deuteronomy*, Pisqa 306)

What is the risk of abandoning Torah? It is more than just ignorance. The loss of Torah is the loss of Judaism's unique thread in the human tapestry that God is weaving. It is the loss of inheritance, the loss of place, like the evaporation of water from the sea of learning. The poem of Moshe Rabbeinu in *Parashat Ha-Azinu* warns of this: "You neglected the Rock that begot you, forgot the God Who brought you forth. The Lord saw and was vexed and spurned His sons and His daughters. He said, 'I will hide My countenance from them, and see how they fare in the end…" (*Deuteronomy* 32:18-20a)

Yet, "Remember the days of old, consider the years of ages past; ask your father, he will inform you, your elders, they will tell you…. For the Lord's portion is His people, Jacob His own allotment." (*Deuteronomy* 32:7, 9) As much as He is our God, we are His people.

No matter the circumstance we find ourselves in, God is present, watching, caring, supporting, and teaching. "He found him in a desert region, in an empty howling waste. He engirded him, watched over him, guarded him as the pupil of His eye. Like an eagle who rouses his nestlings, gliding down to his young, so did

He spread His wings and take him, bear him along on his pinions;
The Lord alone did guide him, No alien god at His side."
(*Deuteronomy* 32:10-12)

Moshe Rabbeinu spent his life in service to the people
Israel, as *'eved Ha-shem'* — a 'servant of God.' At the close of the
previous *parashah*, God informed him that "The time is drawing
near for you to die." (Deuteronomy 31:14) His response was not
to give up, but to teach. As he taught all his life, so he would teach
to the day that he could no longer serve the people.

What we hear in this *parashah* are some of Moshe
Rabbeinu's last words and, true to form, he does not speak of
himself. His own life has meaning from his acts, not his words.
What words are important to him are those words that he speaks
for God. He gathers the people as a whole and recites those words,
and he brings Joshua to him to make the transition complete.

Moshe shared God's vision, and placed it firmly in front of
the Children of Israel with every footprint in the desert. "And
when Moses finished reciting all these words to all Israel, he said to
them: 'Take to heart all the words with which I have warned you
this day. Enjoin them upon your children, that they may observe
faithfully all the terms of this Teaching. For this is not a trifling
thing for you: it is your very life; through it you shall endure on the
land that you are to possess upon crossing the Jordan."
(*Deuteronomy* 32:45-47)

In the end, it is once again the combination of the world,
the Torah, and the generations of Israel that gives his life meaning.
Each generation must be taught, and must teach. Each child must
have words of Torah to articulate their life in the Jewish frame.
Each Jew must have the history of our people clear in their heart to
find the strength to live, pray and die as a piece of God's Jewish
legacy.

To do this takes both a gathering and a gathering place. A
synagogue must be built, but it must have a vision. The *Beit
Kenesset* ("Gathering House") must also be a *Beit Midrash* ("House
of Study). It must be a place to pray, to learn, to grow, and to

teach. Gather the teachers and the pupils, and build them a school. Gather the community and build them a synagogue. Lead them in dreams and prayers.

The legacy of a teacher can best be judged in the mouths and lives of his or her pupils. "A person has to direct heart, eyes, and ears, to teachings of Torah. And so Scripture says, 'Son of man, set your heart and look with your eyes, and hear with your ears all that I say to you, and set your heart to entering the house.' (*Ezekiel* 44:5) He said to them, 'I have to be thankful to you for keeping the Torah after me, so you too must be thankful to your children for keeping the Torah after you.'" (*Sifrei* to *Deuteronomy*, Pisqa 335)

So, "Give ear, O Heavens, and I will speak; And may the Earth hear the utterances of my mouth" (*Deuteronomy* 32:1). "Gather to me all the elders of your tribes and your officials, that I may speak all these words to them and that I may call heaven and earth to witness . . . ." (Ibid. 31:28) "Tell your children about it, and let your children tell theirs, and their children, the next generation!" (*Joel* 1:3)

Robert L. Tobin is a Rabbi at Chizuk Amuno Congregation. Sharing pulpit and teaching duties with Rabbi Zaiman and Rabbi Deborah Wechsler, Rabbi Tobin is Rabbi-in-Residence to the Goldsmith Early Childhood Education Center at Chizuk Amuno and coordinates programs for the Young Adults/Young Families Committee.

Vezot HaBeracha
Dr. Arthur Lesley

This *parashah*, *VeZot HaBracha*, ends the book of *Devarim*, Deuteronomy, and the whole Torah, as well as Moses' life and his career as the transmitter of God's will to the stiff-necked people of Israel. The Humash began with the optimistic creation of a world that God delegated to the governance of a human species created in God's image, that was to be able independently to appreciate God's solitary creativity. Human history continued through steadily disillusioning stories of humans who were rebellious, greedy, silly, lustful, cruel, murderous, deceptive—a list longer than the recitation of *al het* on *Yom Kippur*.

Given everything they could want, let alone need, in the Garden of Eden, the first pair of humans violate the single prohibition in the world. As Ruler of the world and of this free and obstreperous humanity, God tries various remedies, as loving and conscientious parents do: warnings, rewards, punishments of increasing severity; but the humans keep acting like pre-schoolers, early adolescents, arrogant generation somethings, crotchety old geezers—like people.

Then God, recognizing the refractoriness of the "human material," tries to keep alive awareness of the original intention by selecting a vanguard of the populace, the descendants of the few conscientious people, Abraham's family, who will stay separate from the general corruption and exemplify for the others proper obedience to divine will.

But even in this favored group, the human impulses of sibling rivalry, selfishness, incompatibilities of gender and differences of love quickly distract the begats from the do's and don'ts. Joseph's brothers definitively end the family idyll and, in a first, disguised exile, discover God's beneficence in Joseph's survival and forgiveness. God makes them a people, rescues them from slavery, gives them liberating laws at Sinai and a faithful messenger and human interpreter, Moses, as the live-in representative of divinity. These ingenious attempts appear to solve the problem, for a few days.

The chips are still fresh off the stone tablets when the people nevertheless goes and makes its own shiny, lump of a calf, a more conventional and more manageable conception of a sun god —and Aaron ("you, too, are right, my children") helps them! Changing divinities is obviously out of the question, so God considers changing the people. Moses convinces God to keep this group—after all, there aren't any better people, and there is no guarantee that his own family would be an improvement. The winnowing of the people for 40 years in the desert is the next hope. The incident at Baal-Peor, near the end of *Bemidbar*, shows that the stiff-necked people, despite all the special attention that it has received, has still not become much better than the other peoples of the earth. And then Moses, the last best chance for divine rule of humans, must die.

What does Moses say to end his career, his life, the Humash, and this book of Devarim? What kind of summary could there be? Moses tells the people who they are, as tribes, the second time this happens in the Torah. Already in Jacob's death-bed scene, at the end of *Bereshit*, a poem named each son by an emblem of his character. Then, in *Haazinu*, the *parashah* just before this one, the nation of Israel heard again how God had been generous to them and how, nevertheless "Jeshurun grew fat and kicked" (Deut. 32:15) and God acknowledged in exasperation, so to speak, "For they are a folk devoid of sense, devoid of all discernment." (Deut. 32:28) Now in *VeZot HaBracha*, the final parashah, Moses repeats the naming of the separate tribes who are the descendants of Jacob's children.

The way that Moses blesses the Israelites, after all they have endured together, has disturbed me. He tells them who they are as tribes, using some of the same poetic phrases and animal metaphors that Jacob applied to his sons. "All these were the tribes

266

of Israel, twelve in number, and this is what their father said to them as he bade them farewell, addressing to each a parting word appropriate to him," *Ish asher kevirkato berakh otam*. (Genesis 49:28) Moses' blessing differs from Jacob's in several ways: Simeon is omitted and Moses says about several tribes what Jacob had said about different sons. Are Moses' blessings descriptions of character of the tribes' collective identities? Or are they predictions of their behavior? And are his parting words "to each . . . appropriate to him?"

More particularly, I am bothered by the animal metaphors that both Moses and Jacob used, and even more surprised that Moses used them than that Jacob did. When Jacob used frequent animal comparisons to characterize and name his sons, he was perhaps first giving them their coats of arms, which could become tribal emblems. But Moses has tried to turn the tribes into a unified people, organized along the lines of the tribes, but all witnesses to the revelation at Sinai, all subject to divine law, and all experienced in the travail and the miracles of leaving Egypt and of wandering in the desert. Why does Moses now remind them of their separate tribal identities, often through the animal totems? The wolf, viper, wild ass, donkey, and even the gazelle in the tribal emblems are reductive, if apparently flattering, characterizations of tribal groups of human beings, who might instead have been called "little lower than the angels," made "in the image of God," and given dominion over all the beasts.

Perhaps I am troubled by these blessings and their animal images because in the United States Orioles and Ravens, Bears and Hawks, Terrapins and Raptors, Timberwolves and Rattlers are common emblems of commercial sporting teams. Most of these names are taken from powerful, violent animals and birds. The zeal with which apparently normal adults take on the identities of these animals, to the point of costume and impersonation, is worrisome. The names that teams adopt are completely arbitrary and vacuous, merely play. And for the most part, these names suggest the assertion of aggressive, violent impulses that the real teams to which we belong—Commuters, Lawyers, Soccer Moms, Pensioners, Teachers, Garbagemen, Deliverymen, Process-Servers—must never express openly. The playful return of the repressed impulses through these team emblems allows us to expose and stretch the claws that must be retracted in everyday business, so that we can acceptably prowl, menace, roar at, and pounce on our neighbors. Homo homini lupus. Man is a wolf to man. Also women.

The Israeli poet, Yehuda Amichai, called attention to the widespread adoption of such symbols in the modern world: "Beasts of prey are prominent on most emblems: there are lions and eagles and bulls and hawks and all sorts of other predators." He goes on to uncover the same flaw in sacred things: "In the synagogue they have a pair of lions holding up the Tablets over the Holy Ark. Even our own laws, too, can only be kept and preserved by wild beasts." It is disturbing, then, that Moses reminds the Israelites of these subhuman emblems that the tribes are so eager to accept, as if to approve of them. Why flatter the base instincts of the tribes, both their divisive identities and their desire to see themselves as potentially ravenous beasts? It is customary to interpret the reiteration of tribal names and the images that characterize them as something that should make them proud. But this flattering of ancient Israelite tribal loyalty through mention of their totems seems to me to be dubious praise for human beings. If the repetition of the names and characteristic animal emblems of the tribes is not flattering, but insulting, or at least sarcastic, why does it appear?

I think that the answer is connected to one other traditional question about this parashah. Moses is called here, for the first and only time, "man of God," *Ish hae*lohim." Commentators have asked why, and what the epithet means. It is reminiscent of a few other mentions of Moses' character. He is called "the most humble of all men on the face of the earth," (Bemidbar / Numbers 12:3) and "trusted throughout My (God's) household." (Bemidbar / Numbers 12:7) These passages reinforce each other to characterize him. I think that *Ish haelohim* is meant to contrast Moses with the rest of the Israelites, with their animal emblems. He is the one who numerous times has been told what God wanted him to say, and who has said it to the people just as he was told.

With Moses gone, even with the Torah, the people has the potential to undo all the gains and to subvert all the remedies that they have received for human proclivities to selfishness, stupidity, hatred and forgetfulness. When God first told Moses that he would soon die, Moses immediately replied, "Let the Lord, source of the breath of all flesh, appoint someone over the community who shall go out before them and come in before them, and who shall take them out and bring them in, so that the Lord's community may not be like sheep that have no shepherd." (Bemidbar / Numbers 27:16-17) In his reflexive responsibility, Moses does not complain about dying, but immediately thinks of the good of the people. They must not be left passive, helpless sheep, mild animals, just as they also should not be other animals, the wolves, wild asses and lion's whelps who are dangerous to themselves and to others. Moses emphasizes their need for governance by naming the gentlest of animals, but hints at less governable beasts. God has Moses appoint Joshua to be the shepherd of the people.

So why, when the time comes to die, does Moses remind the people of their less peaceable animal emblems?

The Israelites are going to divide the Promised Land by tribes, but they must remember the Torah and their shared experience in the desert; they must subdue their constant inclination to be beasts. Through Moses, God is speaking frankly, reminding them how they are descended from Joseph and his less than fraternal brothers and how they have acted as tribes. God realistically addresses them through the tribal animal emblems that they consider their most flattering conceptions of themselves, as if to say, "I know you, children of Israel. You want to think of yourselves as lions and wild asses, powerful animals, even though you are more like sheep; that is why I have given you the Torah through your shepherd, the one fully human member of the people,

'*Ish haelohim*,' and have chosen another shepherd to continue leading you."

This *parashah*, *VeZot HaBracha*, closes the Torah, the first stage of God's perpetual effort to encourage people to act truly like the humans that were first created, rather than like beasts.

Arthur Lesley has been a congregant at Chizuk Amuno for most of the past fifteen years, when he has been a professor of Hebrew language and literature at Baltimore Hebrew University. He recalls first hearing Rabbi Zaiman preach in Providence, RI on Shabbat Hannuka, 1975.

Biography of
Rabbi Joel H. Zaiman

Rabbi Joel H. Zaiman served as Rabbi of Temple Emanu El of Providence, Rhode Island, before coming to Chizuk Amuno Congregation in the summer of 1980. He and his wife, Ann, are the parents of three children, Elana, Sarina, and Ari.

On the national level, Rabbi Zaiman serves the Rabbinical Assembly, the Conservative Movement and the greater Jewish community in many capacities. He has served as President of the Synagogue Council of America, as Chairman of the United Synagogue Commission on Jewish Education, and as a member of The Rabbinical Assembly's Executive Council.

In his twenty years at Chizuk Amuno, he has been president of both the Baltimore Jewish Council and the Baltimore Board of Rabbis. He is currently chair of the Catholic Dialogue for the Rabbinic Assembly, a member of the Chancellor's Rabbinic Cabinet at the Jewish Theological Seminary of America, a member of the Rabbinical Advisory Council for United Jewish Appeal and Israel Bonds. He serves on the Board of the Institute for Christian and Jewish Studies, and is Chairman of the Education Committee of Krieger Schechter Day School of Chizuk Amuno Congregation, the Conservative Jewish Day School he helped to found in 1981.

As Rabbi of "The Education Congregation," Rabbi Zaiman has helped to institute a variety of childhood and adult education programs at Chizuk Amuno, including the award-winning Stulman Center for Adult Learning. He is also credited with bringing the Florence Melton Adult Mini-School of the Hebrew University of

Jerusalem to the congregation, making Chizuk Amuno the first congregation to house the internationally renowned adult education school. Taking a hands-on approach to Jewish education, Rabbi Zaiman teaches students of all ages at Chizuk Amuno Congregation.

His impact on the spiritual and religious development of his congregants, colleagues, and family is apparent throughout the pages of Find Yourself a Teacher. This celebratory volume is a testament to his dedication to Torah and Jewish learning.

How Judaism Reads the Bible
Professor Jacob Neusner

In asking how Judaism reads the Bible, I spell out the way in which, in the normative documents of Judaism, the Mishnah, the Talmuds, and the Midrash-compilations, Scripture—the Hebrew Scriptures of ancient Israel—becomes Torah, that is, a statement of, an event in, the life of holy Israel with God. For in the faith of holy Israel assembled in the synagogue to hear the Torah and to say prayers, Torah comes to realization in acts of teaching and of learning. Torah-learning finds definition not in intellect alone, in a search for information, for example, about the dead past. Study of Torah forms an act of conscience, character, and conviction, a quest for God in those writings that, in our religion, we maintain convey to us God's will and God's purpose. So, as I shall explain, instead of the secular categories, "Judaism" and "reading" and "the Bible," I invoke different categories. I answer the question, how, in Torah-study, do we, holy Israel of whom the Torah speaks, find in Scripture and tradition what God wishes to tell us today, this minute. As we shall see, for the sages who, in the tradition of Torah revealed by God to Moses at Sinai, studied and taught Torah, the Torah is received as a letter God writes this morning to the here and now of our particular condition: a letter to be taken very, very personally. For, to define matters simply, studying the Torah carries us in search of truth for our circumstance in that revelation of Sinai that the Torah — Scripture, the Mishnah, the Talmuds, the Midrash-compilations all together — presents to us as the heritage of God's meeting with Moses our rabbi.

I.
CELEBRATING A RABBI'S TORAH

This is the right time and the right place to ask so fundamental a question: an event defined to celebrate a rabbi's Torah. That is because rabbis are not professors of Jewish studies or social workers in Jewish agencies, though they are learned like professors and organize community affairs like social workers. Unlike professors, they are rightly expected to profess, not merely to inform; to persuade, to advocate, not merely to enlighten, above all, to exemplify and advocate, not merely to preside and analyze. Unlike social workers they bring to leadership not merely an open-ended agenda of effective action but a very particular set of commitments. They are not Jewish in general, but rabbinical-Judaic in particular. For rabbis synagogues and Torah-study form not only means to an end but a well-defined goal, defined out of the resources of Judaism: commandment, not culture. Specifically, rabbis in the community stand for Judaism, the religion, and not merely for Jewish identity, for Torah as God's message and holy Israel's identification, not merely for Jewish ethnicity. For rabbis, as for Judaism, the continuity of a group, the Jewish community, is not an end in itself. Rabbis serve through the Torah that they teach, in word and in deed. The measure of their success comes to expression in how their disciples, who are the members of the congregation that they serve, grasp the requirements of Torah.

By that criterion, Rabbi Zaiman may derive satisfaction in his twenty years of service. That Chizuk Amuno has asked me to prepare a lesson of Torah — not history, not sociology, not even systematic analysis of theology but Torah — forms the only tribute that, because he is an authentic rabbi, Rabbi Zaiman can accept. That is because the form of this celebration accords with what the Torah requires: to bring honor to the Torah, not to oneself. Specifically, "if you have studied much Torah, do not take pride in that fact, for it was to that end that you were created." Rabbi Zaiman has worked for twenty years that. through him. the Torah find an honorable embodiment, a worthy model for this generation in this time and in this place. You have responded in the only way that matters: as "doing a religious duty brings about doing another religious duty," so study of Torah brings its own reward, which is more and better study of Torah. That defines the challenge set by the Congregation to me. For this occasion, then, I will pay my tribute to Rabbi Zaiman through what I set forth as a lesson in Torah; I will not talk about him; this event bears its own message.

About him I will only tell you this: Rabbi Zaiman comes from the prior Rabbi Zaiman, his father, whom I knew and of whom I can speak, and Rabbi Zaiman's life has been lived as a tribute to the model of that master of Torah who was his father and as a tribute too to his father's counterpart, also an embodiment of Torah, his mother. More praise than that no one has coming in the setting of the nobility of the Torah, from which he descends.

How, then, to realize your resolve of honoring a rabbi in a rabbinical way? It is to show your rabbi what he has achieved by doing yourself what he, as your model, has done for these twenty years. In this congregation, through the coming year, you have determined to celebrate your Rabbi's service by taking up his task and showing what he has taught you by doing the same work on your own. He will then have been your model, just as he drew upon models in Torah-learning. How Rabbi Zaiman studied the Torah in the setting of synagogue worship is how he was taught the Torah in synagogue and in school and in Rabbinical seminary. And that is, Torah as taught by the sages of the Mishnah, Talmuds, and Midrash. My task is to explain to you what he does that some here are going to do, to specify how in the synagogue we receive the Torah week by week, lesson by lesson, as our sages mediate the Torah to us. What I wish now to spell out is how, in the normative and definitive documents of the religion that the world calls "Judaism" and that we call "the Torah," Scripture is received and interpreted and set forth.

II
A SECULAR TITLE FOR A RELIGIOUS MESSAGE

My title, "How Judaism Reads the Bible," intentionally misleads. It is a secular title for a religious message.

275

That is, first, because we in Judaism do not read *"the Bible,"* which is a category of Christianity, not Judaism, and which encompasses what they call "the Old Testament" and "the New Testament." So Judaism does not read "the Bible" — rather, the Torah, by which we mean, God's Teaching.

Second, the title misleads because Judaism does not *"read"* the Torah. The Judaism that we affirm and practice speaks of "Torah-study," not "Bible-reading," and in its classical sources that Torah-study finds very specific definition. We use the language, Talmud Torah, which compares to, but is not the same as, secular study.

Third, if I eliminate from the title "reads" and "the Bible," what is left is "Judaism," and that word serves only as approximately as do "reads" and "the Bible." For "Judaism" stands for pretty much anything any Jew wants it to mean. That is why it is a useless term for the synagogue. Instead of the construction, "Torah did Moses command us," thus "the Torah of Moses," people accept the construction, "my Judaism," as in, "my Judaism teaches" or "...does not require...." So by "Judaism" one can say everything and its opposite. Then what does our religion call itself — for we do not find the word "Judaism" in any of our normative writings, not in Scripture, not in the Mishnah, the Talmuds, or the Midrash-compilations. The word, that we do find, in Judaism, for "Judaism" is none other than "Torah." That encompassing word defines the native category.

When, in the living religion of the synagogue, we wish to speak of the whole of the faith, all its teachings, all together and all at once, we use the word "Torah." Then, if we wish in that same setting to point to our religion, we point to the Torah, an object that serves as embodiment and symbol of all things. So the question becomes, how does holy Israel study — meet God today — in the Torah of Moses that God reveals at Sinai, God whose unity and dominion we accept when we proclaim the Shema?

276

III

How, in Many Synagogues, the Faithful Encounter the Torah:
The Historical Apologetics of Joseph Hertz

Let me start with the known and proceed to the unknown. How, today, in English-speaking synagogues, including Chizuk Amuno, does Judaism read the Torah, that is, how do people encounter Scripture? The answer is, in general, Scripture is portrayed as a one-time historical account of something that really happened; it is defended as reliable by reason of its historical accuracy; it is assessed in terms of historicity. And it is explained in terms of its allegedly original, supposedly historical, setting, long ago and far away: what the original writer meant in the moment of his writing. And by "original writer" God's instruction and Moses's writing — these are rarely meant.

If I had to point to the single most commonly-cited approach to the Torah in synagogue settings of Conservative Judaism, it would be Joseph Hertz's commentary to the Pentateuch. It defines the starting point for Torah-study, because when people hear the Torah declaimed, they follow in the Hertz *Chumash*, and when people prepare a lesson of the Torah, they open Hertz's commentary. But that commentary has two goals, both defined outside the framework of faith. They are, first, to prove that the scriptural narrative is historically reliable, second, to defend the morality of the events portrayed by Scripture. This is done without appeal to a tradition of interpretation — mediation of Scripture to the faithful — represented by Mishnah, Talmud, Midrash — the oral Torah. Those who recall the Qaraite Judaism of early medieval times, which accepted the authority of the written but not the oral Torah, will think of Hertz as a Rabbi of the Qaraite tendency, with his one-dimensional, historical-moralistic reading of an unmediated Scripture. Hertz typifies much of "Bible-scholarship" under Conservative, Reform, and secular auspices: neo-Qaraism in academic garb.

277

What focussed Hertz's attention where it lies? It was his determination to answer liberal-Protestant "Bible criticism," with its debunking of scriptural narrative and its supercilious dismissal of the Torah's morality — and its blatant anti-Semitism and shameless anti-Judaism. When he became chief rabbi of the British Empire, Joseph Hertz determined to meet the crisis by hitting head on the Protestant challenge to the Hebrew Scriptures and their historicity and morality.[1] The liberal Protestant theologians maintained that the Scriptures are not (historically) true, and the religion they set forth is (morally) inferior to the supersessionist Christianity that animated their reading of the Bible. He also took as his task to answer Reform and Liberal Judaism in its British formulation, arguing against its critique of ritual in the name of morality and its articulated policy of compromise and conciliation with (liberal) Christianity. The result was a commentary, the Hertz *Pentateuch*, with its polemics against liberal Protestant anti-Judaism and against Liberal Judaic anti-Orthodox-Judaism.

What Hertz — and through him, much of contemporary Judaism amply represented at meetings of the Society of Biblical Literature today and in the publications of the Jewish Publication Society of America — does therefore is to buy into the liberal-Protestant framing of issues, so he focussed heavily on the historicity of the Torah's narratives. Now, if the issue is, [1] it really happened *or* it didn't really happen, [2] ancient Israel was unique *or* ancient Israel was part and parcel of the ancient Near East — the issue as the Protestant historicists set matters forth in their own context and in ours as well — then the point of declaiming the Torah and studying it is missed. That acutely contemporary reading of Scripture rejects twenty-five hundred years of tradition and a wholly different approach to matters, a different

---

[1] See Harvey Warren Meirovich, *A Vindication of Judaism: The Polemics of the Hertz Pentateuch.* New York and Jerusalem, 1998: The Jewish Theological Seminary of America.

278

way of identifying what matters from the historical one. Hertz had in mind an apologetics against liberal-Protestant "Bible-criticism." But the synagogue in its authentic being is hardly well served by a rehearsal of such an apologetics. The reason is not that Hertz is wrong, but that he is monumentally irrelevant. His commentary misconstrues the Torah in favor of "the Bible" as liberal-Protestant Christianity defined matters.

For Holy Israel at prayer meets God in eternity and receives the Torah as the paradigm, the pattern that conveys God's will for humanity. That is why, win or lose, Hertz's entire framing of matters was simply beside the point. For the Torah is not history and it is not culture. For us, holy Israel, for Judaism, the Torah is God's word. And, by definition, that is to be received as a design for the human condition, not as the record of one-time, one-dimensional events of a secular, historical character. To the discussion of whether or not the Torah is God's revelation to Moses, historical and archaeological facts simply do not register. They do not bear upon the issues of faith, because religion is not history, it is story. And for the synagogue, the Torah speaks in the present, not the past tense: it is proclaimed every time the scrolls are displayed and the community of holy Israel proclaims, "This is the Torah that Moses set before the children of Israel at the command of God." And in the context of the living faith of holy Israel, the Torah is not the story of what happened only once. It is the presentation, through narrative, of eternal truth.

To Judaism realized in synagogue worship and Torah-study, therefore, archaeology proves nothing worth knowing. It is not going to find Eden or Noah's ark, and history cannot evaluate the tangible evidence of the voice of silence that Elijah heard or uncover the cleft in the rock where God sheltered Moses. The Torah, the written mediated by the oral, makes a coherent, systematic statement. But, oblivious of the theological system of Judaism's dual Torah, oral and written, abandoning the oral part altogether except as a source of occasional aperçus, Hertz got it wrong. Specifically, he had not the perspicacity to realize, in

279

engaging with the liberal-Protestant and Reform-Judaic enemy, he was marching onto the battlefield of their choice. He was using weapons they had shaped for their purpose and to their advantage. Historicism, or historical criticism, was originally shaped, within Judaism, as a weapon for Reform Judaism to use against Orthodoxy and for the liberal-Protestant assault on Roman Catholic and Orthodox Christianity and (today) on Evangelical Protestantism alike. Arguments about historical fact therefore did not present a felicitous choice for the defense of the Judaism that in synagogue worship proclaims, "This is the Torah that Moses set...at God's command."

Hertz's basically-historical commentary defies its context, which is the encounter with God in synagogue celebration. For this "Pentateuch" for synagogue use, in its focus on ancient Near Eastern realia, did not even pretend to acknowledge, let alone match its setting in piety. That comes at the moment of full realization of life with God sustained by revelation, when we sing, "this is the Torah...!" To that climactic declaration as the Torah is declaimed, how do the opinions of Driver or Kuenen or Wellhausen pertain? Then in the pews out comes the Hertz Pentateuch, to guide the hearing of the declaimed Torah of God by fulminating against Wellhausen. Invoking "Bible-critics'" authority in support of God's word proves equally beside the point of the occasion. What incongruity! For the (historical, cultural) Scripture that Hertz defended was the Protestant "Old Testament," read as pretty much straight, linear secular history — that and not the Torah of Judaism. That Torah — the Torah holy Israel studies, not the Bible Judaism reads — set forth its own system and structure. That is what formed the natural setting of the written Torah within the profound reading thereof that the oral Torah undertakes. Hertz therefore presented a Judaism in accord with the Protestant fundamentalist framing of matters, that is, the Protestant's uninterpreted, historical record. What is wrong with Hertz is that he does not assign to the Torah that standing proud and unique, congruous with its own proportions and coherence and rationality, that our sages accorded to the Torah.

So the Pentateuch that Hertz presented for synagogue use, for generations of pious and faithful Jews at worship, is not the Written Torah of Judaism, joined for its full and complete meaning with the Oral Torah and presented as a document of a coherent religious system and theological structure. Hertz with his imitators offers, rather, a disproportionate, disjointed, and disagreeable defense of positions never fully set forth in their own right and context, attention to niggling little issues of whether so-and-so really said what Wellhausen said he never said, whether such-and-such a battle was truly just. That the Torah that Hertz represented could not make its statement in such a context becomes clear in the quite desiccated character of Hertz's commentary — disjointed and incoherent. The mark of a true commentary is that it leads us deeper into the Torah. But could we, from Hertz, construct the Judaic religious structure and system in its classical formulation that defines the Torah the world calls Judaism? I think not. From the pages of his commentary one would scarcely suspect that a vast, encompassing, elaborate hermeneutics, that of the sages of the Mishnah, Midrash, and Talmud, has taken over Scripture and transformed the whole into a structure and a system of sublime and transcendent dimensions. Hertz shaped a commentary to address a religious situation of doubt and despair, in which intellectual uncertainty he himself obviously participated. That accounts for the disfiguring vehemence of his rather facile, shallow responses to the enemy, without and within.

But the Judaism that privileges the Pentateuch does so in the context of the Torah, oral and written, and reads the Pentateuch as not the secular history of a small, unimportant nation but as the foundations of the system and structure of God's dominion: Halakhah and Aggadah fused into the design for the social order of the kingdom of priests and the holy people destined for eternal life beyond the grave. That is not the religion for which Hertz formed his apologetics and polemics, and it is not the

281

religion that he served as the first alumnus of the Jewish Theological Seminary of America. But it is the religion of Judaism, as our sages defined it for eternity.

IV
IF NOT HISTORY, THEN WHAT?

If Hertz, and the populous tradition of Scripture-exegesis along one-shot, historical lines represented by Hertz, does not provide us with the right model for receiving the Torah and teaching the Torah in the setting of the faithful of holy Israel in the synagogue, what then? Here I advocate a fresh encounter with an alternative model of how "Judaism" has read and now should "read" "the Bible." It is another approach to the matter of Torah-study altogether, different from the historical one — and one that faithful Israel has taken from the very formation of Scripture itself![2] Other issues than whether the story "really" happened or why, by our standards, the ancients took one position rather than another should precipitate thought, and other questions than those of secular historicity should demand answers. But what these other issues and questions are, and how we are to locate them, remain to be spelled out.

To introduce this other approach, let me start by citing in extreme form a statement of that position that Hertz addressed, the one that regards Scripture as a source of historical fact — bearing self-evident implications of a secular nature:

> A major part of any course in Old Testament is the study of the history of Israel...the fact that [the history of the Israelite people] constituted the context out of which the Scriptures of the Old Testament emerged gives it special significance...How can we really appreciate the messages of the Old Testament authors unless we are

---

[2] For the interpretation of Scripture within Scripture itself, see Michael A. Fishbane, *Biblical interpretation in ancient Israel* (New York: Oxford University Press, 1984).

familiar with the situations which produced them and to
which they were addressed?

George W. Ramsey[3]

The answer to Professor Ramsey's question given by many
centuries of Judaic (and Christian) exegetes of the Hebrew
Scriptures — from ancient Israelite times to our own day in fact —
is, "Without the intervention of secular history, we of holy Israel
appreciate the messages of the Torah very well indeed — just as we
have in the millennia since God gave us the Torah, thank you very
much!"

Without the slightest familiarity with the situations that
produced the laws and stories of Scripture and to which to begin
with they are addressed, we have no difficulty whatsoever in
appreciating the messages of Scripture. That is because in the
synagogue we receive the Torah in the present tense: it takes place
today, when declaimed at the moment at hand. For in fact Judaic
(and Christian) faithful through the ages take as premise that it is
to us and to the faithful of all times and places that the ancient
Israelite Scriptures were and are addressed. God does not speak to
Moses of one generation only, but of all generations to come. That
is the fundamental premise of Judaism, and it explains why we
privilege the Pentateuch to begin with. But that means, for holy
Israel in the synagogue no boundary of time distinguished past
from present; time was understood in a completely different way.
Within the conception of time that formed holy Israel's
consciousness and culture, the past forms a perpetual presence, the
present takes place on the plane of the past, and no lines of
structure or order distinguish the one from the other.

Notice the contrast. History provides one way of marking
time. It is linear, one-dimensional, one-directional. But there are
other ways of marking time, and the encounter with Scripture
embodied in the Mishnah, Talmuds, and Midrash defines one such

---

[3]George W. Ramsey, *The Question for the Historical Israel. Reconstructing
Israel's Early History* (London, 1982: SCM Press), p. xii.

alternative. This other model for receiving the Torah ("reading the Bible") I call a pattern, or paradigm, because by this model interpretation of Scripture appeals for sense to a pattern or paradigm, which imposes meaning and order on things that happened. Hence paradigmatic modes of thought in the worship of the synagogue take the place of historical ones. Thinking by means of paradigms yields a conception of time that elides past and present. It removes all barriers between them, in fact governs the reception of Scripture in Judaism and Christianity until nearly our own time. At stake are [1] a conception of time different from the historical one and [2] premises on how to take the measure of time that form a legitimate alternative to those that define the foundations of the historical way of measuring time. The difference is how time is marked and what the marks signify, so I propose briefly[4] to spell out that difference between historical and paradigmatic thinking and to specify what is at stake in the difference. Now to make concrete this other way of thinking, the paradigmatic way.

V

AN EXAMPLE OF PARADIGMATIC THINKING IN JUDAISM

Judaism reads the Bible by transforming the narrative of Scripture into a pattern that applies to times past as much as to the acutely contemporary world and interprets this morning's newspaper in the light of that paradigm of how things are and what they mean. For Judaism, the past is present, and the present is part of the past, so past, present, and future form a single plane of being. These are matters I shall unpack and spell out. Let me to begin with give a very simple example of this approach to the record of Scripture as a model, much as, in mathematics, we construct models of reality. The character of paradigmatic time is captured in the following,

---

[4] I do so at length in *The Presence of the Past, the Pastness of the Present. History, Time, and Paradigm in Rabbinic Judaism.* Bethesda, 1996: CDL Press.

which encompasses the entirety of Israel's being (its "history" in conventional language) within the conversation that is portrayed between Boaz and Ruth; I abbreviate the passage to highlight only the critical components:

Ruth Rabbah Parashah Five

XL:i.1.A. "And at mealtime Boaz said to her, 'Come here and eat some bread, and dip your morsel in the wine.' So she sat beside the reapers, and he passed to her parched grain; and she ate until she was satisfied, and she had some left over":

B. R. Yohanan interpreted the phrase "come here" in six ways:

C. "The first speaks of David.

D. "'Come here': means, to the throne: 'That you have brought me here' (2 Sam. 7:18).

E. "'...and eat some bread': the bread of the throne.

F. "'...and dip your morsel in vinegar': this speaks of his sufferings: 'O Lord, do not rebuke me in your anger' (Ps. 6:2).

G. "'So she sat beside the reapers': for the throne was taken from him for a time."

I. [Resuming from G:] "'and he passed to her parched grain': he was restored to the throne: 'Now I know that the Lord saves his anointed' (Ps. 20:7).

J. "'...and she ate and was satisfied and left some over': this indicates that he would eat in this world, in the days of the messiah, and in the age to come.

2. A. "The second interpretation refers to Solomon: 'Come here': means, to the throne.

B. "'...and eat some bread': this is the bread of the throne: "And Solomon's provision for one day was thirty measures of fine flour and three score measures of meal' (1 Kgs. 5:2).

C. "'...and dip your morsel in vinegar': this refers to the dirty of the deeds [that he did].

D. "'So she sat beside the reapers': for the throne was taken from him for a time."

G. [Reverting to D:] "'and he passed to her parched grain': for he was restored to the throne.

H. "'...and she ate and was satisfied and left some over': this indicates that he would eat in this world, in the days of the messiah, and in the age to come.

3. A. "The third interpretation speaks of Hezekiah: 'Come here': means, to the throne.

B. "'...and eat some bread': this is the bread of the throne.

C. "'...and dip your morsel in vinegar': this refers to sufferings [Is. 5:1]: 'And Isaiah said, Let them take a cake of figs' (Is. 38:21).

D. "'So she sat beside the reapers': for the throne was taken from him for a time: 'Thus says Hezekiah, This day is a day of trouble and rebuke' (Is. 37:3).

E. "'...and he passed to her parched grain': for he was restored to the throne: 'So that he was exalted in the sight of all nations from then on' (2 Chr. 32:23).

F. "'...and she ate and was satisfied and left some over': this indicates that he would eat in this world, in the days of the messiah, and in the age to come.

4. A. "The fourth interpretation refers to Manasseh: 'Come here': means, to the throne.

B. "'...and eat some bread': this is the bread of the throne.

C. "'...and dip your morsel in vinegar': for his dirty deeds were like vinegar, on account of wicked actions.

D. "'So she sat beside the reapers': for the throne was taken from him for a time: 'And the Lord spoke to Manasseh and to his people, but they did not listen. So the Lord brought them the captains of the host of the king of Assyria, who took Manasseh with hooks' (2 Chr. 33:10-11)."

K. [Reverting to D:] "'and he passed to her parched grain': for he was restored to the throne: 'And brought him back to Jerusalem to his kingdom' (2 Chr. 33:13).

N. "'...and she ate and was satisfied and left some over': this indicates that he would eat in this world, in the days of the messiah, and in the age to come.

5. A. "The fifth interpretation refers to the Messiah: 'Come here': means, to the throne.

B. "'...and eat some bread': this is the bread of the throne.

C. "'...and dip your morsel in vinegar': this refers to suffering: 'But he was wounded because of our transgressions' (Is. 53:5).

D. "'So she sat beside the reapers': for the throne is destined to be taken from him for a time: For I will gather all nations against Jerusalem to battle and the city shall be taken' (Zech. 14:2).

E. "'...and he passed to her parched grain': for he will be restored to the throne: 'And he shall smite the land with the rod of his mouth' (Is. 11:4)."

I. [reverting to G:] "so the last redeemer will be revealed to them and then hidden from them."

The paradigm here may be formed of six units: [1] David's monarchy; [2] Solomon's reign; [3] Hezekiah's reign; [4] Manasseh's reign; [5] the Messiah's reign. So paradigmatic time compresses events to the dimensions of its model. All things happen on a single plane of time. Past, present, future are undifferentiated, and that is why a single action contains within itself an entire account of Israel's social order under the aspect of eternity.

The foundations of the paradigm, of course, rest on the fact that David, Solomon, Hezekiah, Manasseh, and therefore also, the Messiah, all descend from Ruth's and Boaz's union. Then, within the framework of the paradigm, the event that is described here — "And at mealtime Boaz said to her, 'Come here and eat some bread, and dip your morsel in the wine.' So she sat beside the reapers, and he passed to her parched grain; and she ate until she was satisfied, and she had some left over" — forms not an event but a pattern. The pattern transcends time; or more accurately, aggregates of time, the passage of time, the course of events — these are all simply irrelevant to what is in play in Scripture. Rather we have a tableau,[5] joining persons who lived at widely separated moments, linking them all as presences at this simple exchange between Boaz and Ruth; imputing to them all, whenever they came into existence, the shape and structure of that simple moment: the presence of the past, for David, Solomon, Hezekiah, and so on, but the pastness of the present in which David or Solomon — or the Messiah for that matter — lived or would

---

[5]For the notion of the representation of Israel's existence as an ahistorical tableau, see my *Judaism. The Evidence of the Mishnah.* Chicago, 1981: University of Chicago Press. Paperback edition: 1984. Second printing, 1985. Third printing, 1986. Second edition, augmented: Atlanta, 1987: Scholars Press for Brown Judaic Studies.

live (it hardly matters, verb tenses prove hopelessly irrelevant to paradigmatic thinking).

VI
TRANSFORMING HISTORICAL NARRATIVES INTO EXEMPLARY PATTERNS

Now, with the case in hand, let me offer a more systematic presentation of how Judaism reads the Bible. The Hebrew Scriptures of ancient Israel ("the written Torah," to Judaism and "the Old Testament" to Christianity), all scholarship concurs, set forth Israel's life as history, with a beginning, middle, and end; a purpose and a coherence; a teleological system. All accounts agree that Scriptures distinguished past from present, present from future and composed a sustained narrative, made up of one-time, irreversible events. All maintain that, in Scripture's historical portrait, Israel's present condition appealed for explanation to Israel's past, perceived as a coherent sequence of weighty events, each unique, all formed into a great chain of meaning.

But that is not how for most of the history of Western civilization the Hebrew Scriptures were read by Judaism and Christianity. The idea of history, with its rigid distinction between past and present and its careful sifting of connections from the one to the other, came quite late onto the scene of intellectual life. Both Judaism and Christianity for most of their histories have read the Hebrew Scriptures in an other-than-historical framework. They found in Scripture's words paradigms of an enduring present, by which all things must take their measure; they possessed no conception whatsoever of the pastness of the past. So let us consider the full and detailed character of the paradigmatic approach to the explanation of Israel's condition, viewed (to state the negative side of matters) atemporally, ahistorically, episodically, and not through sustained narrative or its personal counterpart, biography, composed of connected, one-time and unique, irreversible events, in the manner of history.

288

The art of the West embodies this other reading of matters. Visually, we grasp the ahistorical perception in the union of past and present that takes place through representation of the past in the forms of the present: the clothing, the colors, the landscapes of the familiar world. But that is mere anachronism, which history can tolerate. Conceptually, we understand their mode of receiving Scripture when we understand that, for our sages of Judaism, as for the saints and sages of Christianity, the past took place in the acutely present tense of today, but the present found its locus in the presence of the ages as well. And that is something historical thinking cannot abide. Not only so, but it contradicts the most fundamental patterns of explanation that we ordinarily take for granted in contemporary cultural life.

Historicism for two hundred years has governed Reform, Conservative and academic Judaism. It defines how "Bible" is taught at Hebrew Union College and the Jewish Theological Seminary and the Reconstructionist Rabbinical College, and it dictates the presentation of Scripture in college and university courses as well. That is why our conception of history forms a barrier between us and the understanding of Scripture and of time that defined the Judaic and the Christian encounter with ancient Israel. The givenness of the barrier between time now and time then yields for us banalities about anachronism, on the one side, and imposes upon us the requirement of mediating between historical fact and religious truth, on the other — hence the approach to scriptural commentary taken by Hertz and a whole century of imitators.

VII
THE PRESENCE OF THE PAST, THE PASTNESS OF THE PRESENT:
THE PARADIGMATIC APPROACH TO SCRIPTURE

So much for the historical approach, what of the paradigmatic one? In the Judaism set forth by principal documents that record the oral

289

part of the dual Torah, particularly those that reached closure from ca. 200 to ca. 600 C.E., both documents of law such as the Mishnah and Tosefta, and documents of Scriptural exegesis, such as Sifré to Deuteronomy, Genesis Rabbah, Leviticus Rabbah, and Song of Songs Rabbah, concepts of history, coming to expression in the categories of time and change, along with distinctions between past, present, and future utterly give way to a conception of recording and explaining the social order altogether different from that of history. It is one that sets aside time and change in favor of enduring paradigms recapitulated in age succeeding age.

The concept of history as we know it, and as Scripture knows it, surrenders to an altogether different way of conceiving time and change as well as the course of noteworthy, even memorable social events. The past takes place in the present. The present embodies the past. And there is no indeterminate future over the horizon, only a clear and present path to be chosen if people will it. With distinctions between past, present and future time found to make no difference, and in their stead, different categories of meaning and social order deemed self-evident, the Judaism of the dual Torah transforms ancient Israel's history into the categorical structure of eternal Israel's society, so that past, present, and future meet in the here and now.

In that construction of thought, history finds no place, time, change, the movement of events toward a purposive goal have no purchase, and a different exegesis of happenings supplants the conception of history. No place in Rabbinic thought, portrayed in successive documents examined severally and jointly, accommodates the notions of change and time, unique events and history, particular lives and biography. All things are transformed by this other way of thinking, besides the historical one that Scripture uses to organize the facts of social existence of Israel.

Here we deal with a realm in which the past is ever present, the present a recapitulation and reformulation of the past. When people recapitulate the past in the present, and when they deem the present to be no different from a remote long ago, they organize and interpret experience in an other-than-historical framework, one that substitutes paradigms of enduring permanence for patterns of historical change. Instead of history, thought proceeds through the explanation of paradigms, the likenesses or unlikenesses of things to an original pattern. The familiar modes of classifying noteworthy events, the long ago and the here and now, lose currency. Memory as the medium of interpretation of the social order falls away, and historical thinking ceases to serve. Universal paradigms govern, against which all things, now, then, anytime, are compared; events lose all specificity and particularity. The characterization of this Judaism as a historical religion and of the medium of that religion as memory in no way conforms to the facts of the Judaism that is studied here.

In this reading of the Torah, with the past very present, the present becomes an exercise in recapitulation of an enduring paradigm, therefore, time and change signify nothing. In its normative statements Judaism is ahistorical because it forms meaning in other than historical ways; it is ahistorical because it is paradigmatic in its structure and sensibility. So, with the loss of the experience of memory in favor of a different kind of encounter with time past, present, and future, time as a conception in the measurement of things ceases to serve. Time is neither linear nor cyclical; it simply is not a consideration in thinking about what happens and what counts. Instead, paradigms for the formation of the social order of transcendence and permanence govern, so that what was now is, and what will be is what was and is. Paradigmatic thinking treats the case not as a one-time event but as an example; it seeks the rules that cases adumbrate; it asks about the patterns that narratives realize in concrete instances. It is what mathematics does when it translates the real world into abstract principles, what social science does when it seeks to generalize about particularities.

VIII

MEMORY IS TO HISTORICAL THINKING
AS DREAM IS TO PARADIGMATIC THINKING

*"For ever after, in every generation, every Israelite must
think of himself [or herself] as having gone forth from
Egypt"*

How does paradigmatic thinking come to realization? As the dance
is the physicalization of music, and as memory is the immediate
realization of history, so is the lived dream the here-and-now
embodiment of Scripture read as paradigm. We are all like Joseph
in Egypt, reading the dream to refer to reality. The task of dance is
to give physical form to music; the assignment of memory is the
contemporary formulation of the past, *and the calling of dream is to
realize the immediacy and concreteness of the model.* The marriage of
music and motion yields dance; the monument and rite of
commemoration produce history; the serene sense of familiarity
with the new put forth in response the lived paradigm — that is
what produces Torah and makes possible Purim in Patagonia,
Exodus in America: "...as if we were slaves to Pharaoh."

These abstract remarks in fact correspond to experience that
all of us have had. The Passover Haggadah asks us not so much to
remember as to experience, ourselves, the moment of Exodus from
Egypt: the present takes place in the past, but the past forms the
present as well.

> *We* were the slave of Pharaoh in Egypt; and the Lord
> our God brought us forth from there with a mightily hand and
> an outstretched arm. And if the Holy One, blessed be He, had
> not brought our fathers forth from Egypt, then surely we, and
> our children, and our children's children, would be enslaved to
> Pharaoh in Egypt. And so, even if all of us were full of
> wisdom and understanding, well along in years and deeply
> versed in the tradition, we should still be bidden to repeat once
> more the story of the exodus from Egypt; and he who delights

to dwell on the liberation is a man to be praised.[6]

To be a Jew means to be a slave who has been liberated by God. To be Israel means to give eternal thanks for God's deliverance. And that deliverance is not at a single moment in historical time. It comes in every generation and is always celebrated. Here again, events of natural, ordinary life are transformed through myth into paradigmatic, eternal, and ever-recurrent sacred moments. Jews think of themselves as having gone forth from Egypt, and Scripture so instructs them. God did not redeem the dead generation of the Exodus alone, but the living too — especially the living. Thus the family states:

> Again and again, in double and redoubled measure, are we beholden to God the All-Present: that He freed us from the Egyptians and wrought His judgment on them; that He sentenced all their idols and slaughtered all their first-born; that He gave their treasure to us and split the Red Sea for us; that He led us through it dry-shod and drowned the tyrants in it; that He helped us through the desert and fed us with the manna; that He gave the Sabbath to us and brought us to Mount Sinai; that He gave the Torah to us and brought us to our homeland — there to build the Temple for us, for atonement of our sins.[7]
>
> This is the promise which has stood by our forefathers and stands by us. For neither once, nor twice, nor three times was our destruction planned; in every generation they rise against us, and in every generation God delivers us from their hands into freedom, out of anguish into joy, out of mourning into festivity, out of darkness into light, out of bondage into redemption.[8]
>
> For ever after, in every generation, *every Israelite must think of himself or herself as having gone forth from Egypt* [italics added]. For we read in the Torah: "In that day thou shalt

---

[6]Maurice Samuel trans., *Haggadah of Passover* (New York: Hebrew Publishing Co., 1942), p. 9.

[7]Ibid., p. 26.

[8]Ibid., p. 13.

teach thy son, saying: All this is because of what God did for me when I went forth from Egypt." It was not only our forefathers that the Holy One, blessed be He, redeemed; us too, the living, He redeemed together with them, as we learn from the verse in the Torah: "And He brought us out from thence, so that He might bring us home, and give us the land which he pledged to our forefathers."[9]

These modes of thought are entirely familiar to holy Israel: we undertake to enter into them every Passover, but every day in our prayers as well, when we enter into God's kingdom, stand at Sinai, receive the Torah in the here and now. We do not venture upon the Passover Seder in order to inform ourselves about domestic politics and foreign policy in ancient Egypt — nor has Judaism ever portrayed a single one of its rites to be limited to one-time, past-tense historical facts.[10]

As essential to historical modes of thought as is memory, so critical to the paradigm that identifies event out of happenings, consequence out of the detritus of everyday affairs is the dream (in sleep) or the intuition (when awake). Then everything is changed. When the model takes shape and takes place in the acutely-, radically-present moment, past and future meet in neither past nor future but paradigm. And then the mode of thought through paradigm accomplishes its enchantment. Paradigm or pattern or model then forms an alternative to historical knowledge, a different way of thinking about the same things and responding to the same questions: O Lord, why? O Lord, how long?

People who see time in the framework of history, past, present, future forming distinct spells, experience the passage of time through the medium of memory. They look backward, into an age now over and done with. Affirming that that was then, and this is now, they evoke memory as the medium for renewing access

---

[9] Ibid., p. 27.

[10] That is not to suggest people did not accept the historical facticity of matters, only that questions of historicity were treated as alien and irrelevant. I return to this matter at the end.

to events or persons deemed or set forth as formative in the present moment. A religion that frames its statement out of the conception of historical time — one-time events, bound to context and defined by circumstance, but bearing long-term effects and meaning — then will evoke memory as a principal medium for the recovery of sense and order out of the chaos of the everyday and here and now. By remembering how things were, or how they have been, moving beyond the barrier of the present moment, people institute a certain order. They form a certain sense for the self-evident and sensible quality of matters.

The Scriptures themselves, seen in isolation from the tradition of interpretation that mediates Scriptures to holy Israel in the synagogue, do cohere as a one-time historical narrative. Israelite Scripture certainly qualifies as a religion of history and memory.[11] It recognizes both the pastness of the past and also invokes the past's power to explain the present. But then, what are we to make of a religion that insists upon the presence of the past and the pastness of the present, instructing the faithful to view themselves, out of the here and now, as living in another time, another place: "Therefore every person must see himself or herself as slave to Pharaoh in Egypt," as the Passover Haggadah-narrative phrases matters? The same invocation of the present into the past also serves to convey the past into the here and now. Once a religious obligation imposes past upon present, shifting the present into a fully realized, contemporary-past, rites of commemoration give way to the reformulation of the ages into a governing paradigm that obliterates barriers of time as much as those of space.[12] Rules

---

[11]That is not to suggest the Authorized History of Genesis to Kings tells us what really happened; at stake here are modes of thought, issues of the social construction of reality, conventions and protocols of interpretation, that are ordinarily classified as historical. That point suffices, and accords with the established facts of scholarship.

[12]I am sure that considerations of space and its divisions are at least as important as those of time. It seems to me necessary that our sages treat as null boundaries of space as much as those of time, but I have not worked on that problem. I should anticipate that Rabbinic Judaism will emerge as not only paradigmatic,

of structure and order apply without differentiation by criteria or time or space. These rules comprise a paradigm. The paradigm not only imparts sense and order to what happens but also — and first of all — selects out of what happens what counts — and is to be counted. The paradigm is a distinctive way of marking time, telling time.

Rites of reenactment with clear focus upon times long gone will form a principal expression of a religion of memory: we do this now in commemoration of that singular ("unique") event long ago, so that we may remember, so that we may draw the right conclusions for today. What makes such rites those of memory and not of a return to an eternal present, of course, finds definition in what distinguishes history from other modes of formulating social organization. It is that defining barrier between present and past, that insistence on the uniqueness of events, but also on their linear and teleological character. We recall in this context the statement of LeGoff, "The opposition between past and present is fundamental, since the activity of memory and history is founded on this distinction."[13] The work of historical imagination, then, is, through the processes of narrative shaping thought, sentimentality and emotion, to move people from here to there, from now to then. The governing proposition of imagination is easily framed: we are here as if we were there; then is as if it were now. The "as if" then embodies in language the working of imagination transcending the barrier of time. Historical imagination forms a powerful tool for the reconstruction of the every day by appeal to the model of another, long-gone but still living age. Memory then is the chosen medium for imagining.

If for our purposes Scripture has supplied the definitions of historical thinking, then the traits of paradigmatic thinking will

---

not historical, but also utopian, not locative. But the shift from bounded space to utopia is to be traced in its own terms.

[13]Jacques LeGoff, *History and Memory* (N.Y., 1992: Columbia University Press). Translated by Steven Randall and Elizabeth Claman, p. xii.

take shape in their opposites and counterparts, and these we find in a few, clear and unmistakable ways in the Rabbinic documents. We simply take the opposites of the indicators of the presence of historical thinking: — [1] linear history, [2] sustained narrative, [3] differentiation of present from past, contrasted against [1] episodic story-telling but [2] no linear, sustained narrative, and [3] the fusion of times into one time.[14] The traits of paradigmatic thinking characteristic of our sages emerge in both what we do not find in those documents and also in what we do find by way of counterpart: how do Rabbinic writers deal with those same themes out of Israel's (alleged) past as are laid out in historical terms in Scripture? Having denied the distinction between present and past, paradigmatic thinking for its part finds the past to be ever-present, and deems the present to form a chapter in the past. The very dilemma of history — bridging the imagined gap between present and past — finds no comprehension at all in thought that finds the principle of order in the model or the pattern that pertains any time and any place; in that setting a distance between here and there, a spell between now and then — both allude to a separation none perceives. That atemporality, we now understand, with its corresponding notion of space, utopianism, derives from a different conception of marking time (or space) from the historical one. Time defined by nature imposes its morphology on time marked by the community and its conventions.

A religion such as Judaism that organizes experience by appeal to enduring paradigms, transcending time by discovering the present in the past, the past in the present, in a process that is reciprocal, will find no more use for memory than it assigns to the concept of "history." Memory matters only to those who organize affairs historically; the barrier between present and past removed,

---

[14]Which is not to be called "eternity." That would represent a profound misunderstanding of the conception of time in Rabbinic Judaism. It is only in the context of history that I have dealt here with the conception of time; the much more interesting problem of time viewed in its own terms in the Rabbinic document remains to be addressed.

memory is assigned no task at all. Once people mark time nature's way, that is, in enduring, recurring patterns, history's insistence on difference between now and then makes no sense. Other questions take priority: identifying the pattern, whether in large things or in small, without reference to scale, but with acute interest in the model or the pattern replicated in no special context. Once we are obligated to see ourselves as if we were not now but then, not here but somewhere else, paradigmatic thinking takes over; and as soon as the subjunctive that expresses a state contrary to fact or condition falls away, so that the "as if" loses its taxonomic power, the paradigm takes over and excludes all considerations of historical specificity: now, not then, but like then. Rabbinic Judaism celebrated Purim not once but many times, not there in particular but everywhere Israel outlived its enemies. This it did not through a process of spiritualization, nor, yet, through rites of reenactment. Rather, the here and now took over the then and there, and also was taken over by the other place, the other time. Without regard to considerations of scale, the same model applied, to give meaning and depth to incident.

IX
FROM UNIQUE EVENT TO EXEMPLARY PATTERN TURNING ONE-TIME HAPPENINGS INTO ALL-TIME PARADIGMS

Then how does this take place, and then what medium in ordinary life corresponds in the experience of paradigm to the medium of memory for history? The question phrased in this way produces an obvious answer, which I gave when I contrasted dreaming with remembering. If we wonder when or where we compare ordinary affairs with an enduring paradigm, it is in dreaming or free-ranging imagination or instinct, what is known through self-evidence and the ineluctable sense for what fits: before thought, besides thought, as much as through ratiocination. Nostalgia is to historical thinking what realized dream is to the paradigmatic kind. How in

298

concrete terms do we see the difference? Yohanan's reading of the passage in Ruth suffices. It is utterly laconic and unemotional, not a narrative meant to elicit feeling, but an exposition aimed at establishing a pattern for us to perceive. Our sages never look back with longing, because they do not have to; nor do they look forward with either dread nor anticipation either; that is what it means to say, the past is present, so there is no looking back, the present is past, so there is no looking forward. Indeed, theirs is a different model for perceived experience from the one that distinguishes past from present, present from future, invoking the one to "make sense" of the next phase in differentiated time. Paradigms or models take over and replace the sense of history with a different sort of common sense.

There we put together, in our own mind's eye, in the undifferentiated realm of night — for the sages' system, for Judaism, the age of sin and exile, to be specific — those patterns and models of experience that coalesce and endure, taking the paradigm of one set of generative experiences and imposing themselves on chosen moments later on. Dream and fantasy select, as much as history selects, out of a range of happenings a few incidents of consequence, history's events, paradigm's models. But in dreaming there is no earlier or later, no now or then, no here or there. Things coalesce and disintegrate, form and reform, in the setting of a few, highly restricted images. In the realm of dreams, paradigms (of experience, real or imagined) come together, float apart, reassemble in a different pattern, unrestricted by considerations of now or then, here or there.[15] Whatever is chosen, out of the chaos of the everyday, to be designated a pattern imposes its order and structure on whatever, in the chaos of the here and now, fits.

---

[15]That explains the aesthetics of the theology of symbolic expression worked out in my *Symbol and Theology in Early Judaism.* Minneapolis, 1991: Fortress Press; reprint, 1999: Atlanta: Scholars Press for South Florida Studies in the History of Judaism.

History strings together event after event, like cultured pearls matched with precision in a necklace. Paradigm's rough, sea-nurtured pearls impose no order or natural sequence in ordered size; being made by nature, they do not match exactly. That is why, in one combination, they make one statement, in another, a different statement — as Ruth Rabbah showed us in a most dramatic manner. And these, I maintain, more precisely correspond to human media for the organization of experience than the historical one: it is how we live out our lives. Our sages formed their conception of time out of the materials of the everyday perceptions of people, for whom past, present, and future give way to the recapitulation of patterns of meaning formed we know not how.[16] Dreams, fantasies, moments of enchantment, occasions or circumstances or places that invoke the model or fit it — these form the medium for the organization of experience. To it time bears no meaning, memory no message. But sages saw matters the way they did because they took the measure of history, not because they ignored it. They formulated another and different reading of history from the historical one; aware of the one, sentient of the other, they transcended history and cast off the bounds of time.

Our sages identified in the written part of the Torah the governing models of Israel's enduring existence, whether past, whether future. And that is precisely why they formed the conception of paradigm, and whence they drew the specificities of theirs, as I shall explain in due course. They knew precisely what paradigms imparted order and meaning to everyday events, and their models, equivalent in mathematics to the "philosophy," then selected and explained data and also allowed prognosis to take place. In place of a past that explained the present and predicted the future, sages invoked a paradigm that imposed structure on past and future alike — a very different thing. And what, precisely, was the paradigm?

---

[16]But that is of course disingenuous. For psychology knows how, and so does theology.

300

Images, in dreaming, form the counterpart to the paradigm's formulations: dream of Eden, dream of Land, nightmare of Adam, nightmare of Israel — and the waking at Sinai and the reawakening in Eden, the paradigm having reached fulfillment. In that dream world formed of the paradigms of Scripture matched against our own immediate and contemporary experience, time stands still, its place taken by form. And in the world of paradigms set forth by Scripture and defined in simple, powerful images by the documents of Rabbinic Judaism, imagination asks of itself a different task from the one performed in a religion of history through the act of memory. Imagination now forms an instrument of selection out of the here and now of those particular facts that count, selection and construction out of the data of the every day a realm of being that conforms to the model that is always present, waiting to be discerned and, not recapitulated once again but, realized — as always, whenever. Seeing the dream in the setting of the everyday defines the task of imagination: not "let's pretend," but rather, "look here...." In that particular vision lies the power of this Judaism to make of the world something that, to the untrained eye, is scarcely there to be seen, but, to the eye of faith, evokes the sense of not *déja-vu* or *temps perdu* but—self-evidence.

IX
GOD IN TIME OR IN PARADIGM

Let us turn, then, to the contrast of history and memory, on the one side, paradigm and realized dream, on the other. This will help us to understand how the very character and mission of Scripture would realize their inner logic in the kind of thinking I am describing.

A document such as Scripture that formulates its statement in historical categories will negotiate data through the medium of memory, on the one hand, and through the doctrine of tradition, on the other. Remembering what was done, handing down the memory — these will formulate the rules for composing the social order in the unfolding present. Memory forms an act of prayer, an effort to overcome the separation from God. For at stake in the historical as against the paradigmatic reading of the everyday in the context of Judaism is the encounter with God: where do we identify the "divine reality...imprinted"? The authentic Bible scholar of our generation, Brevard Childs, formulates what is at stake in memory and in its theological companion, the concept of tradition. What he says carries us to the heart of the matter, which is, Scripture's understanding of memory, concomitant with its selection of the medium of history:

> To remember was to call to mind a past event or situation, with the purpose of evoking some action...To remember was to actualize the past, to bridge the gap of time and to form a solidarity with the fathers. Israel's remembrance became a technical term to express the process by which later Israel made relevant the great redemptive acts which she recited in her tradition. The question of how to overcome the separation in time and space from the great events of the past become the paramount issue.[17]

The premise of Scripture's historical framing of Israel's situation —the pastness of the past — then generates the question that that same framing of matters satisfactorily answers.

Once we recognize that great events belong to the past, we undertake to remember them so as to realize them once more, in Childs's language, "to overcome the separation in time and space...." If to begin with we did not conceive of time in a historical manner, we also should not have to overcome that barrier, to close that separation.[18] First comes the here-and-now

---

[17]Brevard S. Childs, *Myth and Reality in the Old Testament* (London, 1960: SCM Press), pp. 74-5.
[18]In this context I need hardly attempt to explain that powerful sense of the pastness of the past that animates the Hebrew Scriptures. But it seems to me to derive from the perspective of the return to Zion, which conceives of an "Israel"

conception of "exile" and "return,"[19] then comes the utilization of the category, history, to frame matters by explaining them. The insistence on the pastness of the past that defines the concept of history in the Scriptural setting then forms a way of stating that sense of distance or separation — whether from Land, whether from God — that is to be recognized and overcome. "History" then makes a statement that from the perspective of "here," a separation has taken place, and from the viewpoint of "now," there is a then. And "tradition" forms the medium by which that statement's tension is resolved: how to overcome the gap. That is not accomplished by a return to that moment of the past, as Childs says, "...Old Testament actualization cannot be correctly identified with a return to a former historical event."[20] Such a return would violate the first law of historical thinking, as we have noted many times; we can never go back.

Then what kind of history does that thinking yield in Scripture? Childs answers in these terms:

> The Old Testament witnesses to a series of historical events by which God brought the people of Israel into existence. These events were placed in a chronological order within the tradition and never recurred in Israel's history. There was one Exodus from Egypt, one period of wilderness wanderings, one conquest of the land. These events were determinative because they constituted Israel's redemption. in other words, they became

---

once separated from the land but now restored to it, thus conception ("myth") of a return after an interval of time begins with the notion of the separation of space, and that then provokes the sense of the separation in time. A rich account of what is at stake here is set forth in Philip R. Davies, *In Search of Ancient Israel* (Sheffield, 1993: Journal for the Study of the Old Testament Supplement Series 148), especially pp. 113-133.

[19] I say "conception" rather than "experience," since I do not know what experience, if any, comes to expression in the conception; and I say "conception" rather than "myth" or "tradition" since these terms bear weight that would overload the argument here.

[20] Childs, p. 83.

the vehicle for a quality of existence, redemptive time and space.[21]

Then, we ask ourselves, what task is assigned to memory, that is, the medium for the actualization of the statement of history? Childs' reply serves us well:

> Our study of memory has indicated that each successive generation encountered anew these same determinative events...It means more than that the influence of a past event continued to be felt in successive generations...there was an immediate encounter, an actual participation in the great acts of redemption....[22]

Memory then serves as the medium for overcoming the barrier between present and past, opening the way for the present to participate in what happened long ago. By remembering, people were able to relive, regain access to, that time and that event that they knew was once upon a time. How, precisely, does that working of memory craft the world? Childs' final contribution completes this exposition of history, memory, and tradition in ancient Israel's Scriptures:

> Actualization is the process by which a past event is contemporized for a generation removed in time and space from the original event. When later Israel responded to the continuing imperative of her tradition through her memory, that moment in historical time likewise became an Exodus experience. Not in the sense that later Israel again crossed the Red Sea. This was an irreversible, once-for-all event. Rather, Israel entered the same redemptive reality of the Exodus generation. later Israel, removed in time and space from the original event, yet still in time and space, found in her tradition a means of transforming her history into redemptive history. Because the quality of time was the same, the barrier of chronological separation was overcome.[23]

---

[21]Childs, p. 83.
[22]Childs, pp. 83-4.
[23]Childs, p. 85.

304

It would be difficult to imagine a more concise statement of the religious experience of the historical mode of organizing matters than Childs's, since he touches on every element critical to the description of history — the pastness of the past, the singularity and irreversibility of events, but also the power of events in times past to affect the present moment and to effect change therein.

The touchstone, then, is simple: that sense of separation that precipitates the quest for reconciliation, restoration, renewal of relationship. Childs defines the final question to be taken up here: if historical thinking begins with a sense of separation of present from past, then what accounts for the datum of paradigmatic thinking, which forms the union of present and past and abandons any notion that the one is distinct from the other? Where present and past meet, there paradigmatic thinking commences. Now let me spell out the counterpart to Childs's reading of Scripture's disposition of matters: the disposition of Judaism as the oral part of the Torah takes over and recasts the written part.

XI
THINKING IN PARADIGMS:
MATHEMATICS AS THE METAPHOR

A while back I referred to mathematics and social science as two modes of knowledge that appeal to models, translating cases from unique to exemplary, seeking constructions, structures, and patterns out of the detritus of the everyday. This I now offer as the counterpart to the historical thinking characteristic of Scripture but not of Judaism or Christianity in response to that common Scripture.

Since I have used the word "model" as interchangeable with "paradigm" or "pattern," I turn to a brief reference to the use of model in mathematics, since that is the source for my resort to the same word — model — and that mode of description, analysis, and interpretation of data for which it stands. My purpose is to render reasonable a mode of thought that, until now, has been dismissed as "fundamentally ahistorical...insubstantial." But it would be difficult to find a more substantial, a more concrete and immediate mode of addressing events and explaining the concrete here and now than the paradigmatic: ahistorical, yes, and from one angle of vision atemporal too, but far from insubstantial, and, in the context of natural time, profoundly time-oriented.

The paradigm forms a medium for the description, analysis, and interpretation of selected data: existence, rightly construed. In this, paradigmatic thinking forms a counterpart to that of the mathematics that produces models. Specifically, mathematicians compose models that, in the language and symbols of mathematics, set forth a structure of knowledge that forms a "surrogate for reality."[24] These models state in quantitative terms the results of controlled observations of data, and among them, the one that generates plausible analytical generalizations will serve. Seeking not so much the regularities of the data as a medium for taking account of a variety of variables among a vast corpus of data, the framer of a model needs more than observations of fact, e.g., regularities or patterns. What is essential is a structure of thought, which mathematicians call "a philosophy:"

> As a philosophy it has a center from which everything flows, and the center is a definition,...[25]

What is needed for a model is not data alone, however voluminous, but some idea of what you are trying to compose: a model of the model:

> Unless you have some good idea of what you are looking for and how to find it, you can approach infinity with nothing more than a mishmash of little things you know about a lot of little things.[26]

---

[24]Norman Maclean, *Young Men and Fire* (Chicago, 1992: University of Chicago Press), p. 257.
[25]Maclean, p. 261.
[26]Maclean, p. 262.

So, in order to frame a model of explanation, we start with a model in the computer, and then test data to assess the facility of the model; we may test several models, with the same outcome: the formation of a philosophy in the mathematical sense. To understand the relevance of this brief glimpse at model-making in mathematics, let me cite the context in which the matter comes to me, the use of mathematics to give guidance on how to fight forest fires:

> If mathematics can be used to predict the intensity and rate of spread of wildfires of the future (either hypothetical fires or fires actually burning but whose outcome is not yet known), why can't the direction of the analysis be reversed in order to reconstruct the characteristics of important fires of the past? Or why can't the direction be reversed from prophecy to history? [27]

Here the reversibility of events, their paradigmatic character, their capacity to yield a model unlimited by context or considerations of scale, — the principal traits of paradigmatic thinking turn out to enjoy a compelling rationality of their own. Reading those words, we can immediately grasp what service models or patterns or paradigms served for our sages, even though the framing of mathematical models began long after the birth of this writer, and even though our sages lived many centuries before the creation of the mathematics that would yield models in that sense in which, sages' paradigms correspond in kind and function to model-explanation in contemporary mathematics. Before us is a mode of thought that is entirely rational and the very opposite of "insubstantial."

What is at stake in the appeal to "paradigm" or "model" to explain how sages answered the same questions that, elsewhere, historical thinking admirably addresses is now clear. To use the term in the precise sense just now stated, philosophy now took the

---

[27]Maclean, p. 267.

place of history in the examination of the meaning of human events and experience. Forming a philosophical model to hold together such data as made a difference, sages found ready at hand the pattern of the destruction of the Temple, alongside explanations of the event and formulations of how the consequences were to be worked out. And, since the Temple represented the focus and realization of the abstractions of nature — from the movement of sun and moon to the concrete rhythm of the offerings celebrating these events, from the abundance of nature, the natural selection, by chance, and presentation of God's share on the altar — nature's time took over, history's time fell away.

In these two facts — the transformation of event once into pattern by recurrence, the identification of nature's time as the way of keeping and marking time for the social order as well — paradigmatic thinking was born. But in stating my twin-conclusions, I have moved ahead of my story. Let me turn back and unpack the stages of argument, one by one. Precisely why did our sages recast the received historical mode of thinking in such a way as to reread Scripture as a source for not narrative but paradigm? And on what basis did they presume to treat as models what the revealed history of Scripture set forth as a sequence of linear, one-time events? It is time to explain the facts that characterize the documents as ahistorical, atemporal, and non-linear, but rather as paradigmatic: history in quest of philosophy.

XII
THE ORIGINS OF PARADIGMATIC THINKING IN REAL, HISTORICAL TIME

Since, we have seen, our sages subverted the historical thinking they inherited and substituted for it an altogether different kind, recasting the essential of history, the definition of time, in anti-historical terms, we have to wonder how and why sages whose minds were shaped in Scripture and whose souls were cast in its models utterly rejected what Scripture clearly said — and said to other Jews — and substituted modes of thought and patterns of reading of a kind quite alien to the written part of revelation. Here in the Rabbinic documents we have surveyed, we have sustained and systematic thought that shows an alternative to history as a mode of accounting for how things are; that treats as null the most fundamental datum of the historical thinking to which we are accustomed; and that served Judaism (and Christianity) for nearly the whole of its history. If I had to explain why paradigmatic rather than historical thinking predominated, I should have to revert to that very mode of explanation, the historical and contextual, that Scripture set forth but our sages abandoned. Precisely where and when, in the context of Israel's life, did historical thinking emerge? With the answer to that question in hand, we proceed to take up the issue that confronts us.

First, whence the source of the sense of separation of present from past? To answer that question (which is a historical one), we turn to the setting in which, in Israel, history first was set down in a sustained narrative about times past. The Official History of ancient Israel set forth by Genesis through Kings recognizes the pastness of the past and explains how the past has led to the present. That Official, Authorized, or Primary History, came to literary formulation (whatever the state of the facts contained therein) in the aftermath of the destruction of the first Temple of Jerusalem, in 586. Faced with decisive closure, looking backward from the perspective of a radically different present, the thinkers who put together the Primary History took up two complementary premises, the definitive pastness of the past, its utter closure and separation from the present, and, alongside, the power of the past to explain the present and of its lessons, properly learned, to shape the future.

The historical thinking that produced the Authorized History took place at a very specific time and responded to an acute and urgent question by taking account of the facts of the moment. An age had come to a conclusion; the present drastically differed

309

from the now-closed past. History might begin, the sense of closure having taken hold. Since, all scholarship concurs, the Official or Primary History represented by Genesis through Kings came to closure at just this time, the allegation that historical thinking in Israel in particular[28] reaches literary expression in the aftermath of the catastrophe of 586 rests upon solid foundations. Here is when people wrote history-books; here is why they wrote them; here, therefore, is the circumstance in which, for Israel, historical thinking took place.

In this context, we recall Childs's formulation, "The question of how to overcome the separation in time and space from the great events of the past became the paramount issue." The advent of historical thinking and writing became possible precisely when great events from the past receded over the last horizon, and those responsible for the books at hand recognized a separation from those events and so produced a history of how things had reached their present pass. Our sages, however, evinced no sense of separation that precipitates the quest for reconciliation, restoration, renewal of relationship between now and then; therefore they thought in a different manner about the same events. That is the starting point of matters, and it also brings us to a conclusion: why did they think in a different way, what, in particular, led them to this other mode of thought?

Our sages recognized no barrier between present and past. To them, the present and past formed a single unit of time,

---

[28]We are not concerned with the advent of historical thinking in other contexts or in defining historical thinking in Israel by comparison with, or contrast to, historical thinking in either the Near Eastern or Hellenic worlds. Historical thinking in Israel has defined itself in its own writings, and those who received those writings and so radically recast them have responded to the historical thinking they learned in Scripture with this other kind of thinking of their own. Hence I explain not the origins of history or historical thinking in general, or even what is special about Israel's historical thinking, whether in the sixth century B.C. or in the fifth century C.E., but only the circumstances in which in this setting historical thinking took shape, by contrast with the circumstances in which, later on, another mode of thought took precedence.

encompassing a single span of experience. Why was that so? It is because, to them, times past took place in the present too, on which account, the present not only encompassed the past (which historical thinking concedes) but took place in the same plane of time as the past (which, to repeat, historical thinking rejects). How come? It is because our sages experienced the past in the present. What happened that mattered had already happened; an event then was transformed into a series; events themselves defined paradigms, yielded rules. A simple formulation of this mode of thought is as follows:

MISHNAH-TRACTATE TAANIT 4:6

A. Five events took place for our fathers on the seventeenth of Tammuz, and five on the ninth of Ab.

B. On the seventeenth of Tammuz

(1) the tablets [of the Torah] were broken,

(2) the daily whole offering was cancelled,

(3) the city wall was breached,

(4) Apostemos burned the Torah, and

(5) he set up an idol in the Temple.

C. On the ninth of Ab

(1) the decree was made against our forefathers that they should not enter the land,

(2) the first Temple and

(3) the second [Temple] were destroyed,

(4) Betar was taken, and

(5) the city was ploughed up [after the war of Hadrian].

D. When Ab comes, rejoicing diminishes.

We mark time by appeal to the phases of the moon; these then may be characterized by traits shared in common — and so the paradigm, from marking time, moves outward to the formation of rules concerning the regularity and order of events.

In the formulation just now given, we see the movement from event to rule. What is important about events is not their singularity but their capacity to generate a pattern, a concrete rule for the here and now. That is the conclusion drawn from the very passage at hand:

MISHNAH-TRACTATE TAANIT 4:7

A. In the week in which the ninth of Ab occurs it is prohibited to get a haircut and to wash one's clothes.

B. But on Thursday of that week these are permitted,

C. because of the honor owing to the Sabbath.

D. On the eve of the ninth of Ab a person should not eat two prepared dishes, nor should one eat meat or drink wine.

E. Rabban Simeon b. Gamaliel says, "He should make some change from ordinary procedures."

F. R. Judah declares people liable to turn over beds.

G. But sages did not concur with him.

Events serve to define paradigms and therefore, also, to yield rules governing the here and now: what we do to recapitulate.

This brings us back to our question: how an event turned into a series, what happened once into something that happens. The answer, of course, lies in the correspondence (real or imagined) of the two generative events sages found definitive: the destruction of the Temple, the destruction of the Temple. The singular event that framed their consciousness recapitulated what had already occurred. For they confronted a Temple in ruins, and, in the defining event of the age just preceding the composition of most of the documents surveyed here, they found quite plausible the notion that the past was a formidable presence in the contemporary world. And having lived through events that they could plausibly discover in Scripture — Lamentations for one example, Jeremiah another — they also found entirely natural the notion that the past took place in the present as well.

When we speak of the presence of the past, therefore, we raise not generalities or possibilities but the concrete experience that generations actively mourning the Temple endured. When we speak of the pastness of the present, we describe the consciousness of people who could open Scripture and find themselves right there, in its record — but not only Lamentations, but also prophecy, and, especially, in the books of the Torah. Here we deal with not the spiritualization of Scripture, but with the acutely contemporary and immediate realization of Scripture: once again, as then; Scripture in the present day, the present day in Scripture. That is why it was possible for sages to formulate out of Scripture a paradigm that imposed structure and order upon the world that they themselves encountered.

Since, then, sages did not see themselves as removed in time and space from the generative events to which they referred the experience of the here and now, they also had no need to make the past contemporary. If as Childs insists, the Exodus was irreversible, once for all time event, then, as we see, our sages saw matters in a different way altogether. They neither relived nor transformed one-time historical events, for they found another way to overcome the barrier of chronological separation. Specifically, if history began when the gap between present and past shaped consciousness, then we naturally ask ourselves whether the point at which historical modes of thought concluded and a different mode of thought took over produced an opposite consciousness from the historical one: not cycle but paradigm. For, it seems to me clear, the premise that time and space separated our sages of the Rabbinic writings from the great events of the past simply did not win attention. The opposite premise defined matters: barriers of space and time in no way separated sages from great events, the great events of the past enduring for all time. How then are we to account for this remarkably different way of encounter, experience, and, consequently, explanation? The answer has already been adumbrated.

Sages assembled in the documents of Rabbinic Judaism, from the Mishnah forward, all recognized the destruction of the Second Temple and all took for granted that that event was to be understood by reference to the model of the destruction of the first. A variety of sources reviewed here maintain precisely that position and express it in so many words, e.g., the colloquy between Aqiba and sages about the comfort to be derived from the ephemeral glory of Rome and the temporary ruin of Jerusalem. It follows that for our sages, the destruction of the Temple in 70 did not mark a break with the past, such as it had for their predecessors some five hundred years earlier, but rather a recapitulation of the past.

Paradigmatic thinking then began in that very event that precipitated thought about history to begin with, the end of the old order. But paradigm replaced history because what had taken place the first time as unique and unprecedented took place the second time in precisely the same pattern and therefore formed of an episode a series. Paradigmatic thinking replaced historical when history as an account of one-time, irreversible, unique events, arranged in linear sequence and pointing toward a teleological conclusion, lost all plausibility. If the first time around, history — with the past marked off from the present, events arranged in linear sequence, narrative of a sustained character serving as the medium of thought — provided the medium for making sense of matters, then the second time around, history lost all currency.

The real choice facing our sages was not linear history as against paradigmatic thinking, but rather, paradigm as against cycle. For the conclusion to be drawn from the destruction of the Temple once again, once history, its premises disallowed, yielded no explanation, can have taken the form of a theory of the cyclicality of events. As nature yielded its spring, summer, fall and winter, so the events of humanity or of Israel in particular can have been asked to conform to a cyclical pattern, in line, for example, with Qohelet's view that what has been is what will be. But our sages obviously did not take that position at all.

They rejected cyclicality in favor of a different ordering of events altogether. They did not believe the Temple would be rebuilt and destroyed again, rebuilt and destroyed, and so on into endless time. They stated the very opposite: the Temple would be rebuilt but never against destroyed. And that represented a view of the second destruction that rejected cyclicality altogether. Sages instead opted for patterns of history and against cycles because they retained that notion for the specific and concrete meaning of events that characterized Scripture's history, even while rejecting the historicism of Scripture. What they maintained, as we have seen, is that a pattern governed, and the pattern was not a cyclical one. Here, Scripture itself imposed its structures, its order, its system —

314

its paradigm. And the Official History left no room for the conception of cyclicality. If matters do not repeat themselves but do conform to a pattern, then the pattern itself must be identified.

Paradigmatic thinking formed the alternative to cyclical thinking because Scripture, its history subverted, nonetheless defined how matters were to be understood. Viewed whole, the Official History indeed defined the paradigm of Israel's existence, formed out of the components of Eden and the Land, Adam and Israel, Sinai, then given movement through Israel's responsibility to the covenant and Israel's adherence to, or violation, of God's will, fully exposed in the Torah that marked the covenant of Sinai. Scripture laid matters out, and our sages then drew conclusions from that lay-out that conformed to their experience. So the second destruction precipitated thinking about paradigms of Israel's life, such as came to full exposure in the thinking behind the Midrash-compilations we have surveyed. The episode made into a series, sages' paradigmatic thinking asked of Scripture different questions from the historical ones of 586 because our sages brought to Scripture different premises; drew from Scripture different conclusions. But in point of fact, not a single paradigm set forth by sages can be distinguished in any important component from the counterpart in Scripture, not Eden and Adam in comparison to the land of Israel and Israel, and not the tale of Israel's experience in the spinning out of the tension between the word of God and the will of Israel.

The contrast between history's time and nature's time shows that history recognizes natural time and imposes its points of differentiation, upon it. History knows days, months, years, but proposes to differentiate among them, treating this day as different from that because on this day, such and such happened, but on that day, it did not. History's time takes over nature's time and imposes upon it a second set of indicators or points of differentiation. History therefore defines and measures time through two intersecting indicators, the meeting of [1] the natural and [2] the human. As is clear in the foregoing remarks, the

315

context in which "time" is now defined is [1] the passage of days, weeks, months, and years, as marked by the movement of the sun and the stars in the heavens and [2] the recognition of noteworthy events that have taken place in specific occasions during the passage of those days and months and years. By contrast, paradigmatic time in the context of Judaism tells time through the events of nature, to which are correlated the events of Israel's life: its social structure, its reckoning of time, its disposition of its natural resources, and its history too. That is, through the point at which nature is celebrated, the Temple, there Israel tells time.

Predictably, therefore, the only history our sages deem worth narrating — and not in sustained narrative even then — is the story of the Temple cult through days and months and years, and the history of the Temple and its priesthood and administration through time and into eternity. We now fully understand that fact. It is because, to begin with, the very conception of paradigmatic thinking as against the historical kind took shape in deep reflection on the meaning of events: what happened before has happened again — to the Temple. Ways of telling time before give way, history's premises having lost plausibility here as much as elsewhere. Now Israel will tell time in nature's way, shaping history solely in response to what happens in the cult and to the Temple. There is no other history, because, to begin with, there is no history.

Nature's time is the sole way of marking time, and Israel's paradigm conforms to nature's time and proves enduringly congruent with it. Israel conforming to nature yields not cyclical history but a reality formed by appeal to the paradigm of cult and Temple, just as God had defined that pattern and paradigm to Moses in the Torah. Genesis begins with nature's time and systematically explains how the resources of nature came to Israel's service to God. History's time yielded an Israel against and despite history, nature's time, as the Torah tells it, an Israel fully harmonious with nature. At stake in the paradigm then is creation: how come? So long as the Judaism set forth by our sages

316

in the Mishnah, Tosefta, Talmuds, and Midrash-compilations governed, Israel formed itself in response to the eternities of nature's time, bringing into conformity the ephemera of the here and now. That answers the questions, why here? why now? so what? When and where this Judaism lost its power of self-evidence, there history intervened, philosophy and theology, including normative law, gave way to narrative, and the lines of structure and order took a new turning. But that was only recently, and, it now appears, for only a brief spell.

XIII
WHAT IS AT STAKE IN HOW JUDAISM READS THE BIBLE: WHY *HOW* WE THINK MATTERS

A Jewish scholar of Scripture well within the historicist camp states what is at stake in the following language:

> The confessional use of the Bible is fundamentally ahistorical. It makes of Scripture a sort of map, a single, synchronic system in which the part illuminates the whole, in which it does not matter that different parts of the map come from divergent perspectives and different periods. The devotee uses it to search for treasure: under the X lies a trove of secret knowledge; a pot of truths sits across the exegetical rainbow, and with them one can conjure knowledge, power, eternity. Worshipers do not read the Bible with an intrinsic interest in human events. like the prophet or psalmists or, in Acts, the saint, they seek behind the events a single, unifying cause that lends them meaning and makes the historical differences among them irrelevant. in history, the *faithful* seek the permanent, the ahistorical; in time, they quest for timelessness; in reality, in the concrete, they seek Spirit, the insubstantial. Confessional reading levels historical differences — among the authors in the Bible and between those authors and church tradition — because its interests are life present (in the identity of a community of believers) and eternal.
>
> Baruch Halpern[29]

---

[29]Baruch Halpern, *The First Historians. The Hebrew Bible and History* (San Francisco, 1988: Harper & Row), pp. 3-4.

Halpern here characterizes — with a measure of jejune and immature caricature, to be sure — that alternative to the historical reading of Scripture that both Judaism and Christianity selected and faithfully followed eighteen hundred years, until the advent of historical learning in the nineteenth century and its transformation of a powerful instrument of exegesis of Scripture in the twentieth. Until that time another way of reading and responding to events, besides the historical one, governed the way in which the historical writings of ancient Israel were received. I have now explained precisely how an other-than-historical reading of Scripture worked, identifying its premises and showing its results. What is at issue?

At issue is something different from indifference to whether or not things really happened as they are portrayed, and "timelessness" obscures that vastly different conception of time that comes into play in the Judaic and Christian reception of ancient Israel's Scripture, especially its history. For nearly the whole of the history of Judaism and Christianity, a mode of reading Scripture predominated that today is scarcely understood and only rarely respected. In Helper's picture, it is characterized as "confessional," and dismissed as ahistorical. But "confessional" tells us only that faithful practitioners of Judaism and Christianity come to Scripture with reverence and seek there to find what God has told to humanity. The faith of Judaism and Christianity need not insist upon the reading of Scripture as a single, synchronic system — but it does, so the pejorative, "confessional," is both beside the point and accurate. For this "ahistorical" reading means to overcome the barriers of time and space and address Scripture in an unmediated present. And that is what I recommend for the living faith of the synagogue.

The key to the uncomprehending caricature lies in the contrasts, with the climax, "insubstantial." Militant, ideological historicism in that word makes its complete and final statement.[30]

---

[30]I ignore the institutional foundations for the historicistic reading of sacred Scripture, the conduct of that reading under mostly secular (or better,

Faith admittedly is in things unseen, but not in what is "insubstantial," not at all. Still, Halpern speaks for a century and a half of scholarship that has appealed to secular rules for reading documents of religions, Judaism and Christianity, that read the Hebrew Scriptures as the written Torah and the Old Testament, respectively. During the now-protracted spell since the advent of historicism, the holy books of Judaism and Christianity, have been asked to tell us everything but that to which they are devoted: about human events, not about God's perspective on and dealings with humanity. And, in that same long period of time, the reason people have taken up these books and read and studied them — the quest for the written record of God's intervention into human history (for the Torah of Judaism) or of God's footsteps on earth (for the Bible of Christianity) — has been dismissed. After such a long span of time, people have forgotten the religious rules for reading those same holy books and, as Halpern's statement makes clear. They even have lost the capacity even to understand those same rules. But for nearly eighteen centuries those norms governed, and whether or not we accept their discipline, we owe it to ourselves to try to make sense of them.

For there is more at stake than merely understanding a long-ago way of receiving Scripture. The historical way, so long

---

secularizing) auspices, whether in seminaries or in universities. In fact, in such places, though read for historical information, rather than religious knowledge, the Bible is a privileged document, enjoying a central position in the academic study of religion that secular considerations alone will not have accorded it. The upshot is that academic scholarship on Scripture enjoys the sponsorship of the faithful and takes as its task the imposition of secular norms upon the documents of the faith — in the name of the rational labor of the academy. That is why I regard as critical to my venture here the demonstration of the rationality, within the norms of the academy, of the ahistorical, atemporal reading of Scripture that Judaism and Christianity have for most of their histories adopted for themselves, and that means I show the intellectual power of paradigmatic, as opposed to historical thinking. It is not enough to describe how people saw things, I have also to explain their modes of thought within the norms of academic rationality. Willy-nilly, the issue then is theological, though the evidence and argument and thesis merely academic.

319

dominant in the West's reception of its own holy books, proves no longer a secure path to knowledge. For history's premise — the self-evidence of the linearity of events, so that, first came this, then came that, and this "stands behind" or explains or causes that — contradicts the now-articulated experience of humanity. Chaos governs, while from history's perspective, order should reign. Sometimes "this" yields "that," as it should, but sometimes it does not. To the contrary, what happens in ordinary life yields not events that relate to one another like pearls on a necklace, first this, then that, then the other thing, in proper procession. Not at all. Life is unpredictable; if this happens, we cannot securely assume that that must occur in sequence, in order — at least, not in the experience of humanity. That is proven by the irregularity of events, the unpredictability, by all and any rules, of what, if this happens, will follow next. Knowing "this," we never can securely claim to predict "that" as well. The world we seek to understand hardly matches in order and synchronicity the neatly regulated world that history and memory mean to construct for us. Rather, that world corresponds in its deepest being to the disorderly, irregular reality for which paradigmatic thinking — the quest for pattern and order within chaos — serves. If we wish to think about matters of religious fact in full recognition of the uncertainties of knowledge, we are better served by the paradigmatic than the historical reading of the everyday and the here and now.

Jacob Neusner
Baltimore, Maryland
October, 1999
Tishre 5760

The Illustrators

Torah learning is by no means confined to the written word. The Divrei Torah of our artists, Angela Munitz and Ann Zaiman, created through the process of study and devotion, grace this volume with beauty and inspiration.

Angela Munitz (Book Separations) is an artist, designer, and calligrapher who has had numerous exhibitions and has designed for many companies. She attends Rabbi Zaiman's Women's Study group and has participated in programs through the Stulman Center for Adult Learning at Chizuk Amuno.

Ann Zaiman (Cover Design): "I met the father of my children 49 years ago. For 38 of those years, he has also been a Rabbi. This volume is the finest reflection on his life as a Rabbi."